E.T. HORN

Annotations on Ephesians, Philippians, Colossians, and 1 and 2 Thessalonians

Contents

Original Publishing Info

ANNOTATIONS
ON THE
EPISTLES OF PAUL
TO THE
EPHESIANS
PHILIPPIANS
COLOSSIANS
THESSALONIANS

BY
E. T. HORN, D. D.
Pastor of St. John's Lutheran Church, Charleston, S. C.
AND
A. G. VOIGT, D. D.
Professor of Theology, Newberry College, Newberry, S. C.

New York
The Christian Literature Co.
MDCCCXCVI

I

Ephesians

ANNOTATIONS
ON THE
EPISTLE TO THE EPHESIANS

BY
ANDREW G. VOIGT, D.D.

PROFESSOR OF THEOLOGY IN THE
THEOLOGICAL SEMINARY OF THE UNITED
SYNOD
OF THE SOUTH
NEWBERRY, SC

1

Introduction

The Church Addressed. There are some doubts whether this epistle was addressed to the Church at Ephesus. The absence of personal references and of allusions to the previous intimate relations between Paul and that Church is remarkable. The doubts suggested by this circumstance are increased by the omission of the words for "in Ephesus" (1:1) in several of the best manuscripts of the New Testament; for example, the Vatican and the Sinaitic. This omission is confirmed by certain statements of early writers. Tertullian is authority for the statement that the heretic Marcion declared the letter to be addressed to the Laodiceans. The writings of Origen and of Basil contain statements which indicate that they knew of texts which omitted the words for "in Ephesus."

Nevertheless these suggestions of doubt are only sporadic, and the large preponderance of historical proof both in the form of textual evidence and ancient testimony is in favor of Ephesus as the destination of the epistle.

This condition of things has given rise to various theories

in regard to those addressed in this epistle, of which the three following are the chief:

1. It was directed to Laodicea.

2. It was a circular letter intended to be read in various Churches in Asia.

3. It was addressed to the Church at Ephesus.

The last two theories are sometimes combined by making Ephesus the starting-point of the circular letter.

The first of these theories rests upon a conjecture based upon Col. 4:16 and may be rejected. The second is plausible and most generally received now; but it fails to explain the almost unanimous agreement with which the ancient Church regarded the epistle as directed to Ephesus. It cannot be argued from the letter itself (1:15; 3:2) that Paul was not personally acquainted with those to whom he wrote, as he certainly was with the Ephesians. If the writer really was unacquainted with his readers, we might expect some notice of it similar to Col. 2:1. The third theory is best supported by ancient testimony, and on the whole is the most satisfactory. We cannot tell why Paul should have written a letter of such a general character to a Church with which he was so intimately connected. But once admitting that occasion for such a letter might have arisen (and there is no difficulty of conceiving an occasion of this kind), we can easily understand the absence of personal references in so general a letter.

Relations of St. Paul to Ephesus. The city of Ephesus, situated near the mouth of the Cayster and famous for its wonderfully beautiful temple of Diana, was the capital of the Roman province of Asia, which formed the western part of what is generally called Asia Minor, and was the great commercial centre of that region. The relations of

St. Paul to this important city must be learned chiefly from the book of Acts. The founding of the Church there was begun by the apostle himself during a brief visit on his second missionary journey, and was continued by Aquila and Priscilla and afterwards by Apollos (Acts 18:18–28). During his third missionary journey St. Paul returned to the city, completed the organization of the Church, and made Ephesus the centre of a missionary activity extending through the whole province of Asia (Acts 19), and continuing for several years (Acts 19:10; 20:31). Finally, Paul was compelled to leave the city, but by that time the Church was already well established under the direction of "presbyters" or "bishops" (Acts 20:1, 17, 28). At a later period when St. Paul was on his way to Jerusalem, he had a farewell interview with these presbyters at Miletus (Acts 20:16–38).

One of the travelling companions of St. Paul, Trophimus, was an Ephesian (Acts 21:29), and possibly another, Tychicus, also was (Acts 20:4). At a later date St. Paul probably once more came to Ephesus and left Timothy there (1 Tim. 1:3; 2 Tim. 1:18).

The Time and Place of Writing. It used to be generally believed that this epistle was written from Rome, and there is no good reason to depart from this opinion, although in recent times another view has found great favor. It is supposed by many recent scholars that the epistle to the Ephesians, together with those to Philemon and to the Colossians, were written in an earlier period of St. Paul's imprisonment while he was confined at Cæsarea. The famous New Testament scholar Bern-hard Weiss ably advocates this opinion.

This question deserves some discussion. It is certain that

5

the apostle was a prisoner at the time of writing this letter
(3:1; 4:1; 6:20), as well as those to the Colossians (4:3, 18),
Philemon (ver. 1, 9, 13), and also the Philippians (1:7). This
fact as well as the correspondence in style and contents justify
the grouping of these four letters as *the epistles of the captivity.*
The epistle to the Philippians, however, does not bear as
close relations to the other three as these do to each other.
These three must have been written about the same time. The
epistle to Philemon was evidently sent by the slave Onesimus;
and he was a companion of Tychicus (Col. 4:9), the bearer of
the epistles to Colossæ (Col. 4:7) and to Ephesus (Eph. 6:21).
The similarity in style and language of the last two letters,
amounting at times to verbal agreement, also proves that they
were written near the same time. What that time was will
depend upon the decision in regard to the place of writing.

The circumstances under which the apostle wrote must
determine the place of writing. Although a prisoner, he still
enjoyed considerable liberty, so that he was able to continue
his apostolic work (Eph. 6:19; Col. 4:3, 11). This corresponds
with what we know of the condition of St. Paul at Rome
(Acts 28:30), but does not agree with what we learn of his
condition at Cæsarea. For there his liberty hardly extended so
far (Acts 24:23). Again, from Philemon (ver. 22) it is evident
that the apostle expected a speedy liberation, so that he even
appointed a dwelling at Colossæ. It cannot be proved that
the outlook for liberty was ever very promising at Cæsarea.
On the contrary, the gloomy foreboding uttered at Miletus,
in the touching farewell to the elders of Ephesus, could not
have been dismissed from his mind very quickly. Nor is
there anything told about the imprisonment at Cæsarea in
the book of Acts which indicates that Paul *hoped* for a speedy

6

deliverance, whatever he demanded as an act of justice. It is to Rome that we must look for a turn in his affairs which raised his hopes, although we have no narrative of the events which led the imprisoned apostle to expect his freedom. Another argument in favor of Rome as the place of writing is found in what we know of the plans of the apostle. During the captivity at Cæsarea the desire of the apostle, as it had been his long-cherished wish before, was to go to Rome (Acts 23:11) and not to Asia Minor. It is necessary to suppose that Paul changed a long-cherished plan, if he had any intention of going from Cæsarea to Colossæ (Philemon, ver. 22). But in the event of his liberation at Rome nothing could be more natural than that the long-imprisoned apostle should desire to visit his old fields of labor. Accordingly it seems best to regard Rome as the place from which the epistles to the Ephesians, Colossians and Philemon were written.

In accordance with this result in regard to place the time will have to be fixed at about 62 a.d. Assuming, in agreement with the commonly received chronology, that St. Paul arrived at Rome in the spring of 61, some time would necessarily elapse before his case had developed so far as to create a hope of a speedy acquittal (cf. note on Col. 4:3). Hence it is towards the latter part of the "two whole years," referred to at the conclusion of the book of Acts, that the composition of the epistles to Philemon, the Colossians and also the Ephesians must be assigned.

The Contents. The similarity in contents between the epistles to the Ephesians and to the Colossians is at the first glance very striking. A closer examination reveals that the similarity is in details rather than in general argument. In the latter respect the epistle to the Ephesians exhibits much similarity to that addressed to the Romans. In both epistles St. Paul has given a general statement of his gospel. In Romans the apostle argues that salvation is for Jews and Gentiles alike by faith in Christ. He concludes the doctrinal part of that epistle by showing how the manifestation of salvation was all in accordance with an eternal purpose of God. In Ephesians the same system of ideas is presented, but the order is reversed. Beginning with the eternal purpose of God, the apostle proceeds to show how the Gentiles share with the Jews in salvation through Christ. Although the epistle to the Romans is longer, that to the Ephesians is really more comprehensive in scope, exhibiting Christ in His central position in the revelation of God, and in His universal relations to all things and to the Church in particular, the special sphere of the manifestation of His gracious powers. In this respect there is a close affinity between Ephesians and Colossians. For the latter also presents Christ as the head and centre of all things and of the Church in particular. But it does this with a polemical purpose to counteract certain heresies. A controversial purpose of this kind is entirely wanting in Ephesians. There are also some interesting correspondences between this epistle and 1 Peter.

Literature. In a popular commentary like this it would be beyond the purpose to attempt anything like an exhaustive list of the literature on the book under discussion. The class of readers contemplated in this commentary will be best served by the mention of a few of the best books, which will themselves open the way for those who desire to pursue more extensive studies. It is unnecessary to refer to the well-known lives of St. Paul, or to the valuable articles in Bible dictionaries and other works of reference. On questions pertaining to the time and circumstances of writing this, among the other books of the New Testament, the Introduction to the New Testament by *Weiss* is very instructive.

Commentaries written by Lutherans will of course have to be sought in the theological productions of Germany. Among German commentaries we think conservative Lutherans will find those by the following four writers most satisfactory: *Harless, Meyer, Braune* and *Schnedermann.* The work of *Harless* was first published in 1834, but is still valuable. *Meyer's* reputation is so great that it is in vain to commend him. *Braune* furnished the comments on Ephesians in the later editions of Lange's Bibelwerk. *Schnedermann* wrote the annotations on Ephesians in Strack and Zöckler's commentary on the whole Bible.

The leading English and American commentaries are by Eadie, Ellicott, Alford, Hodge, Fausset and Dale. Among these *Ellicott* deserves special attention for grammatical accuracy. For the ordinary reader no book will serve better to lead into the general thought, the line of argument and the historical situation of this epistle than the Lectures on Ephesians by the recently deceased *Dr. R. W. Dale.* In the Notes on Epistles of St. Paul from Unpublished Commentaries by the late *Bishop Lightfoot* there are some very valuable comments on the first fourteen verses of the epistle.

2

Ephesians 1

The Salutation. 1:1–2

This salutation has the general features of the greetings found in most of St. Paul's epistles, but has a special likeness to the salutation in the epistle to the Colossians.

1. Paul, an apostle of Christ Jesus through the will of God, to the saints which are at Ephesus, and the faithful in Christ Jesus:

Christ Jesus. At the present day this sounds like an inversion of names. But Christ is not a mere personal name. It is a title, and here comes first because the appointing of the apostles was a Messianic function.—**Through the will.** From the stress laid upon the will of God in this epistle (1:5, 9, 11; 5:17; 6:6), it might be supposed that an emphasis was intended on these words here. But a comparison of other epistles (1 Cor. 1:1; 2 Cor. 1:1; Col. 1:1; 1 Tim. 1:1; 2 Tim. 1:1) shows that it was customary for Paul to refer to the source of his apostolic office, both as an expression of gratitude and to assure his readers that he spoke divine truth.—**Saints.** A common designation for Christians in the N. T., expressing the special grace received in Christ. Fellowship with Christ makes saints.—**At Ephesus.** It is doubtful whether Ephesus was originally named in the epistle. (Cf. Introduction.) Those who regard the letter as circular of course think it was not. (See on Col. 4:16.) But then they are perplexed to find a reasonable interpretation of the clause without the mention of some destination. "To the saints which are"—it is in vain that commentators have turned these words in every way to find a satisfactory meaning in them as they thus stand. On the other hand, the supposition that the destination of the epistle was purposely left blank so as to be filled in as it went around, is too artificial to commend itself. Some destination must have been originally named; and if any place was mentioned, the best evidence is in favor of Ephesus.—**In Christ.** The sphere within which the epithets "saints" and "faithful" are applicable to Christians.

2. Grace to you and peace from God our Father and the Lord Jesus Christ.

Grace. In this customary greeting of St. Paul **grace** points to the good-will of God as the source of all blessings.—**Peace.** This describes the condition which results when the grace of God has been received. (See on Col. 1:2.)—**Lord Jesus.** Grace and peace come from Jesus as the Mediator, the Lord to whom all authority has been given (Matt. 28:18).

Praise to God for the Blessings of Salvation.
1:3–14

Summary. Praise to God for His blessings in Christ (3)—this
is the theme of the entire following paragraph, which consists
of a single sentence from the third to the fourteenth verse.
Nevertheless it contains the whole plan of salvation in grand
outline. God's blessings in Christ have their origin in the
election of God before the foundation of the world and their
end in the sanctification of believers (4). The nature of this
election is that God embraced us as adopted sons in the love
which He bore to Jesus Christ, the Beloved (5–6). We are
brought into this relation to Christ through His work of
redemption, which secures for us the forgiveness of sins
(7). God's grace enables us to know and apply this truth
(8) and to understand the grand purpose of God, which is to
bring all things into harmony and unity in Christ (9–10). In
accordance with this great purpose the Jewish Christians
were made a heritage for God's glory (11–12), and the
Christians addressed in the epistle received the Gospel and
the seal of the Holy Spirit as an earnest of a final inheritance,
also to the praise of God's glory (13–14).

3. Blessed *be* the God and Father of our Lord Jesus Christ,
who hath blessed us with every spiritual blessing in the
heavenly *places* in Christ:

Blessed. (Cf. 1 Peter 1:3.) The recurrence of the words
blessed, hath blessed and **blessing** should be observed. To
bless means to speak, wish or do good. Men bless God by
word and thought. God blesses men by act.—**The God and
Father of our Lord.** This formula occurs a number of times
in the N. T. The American Committee on Revision give as

12

a marginal rendering: "God and the Father," a translation to be preferred. God blesses us because He is God, and because He is the Father of our Lord and through Him our Father. However, there can be no objection to the expression: "The God of our Lord Jesus Christ." St. Paul uses it in verse 17.—**Spiritual blessings.** Not those which affect our spirit, but those which spring from the Spirit of God. Both good and evil receive blessings from God, but the spiritual blessings are given only to those in Christ.—**In the heavenly places.** God's blessings in Christ are in the region of the heavenly, the domain of spiritual blessings. The nature of God's blessings is described by the addition of this phrase. They descend from heaven. In the sense of this epistle the true Christian is already in heaven, not his future abode, but the heaven that is within and about him. (Cf. 2:6, 19; Phil. 3:20.) Thus Lightfoot beautifully explains.—**In Christ.** More than through Christ. Union and fellowship with Christ are implied.

4. Even as he chose us in him before the foundation of the world, that we should be holy and without blemish before him in love:

Chose us. (Cf. 1 Peter 1:20.) The apostle proceeds to unfold the blessings of God and begins with their origin. This is not in man's goodness, but in God's goodness—a contrast emphatically stated in ch. 2:9. The full meaning of the word translated **chose** is "chose out for himself," implying that God chose out some persons from among others who were left unchosen. From fear of restricting the universality of God's grace, we may be tempted to diminish the force of this word so as to deprive it of its true sense of election. On the other hand is the danger of approaching the word with the preconception of an absolute predestination, and of

carrying into it the idea of arbitrary selection, which it does
not contain. The emphasis of the word is not to be thrown
on the contrast between those chosen and those not chosen.
The entire stress is to be placed upon the positive idea that
the ultimate source and cause of the blessings of salvation
are solely in the will and election of God. The practical
comforting nature of this truth is excellently brought out
in the Lutheran Confession, as the following quotation from
the Formula of Concord (cf. Book of Concord, Jacob's Trans.,
p. 657) will show: "Therefore this doctrine affords also the
excellent, glorious consolation that God was so solicitous
concerning the conversion, righteousness and salvation of
every Christian, and so faithfully provided therefor, that
before the foundation of the world was laid He deliberated
concerning it, and in His purpose ordained how He would
bring me thereto and preserve me therein. Also, that He
wished to secure my salvation so well and certainly that since,
through the weakness and wickedness of our flesh, it could
easily be lost from our hands, or through craft and might of
the devil and the world be torn or removed therefrom, in
His eternal purpose, which cannot fail or be overthrown, He
ordained it, and placed it for preservation in the almighty
hand of our Saviour Jesus Christ, from which no one can
pluck us (John 10:28)."—**In him.** Christ is the sphere in which
we were chosen. When God framed His eternal purpose
to save the world, that purpose so to speak took shape in
the person and work of Christ, everything else finding its
place from the relation it sustained to Him.—**In Christ** thus
denotes the source from which the election and salvation of
God proceed to us. Not because we were in Christ were we
chosen, but in Him is the ground of our election, the power

14

of our salvation and the order in accordance with which we are chosen.—**That we should be holy.** The purpose of the election. It is a question whether this refers to Christ's holiness imputed to us (our justification) or to the holiness which we are to attain by God's grace (our sanctification). Harless argues earnestly for the former view, and Meyer defends the same opinion. But there is such an implication of moral condition in the words **holy and without blemish** that in this and similar passages (5:27; Col. 1:22) the reference to our sanctification seems preferable. As Lightfoot points out, there is a sacrificial metaphor here. **Holy** denotes the consecration, **without blemish** the fitness of the victim for this consecration. (Cf. Rom. 12:1.)—**In love.** Observe the marginal rendering of the R. V., which connects this with the following participle, **having foreordained.** If it is not so connected, it should be joined with **chose** and not with **holy and without blemish.** It is not man's love but God's love which is meant, and which the apostle is making prominent in the entire paragraph.

5. Having foreordained us unto adoption as sons through Jesus Christ unto himself, according to the good pleasure of his will,

Foreordained. The election is carried forward in the form of a decree or regulation made before the foundation of the world. This is the sense of the word **foreordained.** There is more emphatic reference in this word than in the word **chose** to the end for which the election was made. That end is here declared to be the **adoption as sons.—Through Jesus Christ.** All the purposes of God proceed through Christ as the Mediator between God and men. He is God's only son, and God knows no son except in Him. Others can be included

15

in the filial relation only by adoption through Christ (Rom. 8:16).—**The good pleasure of his will.** This expression does not merely assert the unlimited freedom of God's will. It is true that God was determined solely from within Himself to save man, and not by the merit of human works. But the word **will,** which denotes the mere power of volition, is here qualified by **good pleasure,** which refers to the content of the decision of the will as something good. Hence it is not only the freedom but the grace of God's will which we find in the expression.

6. To the praise of the glory of his grace, which he freely bestowed on us in the Beloved:

To the praise, etc. The final end of our predestination. In all of God's blessings two purposes must be distinguished: our good and His glory.—**The glory of his grace.** "The **glory** is not directly termed God's, so far is the author from that view of God's being as the absolute, existing *per se*, from which the Predestinarian view started. Only God's attitude (Verhalten) toward His people is praised, and accordingly in His relation (Verhältniss) to them is **grace** ascribed to Him" (Schendermann).—**Which he freely bestowed.** The marginal rendering is more literal: **Wherewith he endued us.** The verb means "to cause to have grace," namely, God's grace, as is explained in the next verse.—**In the Beloved.** Namely, of God. (Cf. Matt. 3:17; Col. 1:13.) "God, when He gave us His 'Beloved,' gave us all graces with Him" (Lightfoot).

The punctuation of the R. V. correctly indicates the conclusion of a line of thought at the end of verse 6. Having thus explained the origin of God's blessings, the writer proceeds in the next verses to the historical unfolding of God's grace.

7. In whom we have our redemption through his blood,

the forgiveness of our trespasses, according to the riches of his grace,

In whom, etc. Almost the same words in Col. 1:14. Both Ephesians and Colossians treat of the redemption in Christ, the former connecting the doctrine with the gracious will of God, and the latter connecting it with the divine glory of Christ's person.—**Redemption.** Liberation secured by a price or ransom. The price paid for our redemption is indicated in the words: **through his blood.** The idea is sacrificial. Redemption itself is not strictly a sacrificial term, but it easily connects itself with such. (Cf. Rom. 3:24, 25.) The sacrifice removes sin and impurity and thereby delivers from the penalties of sin and impurity. In this way the sacrifice is a means of redemption. The statement in the text is equivalent to that of Christ: "To give his life a ransom for many" (Matt. 20:28). This is shown by a comparison of Lev. 17:11, where atonement is ascribed to the blood, because the life is in it.—**Forgiveness.** The first fruits of the redemption. All other blessings follow this. "Where there is forgiveness of sins, there also is life and salvation" (Luther in the Small Catechism). Forgiveness is in a manner identified with redemption in this place, for forgiveness consists in our redemption from the guilt and punishment of sins. A more complete redemption is mentioned in ver. 14.—**Trespasses.** (See on Col. 1:14.)—**The riches.** "The addition of **riches** we may doubtless explain by the nature of the object, the knowledge of which is disclosed through grace; by that dominion of Christ embracing heaven and earth (cf. ver. 10), the thought of which fills the apostle" (Harless).

8. Which he made to abound toward us in all wisdom and prudence,

Wisdom, Not God's wisdom, but the wisdom which He imparts to men through His Spirit and the Gospel (ver. 17; 3:4, 18). As the writer here combines **wisdom and prudence,** so he combines "wisdom and understanding" in Col. 1:9 and "wisdom and knowledge" in Col. 2:3. All these terms have a moral bearing and not only an intellectual significance. Wisdom is the knowledge of God and His salvation, and as a comprehensive term embraces prudence, understanding and knowledge. **Prudence** here is not simply wisdom applied to practice. That idea is inapplicable to what follows. Prudence denotes a state of mind imbued with wisdom and able to perceive the relation of things to God's truth. Hence the term is closely related to "understanding" as the word is used in Col. 1:9: (See on that passage.)

9. Having made known unto us the mystery of his will, according to his good pleasure which he purposed in him.

Made known unto us. To the apostles, by revelation; to us by the Gospel and the illumination of the Holy Spirit.—**Mystery.** In the N. T. not what is incomprehensible but what is hidden until revealed by God. (See on Col. 1:26.)—**The mystery of his will.** This refers to the purpose of redemption through Christ, the same that is called **the mystery of Christ** in ch. 3:4 and **the mystery of the gospel** in ch. 6:19. "It is Christ as the Great Reconciler, not only of Jew and Gentile, but of heaven and earth" (Lightfoot).—**Good pleasure.** Not only free, but gracious disposition of will. (Cf. note on ver. 5.)—**In him.** Not Christ, but God.

10. Unto a dispensation of the fulness of the times, to sum up all things in Christ, the things in the heavens, and the things upon the earth;

Dispensation. Management such as a housekeeper or

18

steward exercises. "The same metaphor occurs in various relations elsewhere in the New Testament. God is the great 'householder' in not less than five parables (Matt. 13:27; Matt. 20:1, 11; Matt. 21:33; Luke 13:25; Luke 14:21); the Church is the household of God (1 Tim. 3:15; Hebr. 3:2 sq.; 10:21; 1 Peter 4:17); the believers are the members of this household (Eph. 2:19; comp. Gal. 6:10); the ministers are the stewards or dispensers (1 Cor. 4:1 sq.; Tit. 1:7)" (Lightfoot). The connection with the preceding verse should be observed. God purposed His good pleasure unto or with reference to a certain management or arrangement. This arrangement is described as belonging to **the fulness of the times.** The knowledge of Christ and of salvation was given progressively in separate **times,** what we now call dispensations. These times taken together make up a **fulness.** One such fulness is mentioned in Gal. 4:4, when God sent His Son. Whether the present passage refers to that consummation or to the final consummation at the end of the world is difficult to determine. The following clause agrees best with the latter idea.—**Sum up.** This should not be connected with **dispensation,** but with the words **which he purposed** in the preceding verse. The good pleasure which God purposed was to sum up all things, that is, to re-establish universal harmony and unity in Christ. Some suppose that the Greek word used here contains a reference to Christ as **the head over all things,** as this epistle declares Him to be (ver. 22). But this supposition requires that the verb be derived from the Greek noun for "head," which is incorrect. The word simply means to summarize, to recapitulate, just as the summary of a book contains the chief heads. The thought expressed here is that Christ is the summary of

19

all things, rather than their head. It is a mistake to find in
this passage the doctrine of universal restoration, in which
even the fallen spirits are to be redeemed. But there is an
idea of restoration here, namely, the redintegration of the
world from the disturbance of the original order by sin. This
verse is often connected with Col. 1:20 as a parallel, and not
altogether incorrectly. But the difference should be observed.
The phrase **sum up** is more comprehensive than **reconcile**
used in Colossians, and includes it. Christ is the summary
of all things, because in Him universal harmony and unity
are re-established, as explained in Col. 1:16 sq., the one unto
whom all things have been created and in whom all things
consist. All threads of life run together in Christ as a centre.
This summing up is not yet a fully accomplished fact; but
it is being realized in the successive dispensations of God,
and will be completed when in the end all things have been
subjected to Christ. (Cf. ver. 22; 1 Cor. 15:24 sq.)—**All
things.** Not to be limited to persons, but to be taken in
its comprehensive sense.—**The things in heaven,** etc. The
reference is not to angels nor to departed saints. The entire
expression simply denotes the universe. Heaven and earth are
the parts distinguished in the simplest, most natural division
of the world. (Cf. Gen. 1:1; 2 Peter. 3:13.)

11. In him, *I say,* in whom also we were made a heritage,
having been foreordained according to the purpose of him
who worketh all things after the counsel of his will;

Also. To be joined with the relative pronoun or with
the verb, not with the subject **we.** The writer is passing
from the general idea of God's purpose in Christ to its
realization in time. The **also** indicates this progress in the
thought.—**We.** In ver. 12 there is a limiting clause, which

20

indicates that the writer is here speaking of the Jews: **we who had before hoped in Christ.** In contrast with this the Gentiles are described in ver. 13.—**Were made a heritage.** There is much difference of opinion as to the meaning of the Greek word thus translated in the R. V. The word occurs in the N. T. only in this place. Its classical meaning is "to be chosen by lot" or "to obtain by lot." But the idea of a lot is so unsuitable to the purpose of God, described in this connection, that most commentators prefer to discover some other possible explanation. There is a noun of the same root as this verb, which with kindred words is frequently used in Bible language, meaning "inheritance." Assuming that Paul conformed the verb here used to the meaning of this noun, we may find the same thought here which is expressed in Col. 1:12: "Who hath made us meet to be partakers of the inheritance of the saints." In this sense the A. V. has the translation: **Have obtained an inheritance.** Luther's version agrees with this. This interpretation is quite satisfactory, but probably that adopted in the R. V. is to be preferred. According to it there is an allusion here to the O. T. thought expressed in Deut. 4:20 and elsewhere. Israel is called "a people of inheritance" unto God. Taking up this idea Paul says the Jews were thus made a heritage of God in fulfilment of His eternal purpose.

12. To the end that we should be unto the praise of his glory, we who had before hoped in Christ:

Had before hoped. This word plainly means that there was a hope which existed beforehand for something that occurred in the coming of Christ. Hence the only interpretation which is not forced is to refer the phrase to the Jews. Christ was the hope of Israel even though all the Jews did not

21

believe.—**In Christ.** According to the Greek this does not
denote the object toward which hope was exercised, but the
sphere in which the hope was cherished. Ellicott remarks:
"To have hoped **in Christ** was a higher characteristic than to
have directed hope **towards Christ.**" To the faith even of O.
T. believers Christ was not a mere distant future hope, but
a present reality, just as to us Christ is now the judge of the
quick and the dead although the day of judgment is future.
(Cf. 1 Cor. 10:4.)

13. In whom ye also, having heard the word of the truth,
the gospel of your salvation,—in whom, having also believed,
ye were sealed with the Holy Spirit of promise,

In whom ye also. The Gentile readers of the epistle are
now considered in contrast with the Jews. The construction
is irregular, either the verb being implied or the interrupted
construction is resumed in the second **in whom.** In the
former case it is best to supply **were made a heritage.** In the
latter case, and this is preferable, the verb **sealed** expresses
the blessing which the Gentiles received corresponding to
the prerogative of the Jews in being made a heritage of
God.—**The word of the truth.** Something more significant
than **the true word.** Christ is the truth, which is presented
in the word.—**The gospel of your salvation.** In Col. 1:5,
the apostle also joins together in a unity **the word of the
truth of the gospel.** Salvation is effected through the Gospel
as the divinely ordained means of grace.—**Believed.** This
necessarily follows **heard.** The blessings of God are brought
near to all who hear, but are made the possessions of only
those who believe.—**Sealed.** The figure of sealing is used
twice in this epistle and frequently in the N. T. The seal is
the Holy Spirit, because the possession of the gift of the Holy

Spirit is the assurance that we are the adopted sons of God. (Cf. Rom. 8:15; Gal. 4:6.)—**Spirit of promise.** So called because promised in the O. T. and by Christ.

14. Which is an earnest of our inheritance, unto the redemption of *Goa's* own possession, unto the praise of his glory.

Earnest. This like "the first fruits of the Spirit" (Rom. 8:23) is a preliminary gift to impart assurance that more of the same kind will follow. The possession of the Holy Spirit is an evidence that the other possessions intended for God's children will also be given in due time. Bengel has in his terse manner excellently indicated the connection of things discussed here. He says: "Through the word the Holy Spirit had been promised. Therefore when the Holy Spirit was given, those who believed the word were sealed. And those who have the Holy Spirit know that every promise will be fulfilled to them."—**Redemption.** Here as in ch. 4:30, and unlike ver. 7, redemption is represented as something future. Our deliverance from sin is in a certain sense already an accomplished fact through that which Christ has done for us. And yet we wait for the full realization of our liberation from sin and its consequences.—**Possession.** The rendering of the R. V. is a paraphrase rather than a translation of the Greek word here used. There is no word for **God's** in the original. But this explanation which makes the meaning to be **God's own possession,** referring to believers as the people of God, is the best. There is a parallel in 1 Peter 2:9. The Greek noun here used corresponds with the verb in Acts 20:28: "The Church of God which he purchased with his own blood." So here the meaning is the people which God purchased for His own possession.

23

This concludes the discussion of the entire paragraph, verses 3–14. The transcendent importance of this passage demands some general observations in regard to it.

Luther has classed this epistle with the chief writings of the New Testament, "which exhibit Christ to you and teach all that is necessary and blessed for you to know, even if you should never see or hear any other book or doctrine." In this glorious epistle the introductory paragraph is the jewel. The contents of this passage are so rich that it is hardly an exaggeration to say that the whole truth of Christianity is here presented in grand outline from centre to circumference. In all of Paul's letters nothing is more remarkable than the manner in which he here views all things from one centre and contemplates all **in Christ.** This reference is repeated in almost every verse. In ver. 3, it is **in Christ;** ver. 4, **in him;** ver. 6, **in the Beloved;** ver. 7, **in whom;** ver. 10, **in Christ** and **in Him;** ver. 11, **in whom;** ver. 13, **in whom.** So the controlling thought in relation to which everything is considered is Christ, and not an abstract idea of the absolute will or nature of God. Although the range of ideas extends back to **before the foundation of the world,** yet even there the apostle sees all things **in him.** This Christocentric doctrine of St. Paul is of the greatest practical importance. In reading this epistle it must be borne in mind that it is not an abstract theological, much less philosophical discussion of "obstinate questionings about fixed fate, free will, foreknowledge absolute." It is a sad perversion of a passage full of the sweetest consolation and of the highest joy to make it appear in a doubtful light, which only causes uncertainty of mind and anxiety of soul. Bengel rightly remarks that the teaching of this epistle is

24

pathetice exposita, set forth with deep stirrings of emotion. It is not anxious questioning, but reverent, joyful, triumphant contemplation of the wonders of God's grace as revealed in Christ, viewed in their unity and totality as well as in their special applications to God's own people. The apostle wrote not with cool reflection nor quiet abstract reasoning, but with strong pulsations of joy and gratitude, while his gaze was intently fixed upon Christ. In successive waves the combined thought and emotion culminate in the praise of God's glory (ver. 6, 12, 14). The speculations and abstract logical deductions which theologians have connected with this and similar places in the writings of St. Paul are their own, not the apostle's. He does not begin with an abstract conception of God's absolute sovereignty and then reason downward step by step as to what will become of men; but he contemplates and joyfully declares all the glories of divine grace and all the possibilities for a sinful world revealed in Christ. Those seeming contradictions between God's predestination and man's free will evidently did not trouble St. Paul much with Christ before his eyes. In Christ he saw all contradictions vanish; in Him he saw all things reconciled, summed up and harmonized.

Prayer for the Readers of the Epistle. 1:15–23

Summary. The living faith of those addressed is a cause of constant thanksgiving and an occasion for prayer (15, 16). The object of Paul's prayer is the deepening of their knowledge (17), especially of their future hope (18) and of the power of God operative in believers (19). It is the same power of God which effected the resurrection and glorification of

25

Christ, giving Him the supremacy over all things (20, 21),
a headship which Christ exercises in a special manner in
the Church, the body which results from His world-filling
operations (22, 23).

15. For this cause I also, having heard of the faith in the
Lord Jesus which is among you, and which *ye shew* toward
all the saints,

For this cause. (Cf. Col. 1:3, 4.) The blessings described in
the preceding verses are the cause.—**I also.** Presuming that
they themselves gave thanks.—**Having heard.** Nothing can
be inferred from this as to whether the writer was personally
acquainted with the readers or not. Assuming that the letter
was addressed to the Ephesians, it is necessary to understand
him to be speaking of the progress which they made in faith
since his departure from them.—**Faith in the Lord.** The
Lord Jesus was not only the object of their belief, but also its
element. Their faith was grounded in Him. A vital union with
the Lord is implied.—**Which ye shew.** The marginal reading
of the R. V. inserting **the love** is to be preferred. In either
case the practical exercise of faith toward fellow-Christians
is meant.

16. Cease not to give thanks for you, making mention *of
you* in my prayers;

Cease not. (Similarly Col. 1:9.)—**Making mention.** Paul
was more abundant in labors than others, and certainly not
less abundant in prayers. Considering the many churches
and even individuals (Philemon 4) he made mention of, it
is evident that his prayers were very specific and occupied
much of his thought and time.

17. That the God of our Lord Jesus Christ, the Father of
glory, may give unto you a spirit of wisdom and revelation

26

in the knowledge of him;

The God of our Lord Jesus Christ. This is the basis of our relations to God. Jesus Christ is our Lord, and His God is our God. (Cf. John 20:17.) There is no subordination of the eternal Son to the Father implied in this. Each person of the Trinity is God for the other two persons.—**The Father of glory.** Glory is the characteristic quality of God as revealed. When God becomes manifest, that manifestation is glory. The special form of glory to be thought of here is that described in ver. 6, the glory of grace. The believer who through Christ has this Father of glory as his own, may from Him expect glory. (Cf. "riches of the glory of his inheritance" in the next verse.)—**A spirit of wisdom and revelation.** The person of the Holy Spirit is not meant, but that state of the believer which is produced by the imparting of God's Spirit to him. Hence wisdom and revelation are not to be regarded as attributes of the Holy Spirit, but as possessions of the man whom God has blessed. **Revelation** is knowledge of divine truth directly communicated by God. Its addition to the more comprehensive term **wisdom** serves to specify the kind of wisdom meant. The apostle himself enjoyed revelations from God, and he desired that others should receive the same blessing. Nevertheless he was very far from encouraging men to rely upon inner revelations for their knowledge of God, apart from the gospel He preached and taught by word and Scripture while he prayed for the spirit of revelation for others.—**Knowledge of him.** That is, of God, not Christ.

18. Having the eyes of your heart enlightened, that ye may know what is the hope of his calling, what the riches of the glory of his inheritance in the saints,

The eyes of your heart. More than the intellectual

27

faculties. The heart is the life centre. If there is darkness there, the truth of God cannot be perceived. This darkness is the result of a depraved will more than of a deficient understanding. (Cf. 4:18.) The darkness of the heart is sin. Hence **enlightened eyes of the heart** denotes not only an intellectual perception, but a purified spiritual perception, such as indicated in the Lord's words: "Blessed are the pure in heart: for they shall see God."—**May know.** The object to be known is specified in three particulars: a hope, riches, an operation of power.—**The hope of his calling.** The hope which His calling begets in us, not the thing hoped for. God's election in Christ, applied to us through the Gospel, constitutes our **calling.** From this calling springs our hoping. Christians need to learn to hope as well as to love and believe.—**The riches of the glory of his inheritance.** This is the second thing to be known. It properly follows hope, because it is the object hoped for. Certainly it is an object commensurate with the greatest power of hoping the heart can ever attain to. Observe how the apostle heaps up words to express the grandeur of this object. It is an **inheritance.** It is **his** inheritance, that is, it comes from God. It is an inheritance of **glory,** such as "the Father of glory" bestows. The glory is not easily estimated because of its **riches.** The inheritance is future, known chiefly through the hope begotten of God's calling; but at the same time present, because those called have been made partakers of it (Col. 1:12) and have received "an earnest" of it (ver. 14).—**In the saints.** Because the riches just spoken of are in a measure already enjoyed by believers, they are said to be among the saints. The glorious gifts of God are already in the Church. (Cf. 3:16; Col. 1:12; Phil. 4:19.)

28

19. And what the exceeding greatness of his power to us-ward who believe, according to that working of the strength of his might

The exceeding greatness of his power. This is the third particular which the apostle prays may be known. Here is the everlasting foundation on which Christian hope rests. At the basis of all the believer's hopes is God's power or rather separate operations of God's power. For the exceeding greatness of this power is to be perceived as it is displayed in believers and still more in Christ (ver. 20).—**To us-ward.** The change from the second person to the first is significant. The manifestation of God's power might be seen in the readers of the epistle themselves (2:1); but perhaps still more distinctly in the experience of others, notably St. Paul, through whom God wrought so much (Col. 1:29).—**According to.** The connection of the passage beginning thus is variously explained. It is simplest to join it with the preceding clause, but not merely with **believe.** The meaning is not that we believe according to a certain working, but the greatness of God's power toward believers is according to a certain working described in what follows.—**According to** indicates measure. The resurrection of Christ was a signal display of God's power. The greatness of what God is doing towards those who believe is to be estimated by that event and what follows it.—**Working of the strength of his might.** These words trace the operation of God back from the manifestation of His power to its inner source.—**Might** is within; **strength** is might put forth; strength in action is energy or **working.**

20. Which he wrought in Christ, when he raised him from the dead, and made him to sit at his right hand in the heavenly

places,

Wrought in Christ. In the person of Christ God wrought a work which is not limited to that person, but extends to us who believe. The exaltation of Christ is the guarantee or rather the actual beginning of the exaltation of those whose hope is in Him. So the apostle says: "Christ in you, the hope of glory" (Col. 1:27).—**Raised him.** Christ belonged to the category of the dead, but God raised Him out of that class. The quickening power thus displayed continues to act through the living Christ upon those who are dead in sin as well as upon the physically dead. (Cf. 2:5; Col. 2:12; 1 Cor. 15:22.)—**Sit at his right hand.** This refers not to the ascension of Christ, but to His exaltation generally, the fulfilment of the prayer of the Lord given in John 17:5. God's right hand is wherever God is and wherever He reveals Himself. Hence Christ exercises kingly power everywhere. This He does not only according to His divine nature. He sits at the omnipresent right hand of God according to that nature in which He was raised from the dead. In other words, Christ's exaltation belongs to both natures, the human and the divine.—**In the heavenly places.** (Cf. ver. 3.) In this expression the heavenly order of things is contrasted with the earthly order of things. There is no reason to suppose that heavenly places are extensively located in space above or even outside of earthly places.

21. Far above all rule, and authority, and power, and dominion, and every name that is named, not only in this world, but also in that which is to come:

This verse explains the universal sovereignty which belongs to the exalted Christ.—**Rule, authority, power, dominion.** These terms do not designate different orders of angels, for it is impossible to discover a gradation in the list. Angels were undoubtedly prominent in the apostle's thought at this place as in other places, where he uses similar designations. (Cf. 3:10; 6:12; Col. 1:16; Rom. 8:38; 1 Cor. 15:24.) Nevertheless the terms used are general and it is unnecessary to restrict them. The widest reference to anything in the universe that has power, suits best to the leading thought of the supreme and universal exaltation of Christ.—**Every name that is named.** Every name that is given to power of any kind; or better still, more comprehensively, every name that designates anything that exists.—**Not only,** etc. The addition of this phrase makes the preceding clause, if possible, still more comprehensive. The contrast between **this world** and **that which is to come** is not identical with that between earth and heaven. This world denotes the present order of things both on earth and in heavenly places. In the future there will be a new order of the universe. In both worlds, in the present and in the future order, Christ shall have supreme exaltation.

22. And he put all things in subjection under his feet, and gave him to be the head over all things to the church,

And he put, etc. Application of the language of Ps. 8:6 to Christ, as in 1 Cor. 15:27 and Hebr. 2:8. That psalm indeed speaks of man generally, but its utterances only find complete fulfilment in Christ, the second Adam. It becomes manifest in this verse that the exaltation of Christ described in these verses is not one of local transference to a place in heaven, but consists in elevation to a position of supreme authority.—**The head over all things.** Not merely over all persons, but all things in the widest extent, as in ver. 10. The term **head** is not synomymous with ruler. The function of the head is described in ch. 4:16 and Col. 2:19. The head does not merely bear sway. It is the vitalizing and organizing centre of the whole body. As head over all things, all things were created by Christ and consist in Him (Col. 1:16, 17).—**To the church.** The peculiar construction of the sentence must not be resolved into the two ideas that, first, God gave Christ to be head over all things; and secondly, that He gave Him to be head over the Church. The apostle's declaration is that He gave Christ to the Church, and He gave Him in the supreme exaltation over all things described in the preceding verses. More is meant than the idea that the head of all things is also head of the Church. The writer has finished his description of the exaltation of Christ, and now resumes the idea of the power which works among believers (ver. 19). The statement here is that the great power which effected all this glorious and world-wide exaltation of Christ, is in the Church in the person of the Lord. He with His universal power has been given and thus belongs to the Church. Through the Lord the universe is so governed as to redound to the upbuilding of the Church.—**The church.** It consists of those who have been gathered out of the world to be in Christ. In an ancient Greek city the *ekklesia* was the assembly of voters as opposed to the entire population. This *ekklesia* was the essence of the city. In like manner the *ekklesia* or Church of Christ is the quintessence of the world, in which the vital relations of Christ's headship are especially realized.

23. Which is his body, the fulness of him that filleth all in all.

His body. So also Col. 1:18. The term corresponds with **head** in the preceding verse. The same life pulsates through all parts of the body; the same vital principle animates the whole; and this life-principle has its seat and source in the head, Christ.—**The fulness.** The precise meaning of this word is much disputed. The word in its primary signification simply means "that which is filled." From this primary meaning we can easily pass to an idea which corresponds better than any other with the context. That context declares that Christ **filleth all,** and that He is the animating **head.** Then His body, the Church, is that which is filled not only by Him, but with Him. As Christ filleth all things, as He is the head that supplies the body, so He fills the Church and supplies it with the gifts, graces and blessings that come from His person. (Cf. 3:19.)—**That filleth all in all.** Christ is the upholder of all things in all respects. (Cf. Col. 1:16; Hebr. 1:3.) Probably a better translation is: **filleth all things with all.** Christ fills all things, the universe with all that is in it. This world-filling power of the Lord is exercised with special potency in the Church, and herein lie the greatness and the glory of the Church, which the apostle sets forth with glowing fervor in this epistle.

At this point we may ask what has become of the prayer with which the writer began in ver. 17? It has imperceptibly passed over into discussion. And yet it was evidently not lost sight of by the apostle; for in the next chapter he proceeds to make an application to the readers for whom he prayed. The line of thought in the writer's mind was this: he desired his readers to perceive with enlightened eyes the glory of the Church of Christ, so that they might realize the glorious blessings which have come to them in and through this Church.

3

Ephesians 2

New Life freely given in Christ. 2:1–10

Summary.   Those dead through sins (1), being intermingled with the world, governed by the power of evil (2), and thus being by nature children of wrath (3), God in His love and mercy (4) has raised to new life with Christ (5) and exalted with Him (6), in order to exhibit in future worlds His great grace (7). For all salvation is of grace (8). The glory of it is not man's (9), since all human goodness is God's workmanship, effected according to the purpose of God (10).

1. And you *did he quicken*, when ye were dead through your trespasses and sins,

And you. Observe the conjunction.   The connection between this and the preceding paragraph is the very closest. The writer does not begin a new thought. He merely carries forward the thought he has been presenting to its application to the readers.—**Did he quicken.** This verb is not found in the original, but is properly supplied in the English version from ver. 5, where it occurs after the interrupted construction of the sentence is resumed. But the connection with what precedes is so close that it might easily have been supplied from ch. 1:20: "When He raised Him from the dead."—**Ye were dead.** Separated from God, the source of life. Death is first spiritual, then bodily, finally eternal. The new life comes in the same order, first spiritual resurrection, then resurrection of the body, finally life eternal.—**Through your trespasses and sins.** (Cf. Col. 2:13.) The means by which death is brought about are here denoted. The A. V. omits **your** before trespasses. This pronoun is not emphatic, but it is significant. Your trespasses and not another's are the means of your death. Whatever the connection between our death and Adam's sin may be, that connection is made effective through our own sins.

2. Wherein aforetime ye walked according to the course of this world, according to the prince of the power of the air, of the spirit that now worketh in the sons of disobedience;

Ye walked. This term denotes not merely separate outward acts, but an inner moral state as well.—**The course.** The Greek word is the same as that translated **world** in ch. 1:21. It strictly means "age," but expresses not only time but moral quality, the living which belongs to the age.—**The course of this world.** The present order of things in implied contrast with a future order.—**The prince of the power of the air.** (Cf. Col. 1:13.) Looking below the surface of things, it is found that an invisible **power** determines the moral character of the world. This power is not a single person, but a host; for the word in the original is a collective term. At the head of this host is a personal leader or **prince.**

35

The power has its abode about the world, for it does not belong to the mundane order of things. (Cf. 6:12.) Hence it is said to be **of the air—of the spirit.** Not a personal spirit; for the word is not in apposition with **prince** (as might be supposed from the English version), but with **power.** The supermundane nature of this power was described in the words **of the air;** now the power is also described as to the quality in which it is manifested in the world, its spirit, its animating principle. The spirit can be seen in its workings in the sons of disobedience.—**Now worketh.** In contrast with **aforetime ye walked.** The spirit no longer worked in those obedient to the faith.—**Sons of disobedience.** So also 5:6 and Col. 3:6. **Sons** used figuratively does not signify descent or origin, but the class. Those whose actions spring from a certain source, those who belong to a certain class are sons. The class here spoken of are characterized by **disobedience.** This is to be understood with reference to the Gospel, and not only the general laws of God. It is contrary to **the obedience of faith** (Rom. 1:5), as a comparison of Rom. 11:30 shows. Unbelief is the animating principle of the sons of disobedience. The apostle does not refer to the grossly immoral Gentiles as opposed to the more moral, but to the Gentiles and Jews generally as opposed to those quickened with Christ.

3. Among whom we also all once lived in the lusts of our flesh, doing the desires of the flesh and of the mind, and were by nature children of wrath, even as the rest:

We also. The Jews including the writer.—**The lusts of our flesh.** Whatever difference there may have been between Jews and Gentiles in regard to the forms of vice, they were all alike as to the **lusts. Flesh** denotes man both as to body and soul, as separated from the spirit, which is of God. **Lusts** are the desires and appetites which spring from such flesh. Lusts accordingly are those impulses which tend away from God instead of towards Him.—**Doing the desires.** The lusts of the flesh are manifested in certain doings which spring from desires or movements of the will.—**Mind.** Literally **thoughts.** The flesh, embracing both body and soul, really includes the thoughts. But the latter, especially through the imagination, are such a direct source of desires that they receive special mention.—**By nature children of wrath.** The **wrath** is that of God.—**Children of wrath** are those who belong to the class to whom wrath is applicable. They are not only liable to wrath in the future, but are now under wrath. In the words **children of wrath** by themselves nothing is implied as to origin, as if the expression meant that by birth we belong to wrath. But the addition of **by nature** introduces that idea. Here it limits the sphere in which the assertion **were children of wrath** is true. Taken absolutely without this limitation the assertion was not true of the Jews. The fact that they were the people of God with the hope of the Messiah altered their case. But **by nature** the Jews were **even as the rest,**—Nature is opposed to grace (ver. 5). In the state prior to grace, the state in which we were from birth, we were children of wrath. How we came to be in this condition is not stated. Hence there is no direct reference to original, hereditary sin here. But the doctrine of the universal condition of sinfulness is found in this verse, and that doctrine logically presupposes original sin.

4. But God, being rich in mercy, for his great love wherewith he loved us,

His great love. There was nothing lovable in those who

were dead through sins. God was moved by His love alone
to quicken them.

5.   Even when we were dead through our trespasses,
quickened us together with Christ (by grace have ye been
saved),

Quickened us, etc. This is more than being quickened like
Christ. We have here a profound thought which St. Paul
expresses in a number of instances (Col. 2:13; Rom. 6:4–6).
The processes by which a man is renewed through Christ
are not merely moral, giving instruction and prompting to
imitation, but vital. The energies which are active in the
person of Christ continue to act in the persons of those who
become united with Him. When God raised Christ from
the dead (1:20), He potentially quickened all believers. All
that remains is that the act should work out its effects in
mankind. But the effects are accomplished by the operation
of the same energies that were in Christ at His resurrection
and are still in Him. Our new life is already an accomplished
fact in Christ, "who is the beginning, the first-born from
the dead" (Col. 1:18); it is also accomplished in us when we
appropriate what is in Christ by faith.—**By grace have ye
been saved.** In passing, the apostle calls attention to the
fact that all this glory comes in accordance with his central
doctrine, salvation by grace.

6. And raised us up with him and made us to sit with him
in the heavenly *places*, in Christ Jesus:

Raised us up. As in the case of Christ, vivification was a
distinct act from resurrection, so in the believer quickening
precedes resurrection.—**In heavenly places.** The believer's
life, like that of his Lord, belongs to the order of things
peculiar to the heavenly world (Col. 3:1–3; Phil. 3:20).

7. That in the ages to come he might show the exceeding riches of his grace in kindness toward us in Christ Jesus:

The ages to come. Beginning with Christ's resurrection and extending into the ages of ages.—**The exceeding riches.** What the marvellous abundance of God's grace is, no man will realize until it is manifested in the light of eternity.—**In kindness toward us.** Again the apostle repeats the motive of God in salvation.

8. For by grace have ye been saved through faith; and that not of yourselves:

By grace, etc. **Grace** is God's means to save. **Faith** is man's instrument to obtain salvation. Although faith is our act, our holding power on Christ, it too is a part of the riches of grace which God made to abound towards us. "I cannot by my own reason or strength believe in Jesus Christ" (Luther in the Small Catechism).—**Faith.** On this important word Harless has some discriminating remarks which are reproduced here in substance. Faith stands in contrast with sight (2 Cor. 5:7). The name is adapted to the character of its object, which is "things not seen" (Heb. 11:1). It has this object in common with hope (Rom. 8:24.) Christian faith is essentially different from human faith with its uncertainties, because it is an effect of the Holy Spirit (Gal. 5:5; 1 Cor. 12:9; Rom. 12:3); and because it is belief in certain, divinely revealed truth (Rom. 10:17; Col. 1:5; 2 Thess. 2:13).—**That not of yourselves. That** points not to faith (as might be supposed from the English version), but to the main subject discussed, which is salvation. The same remark applies to the next words: **It is the gift of God.**

9. *It is* the gift of God: not of works, that no man should glory.

Not of works. Salvation includes work, as the next verse shows, but as an effect, not as a cause.—**That no man,** etc. God's purpose is that He alone should obtain the glory of salvation. (Cf. 1:6, 12.)

10. For we are his workmanship, created in Christ Jesus for good works, which God afore prepared that we should walk in them.

His workmanship. So far from our salvation being our own work, we ourselves are God's work.—**Created in Christ Jesus.** The time of this creation was not at the beginning of the world, but in our resurrection with Christ. (Cf. 2 Cor. 5:17.)—**For good works.** The end for which we are regenerated.—**Which God afore prepared.** There is a reference here to the eternal purpose of God. The end appointed for believers is holiness (1:4). Good works were foreordained as the sphere in which the regenerate should walk. According to the course of the world, men walk in trespasses and sins (ver. 2); according to God's purpose in Christ, believers walk in good works.

Unity between Jews and Gentiles and Peace with God
through Christ. 2:11–22

Summary. The former condition of the Gentiles was one of separation from God and His covenant (11–12). This separation has been abolished in Christ (13), who removed the division between Jews and Gentiles and made peace with God for both (14–15) by His atoning death (16), which is preached to both alike (17), so that both have access to God together (18). Accordingly the former condition of the Gentiles has been changed into fellowship with God (19) by their faith in Christ, as taught by apostles and prophets (20), whereby they were incorporated into the spiritual temple of

God (21–22).

11. Wherefore remember, that aforetime ye, the Gentiles in the flesh, who are called Uncircumcision by that which is called Circumcision in the flesh, made by hands;

Wherefore. In view of the blessings just described in ver. 1–10.—**Remember.** The memory of their former state of misery would increase their appreciation of their present blessed state.—**The Gentiles in the flesh.** This verse must be interpreted in accordance with the general argument of the passage, which is evidently intended to show how the Gentiles were inferior in advantages to the Jews, but became equal to them through Christ. The words **in the flesh** therefore signify more than mere natural condition. They imply that the Gentiles did not belong to God's covenant, not having its mark in their flesh like the Jews.—**Called Uncircumcision.** Circumcision and Uncircumcision were distinctive names for Jews and Gentiles, and are so intended by St. Paul. But the Jews spoke of the Gentiles contemptuously as the uncircumcised.—**In the flesh, made by hands.** There was no reason for the contempt of the Jews, because their outward circumcision was also in the flesh. It belonged to the domain of the flesh. The advantage of the Jews, which was real, was in the inner circumcision (Rom. 2:28; Phil. 3:3)

12. That ye were at that time separate from Christ, alienated from the commonwealth of Israel, and strangers from the covenants of the promise, having no hope and without God in the world.

Separate from Christ. (Cf. 1 Peter 2:10.) The Gentiles had no hope of the coming Messiah as the Jews had.—**Alienated.** They became such "because knowing God, they glorified him not as God" (Rom. 1:21; Col. 1:21).—**The**

41

commonwealth of Israel. Not the Jewish state. **Israel** has a theocratic, spiritual meaning. It is not "the circumcision in the flesh," but "the Israel of God" (Gal. 3:3; Rom. 9:6). The advantage of the Jew over the Gentile is fully recognized in the use of this name.—**Strangers.** The covenant was framed not to exclude, but include Gentiles. But these having become alienated, made themselves strangers not belonging to God's covenant.—**The covenants of the promise.** The promise is that given to Abraham (Gen. 12:2). The covenants are spoken of in the plural number because the promise was renewed to Isaac and Jacob.—**Having no hope.** The mention of "the promise" suggests a special reference to the Messianic hope. But the phrase ought not to be so limited. The misery of the Gentiles was that they had no hope for the future in general.—**Without God.** More than mere ignorance of God, that is, the true God. Without God means the opposite not only of knowing God, but also of being known by Him (Gal. 4:9). Luther in the Large Catechism, in explanation of the first commandment, says: "What is it to have a God? or what is God? Answer: A God is that whereto we are to look for all good and to take refuge in all distress; so that to have a God is to trust and believe Him from the whole heart; as I have often said that the confidence and faith of the heart alone make both God and an idol."—**In the world.** This completes the desolateness here depicted. The world is out of God lying in wickedness, and those in it are utterly estranged from God.

13. But now in Christ Jesus ye that once were far off are made nigh in the blood of Christ.

Now. Very emphatic.—**In Christ.** The condition "separate from Christ" has been exchanged for a state "in Christ."—**Made nigh.** To God. Equivalent to "reconciled" in

Col. 1:21.—**In the blood of Christ.** The means of bringing the Gentiles near to God. The **blood** is used in a sacrificial sense. We are reconciled to God by the atonement effected by Christ's blood shed as a sacrifice for our sins. (Cf. Hebr. 9:12.)

14. For he is our peace, who made both one, and brake down the middle wall of partition,

He is our peace. The emphasis is on **he,** not on peace. In His person Christ is our peace, for our peace was made in His own body. (Cf. ver. 16; Col. 1:22; 1 Peter 2:24.) Does this mean peace with God or peace between Jews and Gentiles? Both ideas are to be found here, the latter being based upon the former. The general line of thought is not that the Gentiles were "made nigh" to the Jews, nor that the two classes were caused to meet on middle ground; but both were brought near to God through the atonement of Christ, and thereby all enmity between them ceased. Christ became the peace between Jews and Gentiles by becoming first the peace of both with God. This twofold sense in which Christ is called "our peace" is further explained in the following verses in this order: first, the peace between Jews and Gentiles (14–15); secondly, the peace of both with God (16–18).—**Who made both one.** The **both,** as the next words show, are not God and man, but Jews and Gentiles.—**Middle wall of partition.** If there is any allusion to anything in the structure of the temple, it is not very distinct. The figure is so natural that it is unnecessary to trace any special allusion to some particular object in it.

15. Having abolished in his flesh the enmity, *even* the law of commandments *contained* in ordinances; that he might create in himself of the twain one new man, *so* making peace;

In his flesh. In Col. 1:22 more explicitly "in the body of
his flesh through death." By His atoning death Christ made
the cause of enmity between Jews and Gentiles of no effect.
For from that time "neither is circumcision anything, nor
uncircumcision, but a new creature" (Gal. 6:15).—**The law
of commandments contained in ordinances.** This is the
root of the enmity. Not the law itself, for it is good, but the law
externally considered as made up of separate commandments,
which imposed outward ordinances without being attended
with the fulfilling spirit. In this sense the law was the cause
of separation between God and man. It made demands, but
did not give the spirit which secured the fulfilment of them.
This separation from God was the real cause of the enmity
between Jews and Gentiles. Those who love God and thus
fulfil the law are not at enmity with others.—**Of the twain.**
Jew and Gentile. Peace was made not by making Jews out of
the Gentiles (so some Jewish Christians erroneously thought),
much less the reverse; but by making something new, namely
Christians, out of both.—**New man.** A new life as opposed
to the former life of sin, a life wrought by the Holy Spirit.
Hence a life of holiness and spirituality. (Cf. 4:24; Col. 3:10;
Gal. 6:15.)—**In himself.** In Christ's person the old man of
sin and enmity died when Christ was crucified, and the new
man of righteousness and peace was created. The cross was
the potential beginning of all new life (Gal. 2:20).—**Making
peace.** Christ being in His own person our peace with God,
is the peace maker between men.

16. And might reconcile them both in one body unto God
through the cross, having slain the enmity thereby:

Reconcile them. The writer now takes up the primary
point in the peace-making of Christ, namely, with God, of

which the peace between Jew and Gentile was the consequence. The Greek word for **reconcile** in this place is an intensive compound, denoting complete reconciliation. It is characteristic of the language of the New Testament that it never speaks of reconciling God or God being reconciled, but only of man being reconciled and God reconciling. The reason for this usage is by no means that reconciliation is only a change of attitude on the part of man, as if his alienation from God were only a misconception of God's disposition towards him. The enmity of sin is real both on the side of God and of man, and Christ's atoning death was a real atonement, doing enough to satisfy God's demands and to counteract the sins of men. The reason for the peculiar usage of the New Testament, which never makes God the person to be reconciled, arises from the fact that the reconciliation originates with God. He was in Christ reconciling. Even in the Old Testament the sacrifices were God's appointment to show that He provided the way of approach to Himself for man. God is not appeased, as the heathen think their gods are appeased, through gifts and sacrifices. Men cannot win God's favor by their works. God's wrath against sin belongs to His eternal righteousness. That wrath is expressed in His law. From love God changes the relation of men to Him as under the law, by including them (if they will) in the object of His immutable love, Christ, who blotted out the bond that was contrary to us (Col. 1:14). This is the reconciliation.—**In one body.** Not the Church, but Christ's crucified body.—**The cross.** Brief for the death on the cross.—**Having slain the enmity thereby.** The enmity is that between man and God. This enmity, the expression of which was the law, Christ nailed to the cross in His own person and slew by His own

45

death. By making peace through His vicarious death the
enmity was slain.—**Thereby** means by the cross. Some prefer
to translate **in himself** instead of **thereby.**

17. And he came and preached peace to you that were far
off and peace to them that were nigh:

And he came. The grammatical connection of this verse is
with the words **he is our peace** in verse 14. Christ's work of
peace was completed by its announcement and application to
those in need of it. This work was done through the apostles
and other witnesses of Christ. The words **he came** cannot
refer to the incarnation, nor to the resurrection, nor to the
outpouring on Pentecost. Christ came through the Spirit to
those who heard the Gospel and accepted its peace. "Not
only according to John (14:18), but also according to Paul,
Christ Himself came from heaven in the Holy Spirit (since
He is the Spirit of Christ) to those who received the Spirit,
and dwells and rules in them" (Meyer).

18. For through him we both have our access in one Spirit
unto the Father.

This verse gives the proof of the announcement of peace
to both Jews and Gentiles. Both have the one Holy Spirit
and freedom of approach to God through Him. The three
persons of the Trinity are brought together here, as is not
uncommon in the epistles of St. Paul. **Through** Christ as
Mediator, **in** the Holy Spirit as the element of our new life,
we come **unto** the Father.—**In one Spirit.** Not in one mind,
but the one Holy Spirit.

19. So then ye are no more strangers and sojourners, but
ye are fellow-citizens with the saints, and of the household
of God,

Strangers and sojourners. This verse points back to

verse 12, but it is not a mere repetition. There the apostle was speaking of the Old Testament privileges belonging to the commonwealth of Israel; here he is speaking of the kingdom of God as it has come through Christ. In respect to this kingdom they had been **strangers** without citizenship, and **sojourners** without rights and privileges. But the announcement of the peace of Christ had changed that.—**Fellow-citizens with the saints.** Not the saints of the O. T., but of the kingdom of Christ. The thought is the same as in Col. 1:12.—**Of the household of God.** (Cf. Gal. 6:10.) The figure of speech is changed from a city with its citizens to a family.

20. Being built upon the foundation of the apostles and prophets, Christ Jesus himself being the chief corner stone;

Being built. (Cf. Col. 2:7; 1 Peter 2:5.) Again the figure of speech is modified from a household to a house, in which believers are the "living stones" (1 Peter 2:5).—**The foundation of apostles and prophets.** Not the persons, but the preaching of the apostles and prophets, constitutes the foundation. The close connection of prophets with apostles and the order of the words indicates that N. T. prophets are meant, and probably but one class of persons is denoted by the two terms. For the apostles were also prophets, bringing promises to those who heard their message.—**The chief corner stone.** In 1 Cor. 3:11 Christ is called the foundation. The figure is different here. The foundation has already been designated, and Christ is something higher than that foundation. The corner stone determines how the walls of the building are to come together. Christ is the regulating principle determining how all the parts of the house are to be "fitly framed together." (Cf. note on the word **head,** ch.

1:22.)

21. In whom each several building, fitly framed together, groweth into a holy temple in the Lord;

In whom. Not equivalent to upon whom. For the antecedent is not corner stone, but Christ Jesus. This phrase is not figurative, but expresses a reality like **in the Lord** at the end of the verse. By faith Christians are in Christ Jesus. In this relation of union with Him Christian growth and edification progresses.—**Each several building.** The translation of the A. V. is simpler: **all the building.** But the Greek requires the more difficult translation: **every building.** Possibly the reference is to every separate congregation, but it is better to think of individuals. The idea presented is a complex one. Every Christian is a temple (1 Cor. 3:16; 6:19), and at the same time a part of the great temple, the Church.—**Fitly framed together.** The same word once more in 4:16. We may not be able to picture to ourselves the form of the building here described; but the thought is clear. It must be borne in mind that the building and growth here discussed are not outward, but inward and intensive. The more completely any believer has become a temple of God, the more fitly framed is he to join together with others in the Lord. The building of the body of Christ is effected in separate individual souls.—**Groweth.** As a living thing it grows. In Col. 2:7 the apostle also combines the ideas of growing and building.

22. In whom ye also are builded together for a habitation of God in the Spirit.

Ye also. Application of the foregoing truths to the readers. They also are in Christ and in the Church.—**Habitation of God.** The readers are considered individually. God dwells in each one.—**In the Spirit.** The Holy Spirit is meant. He is the sphere or element in which they become a habitation of God. All of God's gracious operations come to us through the Holy Spirit, and when this Spirit abides in us, we abide in Him. (Cf. Rom. 8:9; 1 Cor. 3:16.)

4

Ephesians 3

The Apostle's Ministry to the Gentiles. 3:1–13

Summary. Paul, a prisoner for preaching the Gospel to the Gentiles (1), desires that the readers of the epistle should understand *his* ministry to the Gentiles, committed to him by revelation (2–4). The mystery, revealed now as never before, that the Gentiles participate in the blessings of Christ, was entrusted by special grace to St. Paul (5–7). Unworthy as he deemed himself, it was still his privilege to preach the riches of Christ to the Gentiles, yea, to all men (8–9), so that the manifold wisdom of God should be displayed to the heavenly world (10), in fulfilment of God's eternal purpose in Christ (11), faith in whom gives confidence to approach God (12). The apostle's tribulations should not be a discouragement, since they are an honor to those whose apostle he is (13).

1. For this cause I Paul, the prisoner of Christ Jesus in behalf of you Gentiles,—

For this cause. That given in the verses immediately preceding.—**Paul.** His name had weight and carried authority with it.—**The prisoner of Christ.** (Cf. 4:1; Philemon 1 and 9.) Many think the apostle means that it was really Christ who held him prisoner. We prefer to find here the simpler idea that as a prisoner as well as in all other relations of life the apostle belonged to Christ. Whether at this time he was at Cæsarea or at Rome is a question which we have felt constrained to decide in favor of Rome. (See the Introduction.)—**In behalf of you Gentiles.** His ministry among the Gentiles was the particular cause of his imprisonment. (Cf. Acts 21:28.)

The grammatical construction is now interrupted. Various explanations have been offered to connect this verse with what follows. The easiest from a grammatical point of view is to supply the verb "am" before **prisoner.** But it makes no good sense to say that Paul was a prisoner because the Gentiles became a habitation of God, as this explanation requires. The interpretation most generally received makes the whole passage from ver. 2–13 an afterthought and parenthesis, the regular construction being resumed in ver. 14. But this also is unsatisfactory. Apart from the great length of the parenthesis thus obtained, the contents of ver. 2–13 are too important, too essential a part of the whole epistle, to be an afterthought. Hence we prefer to regard the construction as a true anacoluthon; that is, the construction is broken and its continuity is not resumed. There is, however, a logical connection which binds this paragraph with the general argument of the epistle. Paul desires his readers to appreciate the ministry which has been committed to him, the apostle of the Gentiles, since their place in the kingdom of God depends upon the truth of the gospel which he preached.

2. If so be that ye have heard of the dispensation of that
grace of God which was given me to you-ward;

If so be, etc. Not that they only knew of Paul's ministry
by hearsay, if at all. **If so** indicates not doubt, but on the
contrary emphatic certainty. This is, as Ellicott says, a "gentle
appeal expressed in hypothetical form and conveying the
hope that his words had not been quite forgotten." (Cf. 4:21;
Col. 1:23.)—**Dispensation.** (Cf. Col. 1:25.)—**Stewardship,**
as in the margin of the R. V., is better. Luther translates **Amt,**
office. As a steward (1 Cor. 4:1; Titus. 1:7; 1 Peter 4:10) he
has to dispense grace.—**That grace of God.** A possession
which, as the writer adds, **was given** to him to apply it for
the benefit of the Gentiles.

3. How that by revelation was made known unto me the
mystery as I wrote afore in few words,

By revelation. Their confidence in God was to be remembering that the gospel of their apostle came by revelation,
and not from any secondary source. (Cf. Gal. 1:12.)—**The
mystery.** That stated in ver. 6.—**As I wrote before.** In the
preceding chapters of this epistle.

4. Whereby, when ye read, ye can perceive my understanding in the mystery of Christ;

Ye can perceive. The apostle thus expects independent
judgment on the part of his readers.—**My understanding.**
This epistle is designed to strengthen their confidence in him
as their apostle. What they read here would confirm what
they had previously learned from him.—**The mystery of
Christ.**—The Lord Himself is the mystery. (Cf. Col. 2:2.)

5. Which in other generations was not made known unto
the sons of men, as it hath now been revealed unto his holy
apostles and prophets in the Spirit;

Which. Refers to **mystery.—Other generations.** Expression of time in contrast with **now.—Not made known.** Comparatively, not absolutely. For in a certain manner the mystery of Christ was revealed in the O. T., and St. Paul himself argues the truth of his gospel from it. But the kind and degree of knowledge were not such **as hath now been revealed.—The sons of men.** A peculiar expression not uncommon in the O. T., but rare in the N. T., denoting man in his actual, natural, imperfect state. F. W. Schultz remarks on Ps. 8:5: *"Ben-adam* (son of man) the man of reality as distinguished from *adam* (man) the ideal man." Imperfect mankind is here contrasted with the holy character of the apostles and prophets.—**Holy.** By their office and the inspiration of the Holy Spirit.—**Prophets.** Of the N. T., as in 2:20.—**In the Spirit.** This describes the manner in which it hath been revealed: not merely through the Spirit as the instrument, but the apostles and prophets were located (so to speak) in the Holy Spirit, so that they spoke out from Him.

6. *To-wit,* that the Gentiles are fellow-heirs and fellow-members of the body, and fellow-partakers of the promise in Christ Jesus through the gospel,

That the Gentiles etc. This is the purport of the mystery (ver. 3). Schnedermann has a good analysis of this verse, as follows: "The three members point back, the first to ch. 1:14, 18; the second to ch. 1:23; the third to ch. 1:13; 2:12; and all together to ch. 2:12. The first member [fellow-heirs] emphasizes the relation to future salvation; the second [fellow-members] to the Church, which is already an embodiment of salvation; the third [fellow-partakers] to the word, which from ancient times prepared the way and opened the prospect of salvation. None of the blessings of salvation are withheld from the Gentiles."

7. Whereof I was made a minister, according to the gift of that grace of God which was given me according to the working of his power.

A minister. St. Paul uses three words in speaking of himself as a servant. The word used here and in Col. 1:23 has reference to the work and not to any condition as servile or free. In Rom. 1:1 and other places he uses a word which means bondservant (cf. 6:5), the reference being to the dependence upon the Master. In 1 Cor. 4:1a word is used which denotes an assistant, a subordinate official, such as John Mark was to Paul and Barnabas (Acts 13:5).—**The gift of that grace.** The measure and form of the grace any man receives is his gift. St. Paul tells what his peculiar grace was in ver. 8.—**According to the working of his power.** (Cf. 1:19.) The apostle experienced the working of God's power in his conversion. The grace which was bestowed upon him then made him Christ's apostle.

8. Unto me, who am less than the least of all saints, was this grace given, to preach unto the Gentiles the unsearchable riches of Christ;

Less than the least. Not merely modesty, but a confession of sinfulness. (Cf. 1 Cor. 15:9; 1 Tim. 1:15.)—**The unsearchable riches of Christ.** Not only Christ's grace but also His glory constitute the riches of Christ. This greatness of Christ's glory is one of the special themes of the epistle to the Colossians.

9. And to make all men see what is the dispensation of the mystery which from all ages hath been hid in God who created all things;

Make all men see. Literally "enlighten all." (Cf. 1:18.) This illumination comes by preaching, as the apostle here declares, and not by any direct illumination of the Holy Spirit in the heart without the eternal word.—**All men.** A new feature of St. Paul's ministry. He was the apostle of the Gentiles, but his work was not limited to them. By his gospel he was to enlighten Jews also, so as to make all men, Jews and Gentiles, see the works of God.—**The dispensation.** Not the "stewardship" of Paul, as in ver. 2, but God's "arrangement," as in 1:10. All men were to see how God disposed and regulated events, so that the Gospel came to the Gentiles.—**Which from all ages had been hid.** (Cf. Col. 1:26.) Not absolutely hid, but in comparison with the full revelation of the present, as in ver. 5.—**Who created all things.** Why this reference to creation here? It cannot explain the word **hid.** For although creation is the foundation of all subsequent dispensations of God, it in no way explains why the purposes of God were hidden for a time. Nor will it do to regard this clause as establishing the connection with the next verse, as if the apostle meant to say that God created all things to the intent of making known His manifold wisdom. The connection of ideas is manifestly that the purposes of God were hidden from the beginning, to the intent that now they should be revealed. It is best to regard the clause **who created all things** as an explanation of **dispensation.** At the basis of the entire dispensation lies the act of creation. The plan of redemption is conjoined with that of creation from eternity. "The same Son of God is the Mediator of the creation of the world and the Mediator of the redemption of the world (John 1:3; Hebr. 1:2; Col. 1:20)" (Frank).

10. To the intent that now unto the principalities and the powers in the heavenly *places* might be made known through

55

the church the manifold wisdom of God,

Principalities and powers. (Cf. 1:21.) It is not necessary
to restrict these to the good angels, for the bad angels also
belong to the sphere of the heavenly (6:12). Angels are
capable of an increase of knowledge, and they study the
progress of God's kingdom through the Church. (Cf. Luke
15:10; 1 Cor. 11:10; 1 Peter 1:12.)—**Through the church.**
"The theatre of God's works" (Bengel).—**Manifold wisdom.**
God's revelations are successive, so that each is a fuller display
of the manifold wisdom of God. Especially is this true of the
last revelation which has been given.

11. According to the eternal purpose which he purposed
in Christ Jesus our Lord:

According to, etc. Connect with **might be made
known.—In Christ Jesus our Lord.** (Cf. 1:4.) The purpose
of God was framed in Christ and fulfilled in Him. According
to this purpose God's wisdom is displayed to angels. This
is done through the means of the Church, which consists
of those who belong to Christ and have Him for their Lord.
Through our Lord we are connected with all the glorious
works of God into which angels desire to look (1 Peter 1:12).

12. In whom we have boldness and access in confidence
through our faith in him.

In whom, etc. This is the crowning revelation of God's
wisdom before angels, the preparation of a way by which all,
Jews and Gentiles, could approach Him freely. This way is
through our faith in him. Thus at the conclusion of the
discussion of his ministry the apostle again arrives at the central thought of all his teaching, salvation by faith.—**Boldness.**
Freedom from the constraint of fear. This is produced by the
removal of our guilt through Christ. When our guilt is taken

away we have **boldness,** when our enmity is taken away we have **access in confidence** before God. (Cf. 2:16–18.)

13. Wherefore I ask that ye faint not at my tribulations for you, which are your glory.

Wherefore. In view of the greatness of his ministry, set forth in ver. 1–12, the apostle requests them not to be discouraged at his distressful condition. The comfort of his readers depended upon the truth of his ministry; but the state of the apostle as a prisoner might appear contradictory to the truth of his calling. It might be supposed that if he was God's chosen instrument, the Lord would release him more speedily. This verse anticipates any such doubts.—**Ask that ye faint not.** The object of **ask** and the subject of **faint** are both omitted in the Greek text, and there is some uncertainty as to the way they are to be supplied. Some expositors make "God" the object of **ask,** and others "you"; again, some make "I," and others "you," the subject of **faint.** If we translate "I ask God" in the first clause, there is hardly any doubt that we must translate "I faint not" in the second clause. But we prefer not to believe that the apostle had any doubts about his own constancy, and therefore prays to God in his own behalf to keep him from growing faint under his trials. We think it more probable that the apostle had fears for his readers lest they should become discouraged on account of his afflictions. Hence we prefer the translation: "I ask you that ye faint not." The confidence of the readers of the epistle was to be built on his divine call and not on his personal experiences; although the adversities he endured, properly viewed, were not a disproof of his divine vocation, but rather a confirmation of it. (Cf. 2 Tim. 1:8.)—**Which are your glory.** The grammatical construction is irregular in that it does not clearly indicate

57

what is the antecedent of the relative pronoun **which.** This
may refer to **faint not,** and the thought that it is their glory
not to faint would not be inappropriate in this connection.
But a better construction is obtained by making **which** refer
to **tribulations.** The tribulations of the apostle, so far from
being a cause for discouragement, were their glory, because
they were "the signs of an apostle." (Cf. 2 Cor. 12:12 and the
entire argument from 11:16–12:10 in that epistle.)

A Prayer for the Readers of the Epistle and a Doxology. 3:14–21

Summary. A prayer to the true Father (14, 15) for two gifts:
first, spiritual strengthening (16); secondly, the indwelling
of Christ (17). These gifts are to establish them in love and
further them in knowledge (18), especially in the knowledge
of the love of Christ, with a view to their final perfection (19).

The doxology ascribes to God, the mighty worker of all the
wondrous blessings described in the epistle (20), glory in the
Church and in Christ forever (21).

14. For this cause I bow my knees unto the Father,

For this cause. Not a resumption of ver. 1, as some take
it. (Cf. note on that verse.) The reference is to the preceding
verse, or to the entire preceding paragraph. **Bow my knees.**
Representation of the attitude of prayer.

15. From whom every family in heaven and on earth is
named,

Every family. The translation **fatherhood** must be excluded, because the word does not have that meaning. It
signifies "family, tribe." (Cf. Luke 2:4; Acts 3:25.) But
the etymological connection between the Greek words for

58

"family" and "father" is of importance here. Every family, says the apostle, receives its name from the Father, and this is indicated by the Greek words themselves. The relation of names expresses a relation of facts here. God is the true Father to every family, loving it and caring for it. How is he the Father? Not through creation, but through the new creation in Christ (cf. 2:10). Hence **every family** does not denote all tribes of men, but every group and community of God's children. The apostle is not uttering anything like the idea of Pope's Universal Prayer:

"Father of all! in every age,

In every clime ador'd,

By saint, by savage, and by sage,

Jehovah, Jove, or Lord!"

He is not speaking of a universal fatherhood of God over all creatures, but of the special fatherhood over the sons adopted through Jesus Christ unto Himself; in other words, over every part of the Church, on earth and in heaven. If now God cares for every family as Father, He also cares for that family for which the apostle is praying here. It is with this Christian confidence in the Father that he makes his prayer.

16. That he would grant you, according to the riches of his glory, that ye may be strengthened with power through his Spirit in the inward man;

According to the riches. (Cf. 1:7; 2:4, 7.) "The large ransom paid for our redemption is a measure of the wealth of God's bounty" (Lightfoot).—**His glory.** This includes not only His power, but the whole complex of God's perfections.—**That ye may be strengthened.** The first gift prayed for. It is assumed that they already have the beginnings of faith. These, are to develop into perfection. St. Paul's idea of

59

a Christian was not that he should have just enough religion
to admit him to heaven. He desired to see a constant increase
of spiritual life in his converts. His prayers in this respect
present an example which should be an incentive to Christian
pastors to pray not only for the conversion of men, but for the
growth and strengthening of those already converted. **With
power.** Not the means, but the mode of the strengthening.
He prayed for a mighty strengthening. The means are
expressed in the words **through his Spirit.** The Spirit's
strength is the only strength the Christian has. In all stages of
his life his confession is that of the Small Catechism of Luther:
"I believe that I cannot by my own reason or strength believe
in Jesus Christ my Lord, or come to Him; but the Holy Ghost
has called me through the Gospel, enlightened me by His
gifts, and sanctified and preserved me in the true faith."—**In
the inward man.** The Greek preposition signifies "into,"
thus denoting the direction of the strengthening. God's
Spirit, coming from without, penetrates into the inward man,
carrying His power there. The expression **the inward man**
is not identical with **the new man** (4:24), although somewhat
like it. The new man is the regenerated man. The inward man
does not describe the regenerated man as such, but the part or
sphere within man in which regeneration and all subsequent
operations of grace are effected. (Cf. Rom. 7:22; 2 Cor. 4:16.)

17. That Christ may dwell in your hearts through faith; to
the end that ye, being rooted and grounded in love,

That Christ may dwell, etc. The second gift prayed for.
Where the Holy Spirit is, there is Christ. The indwelling of
Christ, the mystical union as it is often called, is one of the
most comforting realities of Christianity. It should not be
conceived as if Christ were only representatively present in

60

the person of the Holy Spirit. He is personally present in the heart of the believer, so that there is an abiding communion of the believer with his Lord, and the most secret sigh of sorrow or penitence and the most hidden stirring of joy or praise are immediately perceived by him, and need not first be conveyed by the Spirit beyond the skies to Christ. The degree of perfection to which any Christian life has attained is marked by the completeness of this indwelling of Christ.—**To the end that ye,** etc. The designed effect of the gifts, just prayed for, now follows. The grammatical construction is rather irregular; but from this point all until the middle of verse 19 should be combined in one thought, namely, this: By love ye learn the great love of Christ.—**Rooted and grounded.** (Cf. Col. 1:23; 2:7.) The double metaphor expresses firmness, fixedness.—**In love.** Not God's love, but man's love to God is obviously meant. Love is the root and foundation of the Christian life. This by no means conflicts with what is everywhere taught in the Bible of faith as the root and foundation of regenerated life. "Faith worketh by love" (Gal. 5:6). Here love does not denote certain acts or works. In them is not the foundation on which the believer is built up. But underlying the Christian's works is the state or condition of love produced by faith. Herein is the root from which originates the believer's growth; here is the foundation on which his character is built up.

18. May be strong to apprehend with all the saints what is the breadth and length and height and depth,

Strong to apprehend. This strength comes from the Holy Spirit and by the indwelling of Christ, as shown in the verses just preceding. Although the strength referred to is to **apprehend** something, nevertheless its power lies

not in intellectual culture, however valuable this may be
to the Christian, but in love. Here is the one greatest gift
in which all Christians may share and be equal, however
different they may be in other respects. The **strong** Christian
is not he that knows most, nor even he that does most, but
he that loves best.—**With all the saints.** As the power of
apprehension is love, the growth in apprehension will depend
upon the union of believers. A man may pursue knowledge by
himself, but not love. This requires union with all the saints.
There is a knowledge spoken of here, but it is a knowledge
which belongs not to any man by and for himself. It is to
the Church and for it.—**Breadth and length and height
and depth.** Vast dimensions are implied; hence something
extraordinarily great. However, the idea may perhaps be, that
the object should be known on all sides and in all relations,
although this is less likely. But what is the great object
referred to? Perhaps "the mystery," which is the prominent
topic of the whole chapter. But it is not necessary to look far
away for the object implied. It is most easily supplied from
the next clause, **the love of Christ.** The breadth, length,
height and depth of the love which Christ has shown to us,
is an object which demands our greatest strength to know
even as also we are known.

19. And to know the love of Christ which passeth knowledge, that ye may be filled unto all the fulness of God.

To know the love of Christ, etc. A paradox, like 2 Cor.
12:9.

"The love of Jesus, what it is
None but His loved ones know."
Bernhard of Clairvaux.

The love of Christ. Christ's love to us.—**That ye may**

be filled, etc. This is the goal of perfection, and it is set before the Christian to be striven for in this life, and not to be postponed for the life hereafter. The fact that we know that we never will attain to our goal, does not release us from the obligation of constantly moving towards it.—**The fulness of God.** Not the abundance of what God is in His own being, but of what comes from Him to us. Hence this expression signifies the full measure of His gifts, graces and blessings. Of course this is a bounty which no man will ever exhaust in this life, nor even in the life to come. (Cf. note on ch. 1:23.) In the sense of what God is in His own being, "the fulness of the Godhead dwelleth in Christ" (Col. 2:9), but it never will in any other man, not even through the indwelling of Christ.

20. Now unto him that is able to do exceeding abundantly above all that we ask or think, according to the power that worketh in us,

Now, etc. This doxology forms a conclusion to the preceding prayer, and at the same time to the entire first half of the epistle.—**Able to do,** etc. A more literal translation might bring out an idea that does not appear clearly in the rendering of the R. V. The apostle first makes a general declaration of the omnipotence of God: "Able to do above all things." Then he applies this thought to those who pray: "Abundantly beyond what we ask or think." The hindrances to our confidence in God that spring from our own hearts and minds, are overcome by the omnipotence of God.—**The power that worketh in us.** The experience of our own hearts confirms us in our trust in the power of God to do above all things. In ch. 1:19, the apostle already referred to the exceeding greatness of the power that makes us believers. The greatness of the change which is wrought

in the regeneration of a man, points to such a mighty power
as its source, that the Christian should be taught by what he
is, to expect from God everything which is necessary to bring
His new creation to perfection.

21. Unto him *be* the glory in the church and in Christ Jesus
unto all generations for ever and ever. Amen.

In the church. The place where God's fulness is revealed and imparted. There His glory is willingly acknowledged.—**In Christ Jesus.** A true acknowledgment of God's
glory is only possible in union and fellowship with the Lord.
Those out of Christ may be overwhelmed by the majesty of
God, and in the end surely will be. But they will never know,
much less freely acknowledge that magnificent display of
divine attributes, which is experienced by those who have
learned in themselves the love and grace received in Christ
Jesus. All worship of God in spirit and in truth is in the
Church and in union with Christ.—**All generations.** Strictly
speaking, there are no generations in eternity. But creatures
of time cannot express the duration of eternity except by
forms of speech derived from time and the present world.

5

Ephesians 4

Exhortation to Unity. 4:1–16

Summary. With the authority of his bonds, the apostle exhorts to walk worthily of the Christian calling (1), with special attention to those virtues (2) which secure peace and unity (3). For all that belongs to the Church points to its unity (4–6), even the diversity of gifts coming from the one Christ (7), who, as is shown by a quotation from the Old Testament, fills the whole world (8–10). Accordingly, the diversity of offices (11) is intended to contribute to the upbuilding of the body of Christ (12), until the Church attains to unity in perfection (13). Furthermore, this diversity of offices is designed to preserve the members of the Church from all delusions (14) and to enable them to grow into complete communion with Christ, the head (15), from whom the body of the Church, combining unity with multiplicity, effects its own development (16).

1. I therefore, the prisoner in the Lord, beseech you to walk

worthily of the calling wherewith ye were called,

Therefore. Points back to what precedes, either to the last chapter where Paul explains his apostolic relation to them, or to the entire first part of the epistle. On the basis of the doctrines thus far explained, the apostle, as is his usual practice, makes exhortations of a moral and practical nature in the last three chapters of the epistle.—**The prisoner in the Lord.** As a prisoner he stands in fellowship with Christ and His sufferings. Hence he is able to exhort with the authority which comes from his peculiar Christian and apostolic experience. (Cf. 3:1.)—**Walk worthily.** So also Col. 1:10. As was remarked in connection with ch. 2:2, the verb **walk** does not refer merely to separate acts or outward conduct, but expresses a moral condition which manifests itself in a certain mode of action.—**The calling.** The calling was "that we should be holy." (Cf. 1:4; 1:18; 2:10.) This calling is attended and made effective by wonderful operations of God's power. (Cf. 1:19; 2:5; 3:20.) The moral condition of the believer should correspond with the power of the calling and its exalted aim. Note that God's call is not based on our worth; but our worthiness follows our calling.

2. With all lowliness and meekness, with long-suffering, forbearing one another in love;

Lowliness and meekness. The writer now proceeds to detail the positive demands involved in the calling of God, in the first half of this chapter, following this up with negative requirements in the latter half. The virtues mentioned in this verse are those most essential to unity. It is noteworthy how closely the apostle binds the growth of the believer up to the full measure of his calling with the life and unity of the Church. Not in seclusion and separation is the best Christian life developed, but in the fellowship of the Church. **Lowliness** refers more to the inner disposition, **meekness** to the outward attitude.—**With long-suffering.** If these words are not grammatically connected with the following **forbearing,** they at least stand closely related to it in thought. As long as the Church consists of imperfect men, long-suffering and forbearance with the faults of others will always be needed.—**In love.** This is the disposition underlying forbearance, the perfect bond which holds all together, whereas, an uncompromising assertion of rights would tend to drive the members of the Church apart and engender strife and division. Even those who are in the right frequently do much wrong from the want of meekness and forbearance.

3. Giving diligence to keep the unity of the Spirit in the bond of peace.

Keep the unity. This is the central exhortation of the entire paragraph. The unity of the Spirit already exists; hence the exhortation is to keep, to guard it. The unity is ascribed to the Spirit, because He effects it.—**The bond of peace.** Peace is the bond which holds the Church together in unity. In Col. 3:14 "love" is called "the bond of perfectness." **Peace** here is essentially the same as love, since it refers to the inner disposition and not to outward agreement.

4. *There is* one body, and one Spirit, even as also ye were called in one hope of your calling;

The arrangement of the following description of the unity of the Church (ver. 4–6) is by threes. There are three clauses, each with three parts.—**One body and one Spirit.** Unity is a characteristic mark of the Church. Therefore we confess, in the Nicene Creed, "one holy Christian and Apostolic Church,"

and similarly in the Augsburg Confession, Article VII. As man
is body and spirit, so the Church is one body pervaded by
one Holy Spirit. The concession here is that the Church is
not only an organization, but an organism, animated by a
divine power of life. "It is the Spirit that quickeneth." The
body is one; it is not made one by the peace and harmony
of its members. God has made the body one; for this reason
peace should prevail among the members. The one Spirit
is not the unanimity of the members of the Church, but the
one life-giving Holy Spirit.—**Even as ye were called.** The
unity characteristic of the Church may be recognized in the
experience of its members. Every Christian knows that the
hope which his **calling** begets, is one and the same hope that
all have, who are called of God. The one common hope of all
Christians is that of a perfect communion with God and a
perfect fellowship of saints. It is such a body that the Spirit is
bringing into existence by His presence in the Church. When
this one body with one Spirit is fully realized, then the one
hope of our calling will be fulfilled.

5. One Lord, one faith, one baptism,

This is the second group of three which describes the unity
of the Church. The unity of the Church is thus confirmed by
a consideration of what makes men Christians and members
of the Church. **One Lord** is the Saviour of all, and it is
only by Him that men have access to God. This Saviour
is appropriated by all through **one faith,** and there is no
other way of obtaining the benefits of His redemption. **One
baptism** is the means of incorporating all into union with
the one Lord and the unity of the one Spirit.

6. One God and Father of all, who is over all, and through
all, and in all.

One God and Father. The unity of God, in the threefoldness of His relation to all believers, crowns the argument for the unity of the Church.—**All.** All believers, all members of the Church. The universal fatherhood of God over all men is a truth, but it is not spoken of here. All believers have **one Father:** hence there should be peace and unity of spirit among them.—**Who is over all,** etc. All members of the Church acknowledge the same divine majesty **over all,** the same divine energy and activity **through all,** and the same divine indwelling **in all.** The variation of prepositions, over, through, in, expresses the totality of God's relations. It does not reflect the three persons of the Trinity. But it should be observed that the whole arrangement of the series of predicates which mark the unity of the Church is Trinitarian in an ascending order: first, the Spirit in ver. 4; secondly, the Lord in ver. 5; and finally, the Father in ver. 6. And, although it is not stated, the manifest implication is that these three are one.

7. But unto each one of us was the grace given according to the measure of the gift of Christ.

Unto each one. Those things which are individual in the Church need not and should not conflict with the unity just described. On the contrary, they confirm the unity; for, however varied they may be, they all come from one Giver, and all contribute to the one great purpose of God in the Church.—**Was the grace given.** (Cf. 3:2, 7.) The verb is emphatic. The diversity of gifts in the Church is not for the honor or the selfish use of those who possess them, but to profit withal. They were **given.** The gift points to the Giver as the One who determines the design of every given grace.—**According to the measure of the gift of Christ.**

The grace of God which comes through Christ is common to all members of the Church, but it is operative in distinct gifts. These gifts are defined by a certain measure. Both the gift and the measure come from Christ. And the measure is of such a nature that they all fit together to preserve the unity of the Church. The gifts of Christ are not to lead to individualism and segregation, but to supplement each other in the communion of believers.

8. Wherefore he saith,

When he ascended on high, he led captivity captive,

And gave gifts unto men.

He saith. The quotation in this verse is designed to prove that Christ is the Giver of gifts, and it must be considered with this purpose in view. Accordingly the emphasis would seem at first sight to lie on the words **gave gifts.** But since the apostle himself in the next verses comments on the words **he ascended,** the predominant thought should be found in them. And, indeed, there lies the guarantee that Christ is the Giver of gifts. For the significance of this ascension of Christ, as the apostle argues and clearly states in ver. 10, is that **he fills all things.** It is this world-filling exaltation of Christ that proves that the gifts which are possessed in the Church come from Him. The apostle thus recurs to a thought which he already expressed when he said the Church was "the fulness of him that filleth all in all." (Cf. 1:22 and the notes on that verse.)—The citation is from Ps. 68:18, but with alterations. The explanation that these alterations are owing either to the imperfect memory of the apostle, or the Rabbinical method of his use of Scripture, or his adherence to a traditional interpretation in making the quotation, is superficial and satisfactory. St. Paul, doubtlessly, well knew the words and the meaning of the original; but in using them here in his argument, he "succinctly, suggestively and authoritatively unfolds" their Messianic meaning, as Ellicott correctly remarks. The O. T. singer is celebrating the victories and conquests of the people of Israel as Jehovah's triumph and exaltation. The words of the psalm in the R. V. are these: "Thou hast ascended on high, thou hast led thy captivity captive; thou hast received gifts among men." This exaltation of Jehovah St. Paul applies to the exaltation of Christ. The most important change in so doing is that instead of the original **received gifts,** the apostle says, what is apparently just the reverse, **gave gifts.** Nevertheless, he is not departing from the original thought. For the conqueror who has received gifts from his enemies has gifts to bestow upon his own people. As Jehovah's victories brought gifts to His people from His conquered enemies, so Christ's exaltation brought gifts to the Church as the fruit of His victory. Fr. W. Schultz, in commenting on the psalm under discussion, makes the following remarks pertinent to the present passage: "Inasmuch as David and his men received the gifts in question, Paul had a right to see a spiritual antitype to this ascent of Jehovah in the fact that Christ had ascended and had given gifts, charismata, to those that are His (Eph. 4:8). In fact the ascension of Christ first brought the ascent of Jehovah to its consummation, and Paul was all the more justified in referring the latter to the former, because the ascension, as he expressly points out, presupposes a descent, which had never preceded so deeply as in the case of Christ."—**Led captivity captive.** This phrase is equivalent to "subdued his enemies." The abstract **captivity** is placed for the concrete **captives.**

9. (Now this, He ascended, what is it but that he also

descended into the lower parts of the earth?

What is it but, etc. (Cf. John 3:13.) The ascent implies a preceding descent.—**The lower parts of the earth.** Perhaps this means simply the earth, designated thus peculiarly for the sake of the contrast with the heavens, to which Christ ascended. If this is the meaning, the clause refers to the incarnation, when the Lord came to the earth. But a better view is that the apostle did not mean to limit the descent to the earth, but to exfend it to the parts beneath the earth, for his purpose is to show that by His descent and ascent Christ **might fill all things.** Hence it is preferable to understand the expression of Christ's descent into Hades. (Cf. 1 Peter 3:19.)

10. He that descended is the same also that ascended far above all the heavens, that he might fill all things.)

The same. This identity is emphasized because it was the purpose of God that all things should be filled by the one person Christ. (Cf. 1:10, 23.)—**Above all the heavens.** The heaven in which God dwells is beyond the visible heaven. Hence St. Paul can speak of heavens in the plural. So, it is said, Christ our high priest passed through the heavens (Hebr. 4:14). By descending into the regions lower than the earth and by ascending to the highest region, of which we can think, Christ filled all things with His presence and power. It is this exalted Christ that is the Giver of the powers, graces and gifts, by which the Church is built up.

11. And he gave some *to be* apostles; and some, prophets; and some, evangelists; and some, pastors and teachers;

Gave some, etc. A series of gifts, not a gradation of offices, is mentioned here. The reference is not to outward organization, but inner possessions and powers. Naturally

72

the offices resulted from the possession of the gifts. Several of these gifts might be combined in one person. Rom. 12:6–8 and 1 Cor. 12:8–10 are parallel passages. It should be carefully noted here that the apostle speaks of the persons, endowed with the various gifts of Christ, as given to the Church. It would be well if congregations would not consider their pastors so much as men occupying an office, but as men given by the Lord with gifts to edify the Church. For this view would develop a greater respect for the ministry. On the other hand, if pastors considered themselves more in this light, perhaps there would be less inclination among them to change places.

12. For the perfecting of the saints, unto the work of ministering, unto the building up of the body of Christ:

For the perfecting, etc. Luther translates this verse as follows: "In order that the saints be prepared for the work of the office, whereby the body of Christ is to be built up." This is probably the best interpretation of a rather perplexing verse. The difficulty lies in the connection of the three clauses, each beginning with a preposition. Apparently every conceivable arrangement has been proposed. But the progress of the thought is most simply maintained by making the clauses successively dependent upon each other, as Luther's translation does. Christ gave gifts in diversity for the purpose of perfectly fitting the saints. Fitting for what? For the work of service of every kind. And the service is for what? For the ultimate purpose of building up the body of Christ. We have here the idea of a church in which all the members (saints) are workers, an idea to be found elsewhere in the writings of St. Paul. (Cf. 1 Cor. 15:58; 2 Cor. 9:8.)

13. Till we all attain unto the unity of the faith, and of the

knowledge of the Son of God, unto a fullgrown man, unto
the measure of the stature of the fulness of Christ;

Till we all attain. This is the end which the gifts of Christ
serve to bring about.—**The unity of the faith.** It is not unity
of doctrine, of creed that is referred to here. That will be the
outcome of the unity of faith. But the unity of the Church
is dependent upon the growth of the Church in faith, in
the act and state of believing. Hence **one faith** in verse 5.
One faith is a characteristic of the Church, but at the same
time the Church is in a continual state of progress in faith
and in the unity produced by faith.—**The knowledge of the
Son of God.** Nothing essentially different from the faith
of the Son of God. The addition of this clause indicates
the completeness of the apprehension of Christ to which
the Church must attain. For the goal of all Christian life is
to know even as also we are known.—**A fullgrown man.**
Contrast with **children** (ver. 14). Not the members severally,
but the Church collectively is referred to. The Church is to
become a fullgrown man. The body of Christ must develop,
and the end of this development is full maturity.—**The
measure of the stature,** etc. For the words **the fulness of
Christ,** see the note on 3:19. The full measure of gifts, graces
and blessings which come from Christ, is meant. When the
Church has received from Christ as much as it can contain,
then its **stature** is of full **measure.** The question of time,
whether this will ever occur in this world, was probably not
in the apostle's thought when he wrote this verse. His purpose
was to describe the ideal end to be attained, irrespective of the
time when. Undoubtedly the **growth** towards this glorious
consummation belongs not to the future, but to the present
world.

14. That we may be no longer children, tossed to and fro and carried about with every wind of doctrine, by the sleight of men, in craftiness, after the wiles of error;

That we may be, etc. The conditions implied in this and the following verses cannot follow the state of perfection described in the preceding verse. Hence this verse carries us back to verse 12. In the preceding verse the writer stated positively what must be the end of the development to be brought about by the work of ministering of the saints. In this verse he states negatively what the development must not be.—**No longer children.** It is no disgrace to be children in faith in the beginning; but the time must come when the Church will be children no longer. (Cf. 1 Cor. 13:11.)—**Tossed to and fro,** etc. A similar figure occurs in James 1:6 and in Hebr. 13:9. A lack of steadiness is characteristic of youth.—**Every wind of doctrine.** There is nothing in this expression to imply that the doctrine is bad; but the context implies this.—**The sleight of men.** An expression derived from the use of dice in gaming. The unsettling of believers by evil doctrines is carried on with design. The real author of such designs and sleights is the unseen power of evil.—**The wiles of error.** There is a kind of personification in the word **error.** The word translated **wiles** is connected with the English word **method.** The thought is that error as a power of deceit has its agents at work among believers, who methodically practise fraud upon the unwary and the unstable.

15. But speaking truth in love, may grow up in all things into him, which is the head, *even* Christ;

Speaking truth. This is one word in Greek. Interpretations of this word, and indeed of the entire sentence,

75

have varied. The contrast with the preceding verse should
be carefully observed.—**Speaking truth** stands opposed to
wiles of error. It has reference not only to speech, but
to that truthfulness of the Christian spirit which begets
truth in speech. This spirit of simple truth must disarm
the crafty agents of error, and secure the true growth of
the Church through us.—**In love.** Some connect this with
the verb **may grow up,** which follows. But the connection
with the participle, **speaking truth,** presents less difficulty.
Love must not be identified here with mildness, leniency, as
if the exhortation were to speak gently and indulgently of
error. Love in speaking the truth must sometimes use the
very opposite of gentle tones, because it "rejoiceth not in
unrighteousness, but rejoiceth with the truth" (1 Cor. 13:6).
Love here denotes that inner state of the heart from which
truthfulness springs. "Rooted and grounded in love" (3:18),
those who are children in faith will keep the spirit of truth and
thereby be protected against the delusions of error.—**Grow
up.** A contrast with **children** (ver. 14).—**Into him, which
is the head.** All the vitality, all the powers of growth are in
Christ, the head. Hence the growth must be into this sphere
and element of vitality, just as the tree strikes its roots deeply
into the soil. In other words, the condition of all growth in
the Church is union with Christ.

16. From whom all the body fitly framed and knit together
through that which every joint supplieth, according to the
working in *due* measure of each several part, maketh the
increase of the body unto the building up of itself in love.

From whom all the body. The figure of a body, representing the Church perfecting its unity, is now carried out in detail. The source of all the increase is the head. In Col. 2:19 we

find a parallel which throws much light on this verse.—**Fitly framed and knit together.** (Cf. 2:21.) The organization of the Church by the spiritual relations of the various parts (for the mere outward organization is not referred to here) makes it a harmoniously and compactly joined body, and thus adapts it for growth in unity.—**Through that which every joint supplieth.** There is some uncertainty as to the meaning of the clause thus translated. The margin of the Revised Version gives a literal translation: "Through every joint of the supply." The supply comes from Christ. All His gifts contribute to the unity of the Church. These gifts which form the supply might be regarded as forming joints, and thus the clause might be taken in its literal rendering. But it is very awkward to speak of the supply forming joints. It is much better to consider the supply as passing through all the various joints, thus contributing to the growth of the body. This is the thought contained in the translation of the R. V. and confirmed by the parallel passage Col. 2:19.—**According to the working,** etc. In the body each several part has a measure of work to perform to sustain the whole. If any part fails to contribute its "supply" to the other parts, then the growth is hindered.—**Maketh the increase of the body.** The subject is **all the body.** The body effects its own increase, of course, only through the joint operation of all the various members. While the growth has its source in the head, Christ, at the same time it is carried on through the action of each several part of the body. Endeavoring to form a detailed conception of the ideas of this verse, we would view the matter as follows: The believers in Christ are the members of the body; the gifts which Christ bestows constitute the supply; the joints would then naturally be found in those

functions and offices, which the supply of gifts develops; by
the interaction of the members through their various offices
and functions, according to the measure of each, the supply
is carried through the whole body for its increase.—**Unto
the building up of itself.** Edification is the great end of the
activities of the Church.

Exhortation to Forsake the Vices of Heathenism. 4:17–24

Summary. This exhortation is in three parts. First, to
put off the old man and to put on the new man (4:17–24).
Secondly, to exercise Christian virtues in place of heathen
vices (4:25–32). Thirdly, especially to avoid the predominant
vices of carnal impurity and covetousness (5:1–14).

The first part of the exhortation, demanding the putting
off of the old man and the putting on of the new, is a solemn
appeal to walk no longer as the Gentiles do (17), who through
alienation from and ignorance of God (18) gave themselves
up to all uncleanness (19). The readers of the epistle had
learned that the truth of Christ (20–21) required the putting
off of the old man of heathenism (22) and the putting on of
the spiritual man (23–24).

17. This I say therefore, and testify in the Lord, that ye no
longer walk as the Gentiles also walk, in the vanity of their
mind,

This I say therefore. The general thought of ver. 1 is
resumed and now unfolded negatively.—**In the Lord.** In
fellowship with the Lord. The appeal gains in solemnity by
being based not on human motives, but on the fellowship
of Christ.—**Vanity of their mind.** (Cf. Rom. 1:21.) This

vanity was the loss of the one great reality, God. From this resulted general depravation.

18. Being darkened in their understanding, alienated from the life of God because of the ignorance that is in them, because of the hardening of their heart;

Darkened in their understanding. This accounts for their conduct. They lost the light to guide them. **The life of God.** Not a coarse life, but actually the life which is in God and which comes from Him. (Cf. John 1:4.) The Holy Spirit is the Lord and Giver of life. The loss of the gracious operations of the Spirit of God signifies the loss of life and spiritual death.—**Ignorance that is in them.** That is, abiding, indwelling ignorance. But was not this an excuse for them rather than an aggravation of their guilt? By no means. The connection with the next verse shows that not mere intellectual lack of knowledge, but a moral incapacity to know, is meant. This moral condition, which precluded knowledge of the truth, was the cause of heathen alienation from God.—**Hardening.** Spiritual callousness, insensibility. How this awful ignorance and callousness came about is described in Rom. 1:21. The implication here is, that it was their own fault.

19. Who being past feeling gave themselves up to lasciviousness, to work all uncleanness with greediness.

The preceding verse described their depraved condition, this their depraved conduct.—**Past feeling.** The extremity of wickedness; the state where no compunctions of conscience are any longer experienced.—**Gave themselves up.** Their own choice made them the slaves of vice. This is their condemnation. Because they gave themselves up, God also "gave them up" (Rom. 1:24).—**Lasciviousness.** Not only sensual sins, but all kinds of wanton conduct are included in this term.—**To work all uncleanness.** With conscious purpose, as the business of their lives. Further than this it is impossible to go in sin.—**Uncleanness.** Pre-eminently sensual filthiness, of which heathenism developed most unnatural forms.—**With greediness.** This addition, after the reference to such gross sins, is so peculiar that many have thought that the word does not have its usual meaning of "covetousness" here, but that it denotes some excess of uncleanness. But there is no sufficient reason to ascribe any other than the true meaning to the word. Covetousness is brought into close connection with impurity in other passages of the N. T. (Cf. 5:3; Col. 3:5; 1 Cor. 5:11.) Slaves of lust as they are, their minds are at the same time dominated by covetousness. No vices seem to have such general and complete control of men as these two. Indeed, these are the salient features of a worldly spirit, uncleanness and greediness.

20. But ye did not so learn Christ;

Learn Christ. Not merely the doctrine of Christ. The substance of Christian truth is what Christ is in His own person. (Cf. 1 Cor. 1:23; Phil. 1:15.) What He is in Himself, shows what He should be in us. The truth that appears in Christ is all purity and holiness, so that it is utterly opposed to every form of uncleanness and selfishness.

21. If so be that ye heard him, and were taught in him, even as truth is in Jesus:

If so be, etc. (Cf. note on 3:2.) The apostle emphatically implies that they had heard.—**Taught in him.** They were taught not only about Christ, but were in communion with Him, when they were taught.—**Even as truth is in**

80

Jesus. The simplest explanation of this troublesome clause is to connect it with the preceding words **were taught.** It describes the manner in which they were taught. From 5:6 it is evident that another manner of teaching had come in among them. Dale gives a good statement of the meaning of ver. 20 and 21 which we repeat here: "*Ye*—he places them in emphatic contrast with their fellow-citizens who were outside the Christian Church and who had not received the Christian Faith.—Ye *did not so learn Christ.* He means that they did not *learn Christ* in such a way as to suppose that they could continue to be guilty of lying, of theft, of drunkenness, of sensuality, and all the vices of heathenism. The knowledge of Christ which they had received might be imperfect, but it did not leave them ignorant of the necessity of righteousness. For, as the apostle hopes and believes, they had not merely listened to human teachers whose conception of Christian truth might be false and who might be unable to convey the truth they knew to others; Christ's own voice had reached them; when they became Christians they *heard* HIM. Truth, the highest truth, the truth it most concerns Christian men to know, is *in Jesus.* Truth can never be rightly known when separated from Him. All real and effective teaching must be in harmony with truth as truth is in Him. But this was precisely the teaching which the apostle trusts had been given to the Ephesian Christians. For they themselves were *in Him* and *were taught ... even as truth is in Jesus.*"

22. That ye put away, as concerning your former manner of life, the old man, which waxeth corrupt after the lusts of deceit;

That ye put away. This is what they **were taught.** The beginning of all Christian morality is a thorough conversion.

The pronoun **ye** is emphatic, as in ver. 20: ye as Christians, no longer Gentiles. The readers had need of being reminded of the necessity of a complete moral transformation, since much of their **former manner of life** doubtless still adhered to them.—**The old man.** Not only certain features of their former life were to be dropped, but the whole mind, will and nature, underlying all the manifestations of sin, were to be put away. The term **the old man** designates more than certain acts or habits. In Col. 3:9 the apostle says, "The old man with his doings," so that the doings are distinct from the old man. The term denotes the nature (cf. 2:3) which underlies actions. This nature should no longer be theirs, for it belongs to a time previous to the new birth (Tit. 3:5; John 3:3) by which the old man died (Rom. 6:6). For this reason it is called **old.** This old man being dead should remain dead and not be revived.—**Waxeth corrupt.** The old man represents a nature which is not only partially bad, but entirely bad. Nevertheless there is a growth in corruption. The depravity may become more and more intense, and this is the tendency of the evil nature of men.—**The lusts of deceit.** Sin is deceit (Hebr. 3:13.) The lusts which spring from sin cause an increase in corruptness. That is the nature of these lusts; they necessarily tend to corruptness. So they are properly ascribed to **deceit,** which as a power makes slaves of evil men without their perceiving the bondage they are in.

23. And that ye be renewed in the spirit of your mind,

Renewed. In the Greek word there is an idea of rejuvenation or restoration to a former condition. The apostle sees the original nature of man shine through all the corruptions which come upon him, God's work which underlies all man's marring. This original nature he desires to see restored.—**In**

the spirit of your mind. Not simply the inner nature, as if the expression were equivalent to "the inward man" (3:16). **Mind** here is the organ of moral thinking. **Spirit** is the life-principle. The life-principle of all true moral thinking and living is not original with man, least of all in his fallen condition; but it is derived from the Holy Spirit. The renewal therefore is to be in that spiritual power of the mind which is effected by the Holy Spirit. The expression forms a contrast with the words **former manner of life** (ver. 22). In their former condition they were without the spirit of mind, because they were without the Holy Spirit, who imparts true spiritual power to man. Their renewal consists in the attainment of that spiritual power of mind which originally belonged to man.

24. And put on the new man, which after God hath been created in righteousness and holiness of truth.

Put on. In putting away the old man the new is put on. There are not two acts, but a positive and negative side to the same act.—**The new man.** The nature opposite to that designated by the old man, the nature that manifests itself in deeds of holiness. The new man is not something fashioned by man. It is given to him. Its existence is assumed here, and the exhortation is to bring to perfect development the life of the Spirit which is given in regeneration. This is done in the progress of sanctification.—**After God.** God Himself is the pattern of the new man. (Cf. Matt. 5:48.) There is a reference here to the image of God, in which man was originally made (Gen. 1:27). This is clearly proved by the parallel passage, Col. 3:10.—**Created.** God's works in man, not man's own production. (Cf. 2:10.)—**In righteousness and holiness of truth.** As **deceit** (ver. 22) is productive of evil lusts, **truth** is

the source of inner purity or **holiness,** and just conduct or
righteousness.

Exhortation to forsake the Vices of Heathenism continued.

4:25–32

Summary. The second part of the exhortation is an appeal
to practise Christian virtues instead of heathen vices. This
presents the workings of renewal in contrast with the evil
habits of their old nature. Falsehood must give way to truth
(25); anger must be restrained (26–27): theft must cease, and
work with beneficence begin (28); impure speech must be
exchanged for speech that is profitable (29); the indwelling
Spirit must not be grieved (30); every form of bitterness must
yield to kindness, according to the example of God in Christ
(31–32).

25. Wherefore, putting away falsehood, speak ye truth each
one with his neighbour: for we are members one of another.

Special manifestations of the old man are now considered.
In the exhortations which follow in rapid succession, the
apostle evidently has the relations of Christians to each other
in the Church in view.—**Speak ye truth.** Already in ver. 15
the apostle has spoken of truthfulness as a condition of the
growth of the Church. Truth lies at the basis of all Christian
life. Men become Christians by learning the truth, as it is in
Jesus, Nor can any true union between man and man, such
as is essential to the Church, exist, except on the basis of
truth.—**Each one with his neighbour.** Fellow-Christians
are referred to, as the next words show.—**Members one
of another.** Here is the motive for speaking the truth,
and indeed for all the virtues recommended in the entire
paragraph. Christians are members one of another in the
Church. They are parts of the body of Christ, held together in

84

that unity which God has created through the Holy Spirit, and which is described in verses 4–6. Falsehood breaks down this unity, for it sets up between members that power of "deceit" (ver. 22) which brings forth the lusts that cause wars and fightings (James 4:1).

26. Be ye angry, and sin not: let not the sun go down upon your wrath;

Be ye angry, etc. A quotation from Ps. 4:5, according to the Septuagint translation. The negative belongs only to the word **sin.** The strange imperative, **Be ye angry,** has caused much perplexity. To regard the imperative as merely giving permission, is doubtful grammatically and, what is worse, as to the thought obtained. For it would imply a concession to what in itself is not right. By the imperative the apostle does not conceive what is really wrong, but requires them to do what is right. But even with the knowledge that there is a just indignation, it seems unnecessary to command people to be angry. The best explanation is this. The force of the first imperative is limited in its application by the second imperative, containing a negative. The idea then is that we are to be angry only in the right way; that is, in such a way as not to sin. In short, be angry so as not to sin.—**Let not the sun,** etc. The day of provocation should also be the day of forgiveness and reconciliation.

27. Neither give place to the devil.

In the display of anger and all the passions associated with it, the devil finds a fine opportunity to do his evil work. In this connection we must think not only of the mischief which he does among individuals, but the evil he inflicts on the Church. For as it is the Holy Spirit who holds the Church together in unity, it is the evil spirit who destroys the unity of the Church through the evil passions of men. Resentment is in itself a separation of fellowship.

28. Let him that stole steal no more: but rather let him labour, working with his hands the thing that is good, that he may have whereof to give to him that hath need.

Steal no more. However strange this exhortation may sound when addressed to Christians, it was not superfluous for those recently reclaimed from heathenism and its loose moral ideas.—**Working,** etc. Self-supporting; not living by the labors of others.—**The thing that is good.** Not only what is legally allowed, but what is positively beneficial. Some forms of business allowed by law a Christian should not follow.—**Have whereof to give.** The Christian should work, not to accumulate wealth, but to be a benefactor. Herein lies the strongest contrast to being a thief.

29. Let no corrupt speech proceed out of your mouth, but such as is good for edifying as the need may be, that it may give grace to them that hear.

Corrupt. Whether obscene or malicious. The Greek word is the same that is used to designate a corrupt tree in Matt. 7:17.—**As the need may be.** Seasonableness is an important element in edifying speech.—**Give grace.** Bestow a favor or benefit. In other words, be helpful.

30. And grieve not the Holy Spirit of God, in whom ye were sealed unto the day of redemption.

And. Connects this verse closely with the preceding, so that what follows is not a new exhortation, but a continuation of that begun in the last verse.—**Grieve not the Holy Spirit.** Corrupt speech is more than an offence against man; it is an offence against the indwelling Holy Spirit. If the Holy Spirit were not a person, He could not be said to be grieved. There is therefore in this statement an argument against the Unitarian idea of God.—**Sealed unto the day of redemption.** (Cf. 1:13.) This fact makes the admonition more serious. For the Holy Spirit will forsake the person that grieves Him, and thus the seal with all its glorious hopes will be lost.

31. Let all bitterness, and wrath, and anger, and clamour, and railing, be put away from you, with all malice:

The sins enumerated in this verse are all manifestations of hatred. The series begins with the inner source of this form of sin and proceeds outward to the works in which it is manifested.—**Bitterness.** A state of mind which must be exchanged for sweetness of temper before the sins which follow can be avoided.—**Wrath.** Agitation of bitter feelings.—**Anger.** Not mere provocation, but resentment.—**Clamour.** Outbreak of anger in speech.—**Railing.** The form which the clamor is apt to take. The Greek word is **blasphemy,** but here directed against man, not God.—**Malice.** Not wickedness generally, but in accordance with the context the malicious act, which is prompted by wrath.

32. And be ye kind one to another, tenderhearted, forgiving each other, even as God also in Christ forgave you.

This verse forms the contrast with the preceding, and recommends the fundamental Christian virtue, love, but in the special form of forgiveness.—**Kind.** The opposite of bitterness.—**Tenderhearted.** Contrary to wrath and anger.—**Forgiving.** Opposed to clamor, railing, and malice.—**Even as God,** etc. The relation which Christians sustain to each other in God and Christ is to be the motive for their conduct. The forgiveness of sins through Christ is what brought Christians together into the unity of the Church.

The experience of this forgiveness should keep alive in them the spirit of forgiveness towards others. How God forgave in Christ, was shown in ch. 1. The details of conduct into which the apostle has entered here are based on the great doctrines exhibited in the first part of this epistle. Without faith in all those great and wonderful truths which show how God forgave us in Christ, how He blessed us in Him, and how He created us in Him for good works, it is impossible to attain to the virtues here recommended. Thus does Christian doctrine, through the medium of faith, lie at the basis of all Christian life.

6

Ephesians 5

Exhortation to forsake the Vices of Heathenism continued. Ver. 1–14

Summary. The exhortation against the special vices of heathenism, impurity and covetousness begins with the highest moral principle of imitating God in love according to the example of Christ in His sacrificial death (1–2). In pursuance of this general principle, the predominant vices of heathenism, impurity in every form and covetousness are to be shunned (3–4); for these vices exclude from the kingdom of God (5), notwithstanding vain and sophistical objections (6). Ceasing from these vices (7–8), the children of light should exhibit the power of light (9–10), reproving the works of darkness, the shameful deeds of secrecy (11–12); for this is the function of light (13); as God in His word also reproves those dead in sins (14).

1. Be ye therefore imitators of God, as beloved children;

The first series of exhortations against the vices of the

heathen (4:17–24) and also the second (4:25–32) ended by leading up to the thought of taking God for a pattern of correct conduct. This third series begins on the same plane. The highest expression which can be given to Christian duty, is that it is imitation of God.—**Imitators of God.** The language of the text seems almost too strong. Is it possible for man to be an imitator of God? In an absolute sense it is not possible; but in the sense explained in the next verse it is possible.—**Beloved children.** It is this filial relation to God, which, while relaxing nothing of the obligation, facilitates the imitation of God. Love calls forth love. Being **beloved** of God, we are inwardly impelled to do to another as has been done by us. (Cf. 1 John 4:11.)

2. And walk in love, even as Christ also loved you, and gave himself up for us, an offering and a sacrifice to God for an odour of a sweet smell.

Walk in love. In this respect we are to imitate God. Of course there can be no comparison in the degree of divine and human love. But in however limited a degree, man can exercise the divine privilege of love.—**Christ also loved.** The love of God which is our pattern is presented to us in human form in Christ. In this form we can imitate it.—**Gave himself up.** So also ver. 25. In expressions of this kind the manifest meaning is to death: "Greater love hath no man than this, that a man lay down his life for his friends" (John 15:13).—**For us.** Not merely for our benefit, but in our stead. The relation between Christ and us is distinctly shown in the next words. If Christ died as a sacrifice for us, the meaning must be that He died instead of us.—**An offering and a sacrifice.** It is manifest that the apostle is not merely using O. T. sacrificial terms with a strict O. T.

signification. Hence in explaining the difference between these two terms, **offering** and **sacrifice,** distinctions like bloody and unbloody sacrifices, or sin-offerings and peace-offerings, are inapplicable. Both terms must refer to the death of Christ, just before mentioned. According to Hebr. 5:1, even in the ceremonial of the O. T. gifts as well as sacrifices were offered for sin. Christ's offering and sacrifice were the fulfilment of what was prefigured not only in certain, but in all the gifts and sacrifices of the O. T. The offering and the sacrifice were both for sin. Accordingly we find here the idea of atonement. In His death Christ was a **sacrifice;** in that He gave Himself up, He made an **offering** of Himself. By both sacrifice and offering He became our peace (2:14) and the propitiation for our sins (1 John 2:2).—**Odour of a sweet smell.** Indicating acceptance with God. The expression is derived from the O. T. (Exod. 29:18; Levit. 1:9).

3. But fornication, and all uncleanness, or covetousness, let it not even be named among you, as becometh saints;

But. Having stated the principle of morality in its highest form positively, the writer proceeds to state some negatives. In doing so he passes from the supreme virtue directly to the worst vices of heathenism, those which would present the strongest temptations to men who had recently emerged from heathenism. No stronger contrast can be conceived than that between the imitation of God in love and the practice of the grossest sensuality. Hence this verse properly begins with a very emphatic **but.—All uncleanness or covetousness.** The same combination in 4:19. In regard to uncleanness the moral sense of the heathen was very obtuse. Next to uncleanness probably covetousness was the most prevalent vice.—**Not even be named.** Much less done.

91

Impure speech is proof of an impure mind.—**As becometh saints.** This appears like a mild statement of the ground for purity. But properly considered this propriety is a higher obligation than any legal restraint. For the sense of what is becoming must have its roots in the heart. St. Paul evidently attached much weight to decency and propriety, as the following instances show. "Not befitting" (ver. 4); "worthily of the calling" (4:1); "this is right" (6:1). (Cf. also 1 Cor. 11:13; 1 Tim. 2:10; Tit. 2:1.)

4. Nor filthiness, nor foolish talking, or jesting, which are not befitting: but rather giving of thanks.

Filthiness. Everything shameful, whether in word or deed.—**Foolish talking.** Not to be limited to obscenity. Holiness requires a serious mind. "As the pride of the Roman people was justly offended when they saw an emperor descend into the arena with charioteers and gladiators, so the finer feeling of the Church is justly offended when Christian men indulge in buffoonery and play the fool" (Dale).—**Jesting.** This refers to refinements of speech which gild vice.—**Not befitting.** The sinfulness and danger of these subtler forms of impurity are easily overlooked.—**Giving of thanks.** (Cf. ver. 20.) This one thing is placed in opposition to all the sins just referred to. The Christian is to live in a state of gratitude, and thereby to counteract the entire state of sin. It is this state of mind which will give to the Christian mind that cheerfulness which is befitting as opposed to worldly merriment.

5. For this ye know of a surety, that no fornicator, nor unclean person, nor covetous man, which is an idolater, hath any inheritor in the kingdom of Christ and God.

Which is an idolater. Probably the **covetous man** alone is thus characterized (cf. Col. 3:5), and not the unclean person. However, it is true that the other classes referred to also serve another master besides God. (Cf. Phil. 3:19.) The seriousness of this charge would be deeply felt by those who had recently escaped from idolatry.—**Hath any inheritance.** (Cf. Gal. 5:21; 1 Cor. 6:9.) Not only will not have in the future, but has not and cannot have. The inheritance is indeed future, but the seal of the Spirit, which is the assurance of the inheritance, is a present possession. The sins referred to cause the loss of this assurance. (Cf. 4:30.)—**The kingdom.** This is a fundamental conception in the doctrine of the New Testament. The kingdom of God is the sphere of God's gracious operations through Christ. Only that which is wrought by the Holy Spirit has place in it. Whoever is not led by the Spirit, and in whomsoever the redemption of Christ is not effective to put down sin, can have no share in it.—**Of Christ and God.** This may be one of the few cases in which St. Paul calls Christ God directly. (See Rom. 9:5.) But it is more in accordance with the usage of St. Paul to refer God not to Christ, but to the Father.

6. Let no man deceive you with empty words: for because of these things cometh the wrath of God upon the sons of disobedience.

Deceive you with empty words. Sophists who "call evil good and good evil" are to be found in every age.—**Cometh the wrath.** (Cf. Col. 3:6.) Not merely in the future. That the wrath of God also comes in the present world is clear from chap. 2:3 and many passages of the Bible.

7. Be not ye therefore partakers with them;

Partakers. The reference is not to the wrath, but to the sins spoken of. The allurements of old associations might easily tempt them.

8. For ye were once darkness, but are now light in the Lord:
walk as the children of light

Ye were. Emphasis on this word. It is now a thing of
the past.—**Once darkness ... now light.** The change is not
merely one of condition, but of nature. They are not only in
light, but are light. Those who have been "enlightened" (cf.
1:18) through Christ, must themselves emit light.—**Children
of light.** Those who belong to the principle of light. Not his
deeds make a Christian a child of light, but God's grace does
this. The walk must correspond with the grace received.

9. (For the fruit of the light is in all goodness and righteousness and truth),

This verse adds an explanation to the exhortation just given,
thereby adding emphasis to it, an emphasis which is all the
stronger because the verse is only a reminder of what they
well knew was so.

10. Proving what is well-pleasing unto the Lord;

The Christian life requires continual proving, testing,
examining of what is good, right and true. The test-question
is in all cases: "Is it well-pleasing unto the Lord?"—**Lord.**
Christ is referred to. The Christian's relation to Christ is his
chief concern, and his walk is to be judged by its effect upon
this relation.

11. And have no fellowship with the unfruitful works of
darkness, but rather even reprove them;

Have no fellowship. Not even by countenancing or
conniving.—**Unfruitful works of darkness.** A contrast
with "fruit of the light" (ver. 9). But the writer does not
say "Fruit of darkness," but **works,** because darkness is not
productive. Similarly in Gal. 5:22, "The fruit of the Spirit;"

but in ver. 19, "The works of the flesh."—**Unfruitful.** Not productive, only tending to destruction.—**Reprove them.** In words and not merely by silent conduct.

12. For the things which are done by them in secret it is a shame even to speak of.

For. This verse gives a reason for the reproving recommended in ver. 11.—**Done by them in secret.** The works of darkness tend to such extremes that even the sons of disobedience do them in secret.—**Shame.** The very mention, much more the doing of them, is a shame. Of course this does not include the mention of them in reproof. Quiet discountenancing is not enough. They must be brought to light by energetic reproof, because they are so exceedingly shameful. St. Paul himself sets an example, how this is to be done in this chapter and elsewhere in his epistles.

13. But all things when they are reproved are made manifest by the light: for everything that is made manifest is light.

All things. All those things of which he is speaking, the things done in secret.—**Made manifest by the light.** Reproof brings evil deeds out from darkness and into the light where they can be seen.—**For everything,** etc. A general proposition to confirm the preceding statement. An object when illumined is itself light. Evil deeds are made light by reproof, and thereby stand condemned.

14. Wherefore *he* saith. Awake, thou that sleepest, and arise from the dead, and Christ shall shine upon thee.

He saith. A formula used in introducing quotations from the O. T. (Cf. 4:8.) But commentators have been puzzled where to find the verse which St. Paul quotes. The general opinion is that the citation is from the beginning of chapter

95

60 of Isaiah, but that the apostle introduces into the passage a
N. T. interpretation. So where the original says: "Arise, shine,"
the apostle explains that those who are to arise are sleepers
who are to awake, and the dead who are to arise. And where
the original says: "The glory of the Lord is risen upon thee,"
he explains that this glory of the Lord is Christ. But after the
source of the quotation is thus determined, another difficult
question arises, namely, as to its application. The writer has
been admonishing his readers to be reprovers of evil. But the
quotation which he adds, is not an admonition to reprovers,
but to the reproved themselves. The best explanation is
that the apostle is presenting an example, a model for the
Christian reprover of sinners in the action of God. The verse
in this way becomes a crowning reason for the propriety
and necessity of reproof, since God Himself reproves man in
order to enlighten him through Christ.

Exhortation with Respect to Various Relations of Life. 5:15–6:9

Summary. This exhortation is subdivided into four para-
graphs. First, a general exhortation to wise living (5:15–21).
Secondly, an exhortation in regard to the duties of husband
and wife (5:22–33). Thirdly, an exhortation in regard to the
duties of parents and children (6:1–4). Fourthly, the duties
of servants and masters (6:5–9).

In the general exhortation to live wisely the apostle advises
to walk with caution, as wisdom requires (15), making full
use of the opportunities of life, according to the will of the
Lord (16, 17); avoiding excess, full of the Spirit (18), edifying
others as well as themselves with song (19), always rendering

thanks to God (20), with mutual subjection in Christ (21).

Continuing the general thought of mutual subjection the apostle takes up the duties of wife and husband. He requires that wives should show obedience to Christ by being subject to their husbands in a way similar to that in which the Church is subject to Christ (22–24). As Christ loved the Church, making it glorious for Himself, so husbands should love their wives, who are their own bodies (25–28). This is an unselfish kind of self-love, just as Christ loves the members of His own body (29–30). Such love was contemplated in the original institution of marriage, which established that close relation of man and wife that prefigures the relation of Christ to the Church (31–32). Severally and individually they are to realize this intimate relation, the husband by love, the wife by fear (33).

The respective duties of children and parents require, in accordance with the general principle of mutual subjection, that children render Christian obedience to their parents, as both nature and the divine law demand (6:1–3); and that fathers do not make it difficult for their children to obey, but bring them up with the consciousness that they themselves are governed by Christ (4).

Finally, in regard to servants and masters, it is the duty of the former to serve their earthly masters so as to serve Christ at the same time (5), with sincere hearts doing the will of God and not mere service unto men (6–7), looking to the Lord for reward (8). On the other hand, it is the duty of masters to forbear threatening, and on their part to fear the impartial Master of all men (9).

15. Look therefore carefully how ye walk, not as unwise, but as wise;

Many commentators regard the paragraph which begins here as a conclusion of the preceding exhortation. But the close connection between verses 21 and 22 rather requires that it be considered as a transition from what precedes to the special exhortations which follow.—**Carefully.** The translation of the R. V. connecting this with **look** instead of with **walk,** as in the A. V., is based on a more accurate Greek text. The Christian dare not allow himself to go to any place to which inclination or circumstances would carry him. He must look before he sets his foot down anywhere.—**Wise.** It is assumed that God has given them wisdom. (Cf. 1:8, 17.)

16. Redeeming the time, because the days are evil.

Redeeming the time. (Cf. Col. 4:5.) Making the opportunity your own by using it for good.—**The days are evil.** The time and surroundings in which the Ephesians lived were very unfavorable to righteousness. Hence the need for a careful use of opportunities.

17. Wherefore be ye not foolish, but understand what the will of the Lord is.

Foolish. The folly referred to here is wickedness, as everything is that is against the will of the Lord.—**Understand,** etc. This understanding is at the bottom of all truly wise living. Just as soon as we act without regard to the will of our Lord, we fail to do right. The **Lord** spoken of here is not God the Father, but the Lord Christ. The exhortation is this: not to fall away from the knowledge of what Christ, their Lord, wills; for if they do so and lapse into their old life, they will prove themselves foolish, wicked and unworthy of Christ.

18. And be not drunken with wine, wherein is not, but be filled with the Spirit;

Drunken, One notorious way of playing the fool.—**Riot.**

Release from all moral restraint. Drunkenness produces such an unsettling of the moral nature.—**Be filled,** etc. A contrast with the preceding clause. But the contrast is not, as would appear at first sight, between **wine** and **the Spirit,** as if the apostle meant to say Spirit-filled as opposed to wine-filled. These two words are not in the same construction in the Greek text. **Filled with the Spirit** does not denote a state of intoxication, but of soberness, whatever exaltation of mind may be produced by it. Compare St. Paul before Festus, Acts 26:25: "I am not mad, most excellent Festus: but speak forth words of truth and soberness." This soberness produced by the Spirit is the corrective of being drunken.

19. Speaking one to another in psalms and hymns and spiritual songs, singing and making melody with your heart to the Lord;

This and the two following verses indicate various ways in which their being filled with the Spirit is to be manifested. First it is to show itself in relations of fellowship with others. There is a reference in this verse to gatherings, religious or social, or probably both.—**Psalms,** etc. No very marked distinction need be made between psalms, hymns and spiritual songs. The last designation is general; hymns are praise songs, and psalms are such compositions as are called by this name in the O. T. The variety of designations here employed indicates that any song, pervaded by the Holy Spirit, is suitable for mutual edification and enjoyment. (See on Col. 3:16.)—**With your heart.** In the second place, their being filled with the Spirit must show itself in inner joy and self-edification. When not in company, or if unable to sing, the heart of the Christian is still to be lifted up to the Lord in inner melody.

20. Giving thanks always for all things in the name of our
Lord Jesus Christ to God, even the Father;

Giving thanks. This is a third form in which being filled
with the Spirit is to manifest itself.—**All things.** Not only
certain things, but all things; things unpleasant as well as
things pleasant; things withheld not less than things received.
All things work together for good for the Christian.—**In
the name,** etc. God blesses us through Christ, in whom
is our access to God. His name makes our thankgiving
acceptable.—**God, even the Father.** Literally translated in
the margin of the R. V.: "the God and Father." (Cf. 1:3.) By
the designation of God as the Father the filial relation of the
Christian towards God is emphasized.

21. Subjecting yourselves one to another in the fear of
Christ.

A fourth mode of exhibiting fulness of the Spirit, and at
the same time a direct transition to the special exhortations
which follow. God's Spirit teaches love and humility as the
governing principle of Christian conduct and courtesy.—**In
the fear of Christ.** Reverence for Christ and dread of His
judgment inspire a fear of offending Him in the persons of
fellow-believers and fellow-men generally.

22. Wives, *be in subjection* to your own husbands, as unto
the Lord.

A general remark in regard to the entire paragraph which
begins here will clear the way for the understanding of some
of the details. The apostle presents an analogy between
the relations existing between husband and wife, and those
existing between Christ and the Church. But in part the
writer does more than this; for he exhibits the relations
between Christ and the Church independently of the analogy.

Hence some features in the relation of the Lord and the Church are referred to for which there is no counterpart in the relation between husband and wife.—**Be in subjection.** (Cf. 1 Peter 3:1.) This verb is not contained in the Greek text, but is very naturally supplied from the preceding verse. Dale lays great stress on the fact that the apostle does not say "obey" in describing the duties of the wife towards her husband. But some kind of obedience seems to be implied, although all servile, obedience of wife to husband is excluded in this exhortation.—**Own husbands.** So called not in contrast with other men. But their husbands are their own; they possess them and love them; and in this intimate relation to them should be founded their subjection to them.—**As unto the Lord.** Faithful performance of this duty, as of every other, is subjection to the Lord Jesus Christ.

23. For the husband is the head of the wife, as Christ also is the head of the church, *being* himself the saviour of the body.

The husband is the head. Not the Lord, not the absolute master of the wife. The dependence of the wife upon the husband is indeed expressed here, but that dependence is not of the nature of abject submission. There is an assertion of the superiority of the husband here; but that superiority consists in the ability to care for the wife, as the head cares for the body, and as Christ cares for the Church.—**Christ also is the head.** From ch. 4:15 it is evident that Christ is for the Church the head of supply, which regulates the growth of the whole body. The connection between Christ and the Church is a living one. Not force, but the power of love, unites the Church to its Lord. So it should be between husband and wife.—**Saviour of the body.** By His salvation He made the body His own, and thereby became its head. It is useless to try

to find anything in the relation of husband and wife parallel
to this work of salvation. Here is one of the places where the
analogy of Christ and a husband fails. The apostle's thought
drops the relation of husband and wife for a moment, and
lingers on the wonderful relation of Christ and the Church
alone.

24. But as the church is subject to Christ, so *let* the wives
also *be* to their husbands in everything.

But. Resuming the analogy after a momentary interrup-
tion.—**Subject.** The relation of dependence described in the
preceding verse makes subjection necessary. The Church
must obediently allow its head to care for it, and the wife
must obediently accept the care of her husband.

25. Husbands, love your wives, even as Christ also loved
the church, and gave himself up for it;

Gave himself up. (Cf. 1 Peter 3:7.) To death as a sacrifice.
(Cf. ver. 2.) Here again the apostle goes beyond the analogy
between Christ and a husband, and dwells upon what is true
of Christ alone.

26. That he might sanctify it, having cleansed it by the
washing of water with the word,

Sanctify it. As in 1:4 sanctification is made an end
of election in Christ, so here it is an end of His atoning
death.—**Cleansed it.** This purification is the first step in
the sanctification.—**The washing of water with the word.**
The more literal translation "in the word" would be preferable
for a reason indicated below. This peculiar phraseology of
the apostle could be understood by the readers of the epistle
of nothing else but of a washing that was well known to them,
namely, baptism. The language here used calls to mind the
familiar definition of baptism in Luther's Small Catechism:

"The water comprehended in God's command and connected with God's word." The washing is not one of water alone nor of the word alone, but of water in the word. The water is joined with the word, so to speak encased in it, and thus applied for purification. The word is that of the Gospel. This word applied with the water brings the blessings of the Gospel, without which there is no purification from sin, namely, the forgiveness of sins and the beginning of a new life by the power of the Holy Spirit (Acts 2:38; 22:16; Titus. 3:5). The Church is cleansed by baptism because its members are purified by this washing on their entrance into it.

27. That he might present the church to himself a glorious *church,* not having spot or wrinkle or any such thing; but that it should be holy and without blemish.

This verse contains a fuller statement of the process of sanctification. It is common to regard it as a figure of speech drawn from the custom of preparing a bride and bringing her to her bridegroom. The context, which discusses the marriage relation, readily suggests this idea, and the language of 2 Cor. 11:2 seems to confirm it. Nevertheless this interpretation is objectionable. Here is a point at which the general principle about this whole paragraph stated above (see on ver. 22) is especially applicable. The apostle does not only think along the line of the analogy between Christ and a husband; but sometimes he follows out thoughts which are applicable to the relation of Christ and the Church alone. To interpret this verse as a figure derived from matrimony is liable to open the way for a use of the imagination which runs into fanciful details, and is hardly consistent with a sober understanding of the Scriptures. But even if fanciful details are avoided, nevertheless it is objectionable to find here a

figure derived from the purification of a bride preparatory
to being led to her husband. It would make of the passage
an allegory, representing the relation of Christ under the
forms of marriage. Now it should be observed that the
apostle is doing the very reverse of this. He is deriving the
relations which should exist between husband and wife from
the relation of Christ to the Church. The whole passage,
beginning with the latter part of verse 25 and extending to
the end of verse 27, describes features in the love of Christ
which display its greatness, but for which there is no parallel
in the love of a husband.

But while we exclude the figure of matrimony, we recognize that the language of this verse is indeed figurative; but
only as sacrificial language in the N. T. generally is figurative.
For the terms here used, "not having spot or wrinkle or any
such thing," and "holy and without blemish," are such as are
commonly used to describe a perfect sacrifice. (Cf. Col. 1:22;
Rom. 12:1; 1 Peter 1:19.) The truth of this verse briefly stated
is this: Christ offered Himself in order to make the Church a
perfect offering to Himself.

28. Even so ought husbands also to love their own wives as
their own bodies. He that loveth his own wife loveth himself:

As their own bodies. An additional argument why they
should love their wives; they are their own bodies. Hence
not to love them is to sin against nature.

29. For no man ever hated his own flesh; but nourisheth
and cherisheth it, even as Christ also the church;

Nourisheth and cherisheth. As with a mother's
love.—**As Christ also,** etc. The Church is not the flesh,
but the body of Christ. Nevertheless the relation of Christ to
the Church teaches the same truth that nature teaches in this

matter.

30. Because we are members of his body.

The oneness of man and wife has its analogy in the oneness of the Church and Christ's person. For the profound meaning of this verse is not merely that we are members of that body which Christ acknowledges as His, the Church; but that the members who constitute the Church are in some sense members of His personal body. The A. V. adds the words: "Of his flesh and of his bones." The textual authority for these words may not be sufficient to retain them; nevertheless the idea they express is in perfect harmony with the thought of the verse. The same life that is in the person of Christ is in us. The same life is in the branches and in the vine. It is in harmony with this intimate union between Christ and believers that the Lord communicates His own body and blood in the Holy Supper.

31. For this cause shall a man leave his father and mother, and shall cleave to his wife; and the twain shall become one flesh.

For this cause. The thought is not that because believers are members of the body of Christ, therefore husband and wife are one. The verse is a free citation of Gen. 2:24. But the connection in which the apostle places it, both with the preceding and the following verse, shows that he had more in mind than the marriage relation. It is true that inasmuch as marriage is an analogous relation to the union of Christ with His members, a man must cleave to his wife even if other tender ties, like filial relations, are thereby severed. But the apostle is not only speaking of human relations. In the words he quotes, he somehow saw the wonderful union that exists between Christ and the Church. Because we are members of

His body, for this cause (as the text says) the principle stated in Gen. 2:24, of marriage, is true also of Christ and the Church. The apostle himself declares that he finds this "mystery" in it. But the words are not an allegory requiring that an antitype be found for every detail. Hence it is fanciful and vain to try to show how Christ left His father and mother. The details of the quotation belong only to the human relation; but the principle, the underlying idea of unity, of cleaving together, is true of Christ and the Church.

32. This mystery is great: but I speak in regard of Christ and of the church.

"While the words of the quotation from Genesis are on his lips and he is dictating them to the friend who is writing the epistle for him, I think I see a look of dreamy abstraction come over his face, showing that his thoughts have passed from earthly to heavenly things. He is in the presence of the transcendent unity of Christ and the Church.... Forgetting that he was writing about marriage, he exclaims, *The mystery is great*" (Dale).

33. Nevertheless do ye also severally love each one his own wife even as himself; and *let* the wife *see* that she fear her husband.

In conclusion the apostle makes an individual application of the general truth of the whole paragraph.—**Fear.** Not slavish fear, but fear inspired by love; fear of causing offence.

7

Ephesians 6

1. Children, obey your parents in the Lord: for this is right.

It was natural for the apostle to pass from the duties of husband and wife to those of children and parents. (Cf. Col. 3:20.) **Obey.** This is the form in which the general rule of 5:21 applies to children. It is evident that the apostle is especially addressing children who are not small.—**In the Lord.** Their obedience to parents was to be a service to the Lord Christ, to whom they belonged.—**This is right.** The nature of the case requires such obedience. Luther translates well: *Das ist billig* (that is proper). Here again the apostle insists on propriety.

2. Honor thy father and mother (which is the first commandment with promise),

3. That it may be well with thee, and thou mayest live long on the earth.

Not only natural propriety, but God's express commandment, requires, obedience to parents. The importance of this commandment is emphasized by referring to the unique promise connected with it.—**The first commandment.** The fourth is the first with a specific promise attached to it,

and indeed in this respect it is unique in the decalogue. The
first commandment also has a promise added to it (cf. Exod.
20:6); but the promise is quite general, and moreover belongs
to all the ten commandments, as Luther clearly shows in his
Catechism.—**It may be well,** etc. The promise of longevity
and temporal prosperity is fulfilled collectively rather than
individually. The temporal welfare of nations depends upon
nothing more than well-regulated family life, and the fourth
commandment aims to secure this.

4. And, ye fathers, provoke not your children to wrath: but
nurture them in the chastening and admonition of the Lord.

And. The conjunction is of much force. The re-
ciprocal duty of parents immediately follows that of
children.—**Fathers.** The mothers are not mentioned,
because their position has already been defined in 5:22.
In virtue of this position they are included in the term
"fathers."—**Provoke not,** etc. Children cannot honor their
parents in wrath, even if they outwardly obey. Hence
parents must not exercise their authority so as to provoke
rebellious feelings in their children. This exhortation applies
both to moody conduct of parents and to false ideas of
discipline.—**Chastening.** Not mere chastisement, although
this may form a part of what is intended. That which is
required here is the training and moulding of the child-nature
generally.—**Admonition.** A special feature of "chastening."
It consists in encouragement of the child when it is right, as
well as setting it right when it is in danger of going wrong or
has gone wrong.—**Of the Lord.** The chastening is the Lord's
chastening. Much attempted bringing up of children is not.
The parent, according to the apostle's view, is the minister of
the Lord Christ. In this view there is a grave responsibility

for the Christian parent, but also a great comfort. For Christ is present in the household to give to the training done under Him effect and success. If children grow up well, it is not owing chiefly to parental wisdom, but divine grace.

5. Servants, be obedient unto them that according to the flesh are your masters, with fear and trembling, in singleness of your heart, as unto Christ;

After discussing the duties of parents and children the apostle proceeds to address those who belong to the family in a wider sense, the domestics or slaves. So also Col. 3:5. (Cf. 1 Pet. 2:25.)—**According to the flesh.** Describes their human masters in contrast with Christ the Lord. There is in these words the recognition that inwardly in their spirits they are not bound, but free in the bondage of Christ.—**Fear and trembling.**—Not dread of their earthly masters, but such a regard for them as the fear of Christ inspires. (Cf. Phil. 2:12; 1 Cor. 2:3.)—**Singleness.** Best understood from its opposite, duplicity.—**As unto Christ.** The true Master, for whom all service should be rendered. If a slave might have doubts what kind of service his earthly master had a right to claim from him, he could have no doubt about what kind of service he owed to Christ.

6. Not in the way of eyeservice, as men-pleasers; but as servants of Christ, doing the will of God from the heart;

Eyeservice. Only to please the master's eye, not to do their duty.—**Men-pleasers.** It is not wrong to desire the approval of men; but flattery and fawning service is beneath the dignity even of a Christian slave. Christian servants are to be God-pleasers.—**Servants of Christ.** St. Paul everywhere represents the Christian as the **servant** of God and Christ. From this relation of service arise all his earthly obligations.

Chrysostomos aptly says: "This is the servitude that even
Paul, the free man, serves.... Look how he divests thy slavery
of its meanness."—**From the heart.** Even slave's work is to
be soul work. Not that a master possesses his servant's soul.
But God binds the soul of the servant to his master's service.

7. With good will doing service, as unto the Lord, and not
unto men:

There is a kind of paradox here; for doing bond-service
rests not upon will, but compulsion. The exhortation is that
the servant's good will is to anticipate all compulsion.

8. Knowing that whatsoever good thing each one doeth,
the same shall he receive again from the Lord, whether *he be*
bond or free.

Receive again. Good works are like a deposit with Christ.
When He comes again to judge He will give back to each his
own. This verse anticipates any objection which might arise
from the injustice of a human master.—**Bond or free.** In this
way the apostle lifts the servant to a higher plane on which
he is the equal of others.

9. And, ye masters, do the same things unto them, and
forbear threatening: knowing that both their Master and
yours is in heaven, and there is no respect of persons with
him.

And. The. conjunction forcibly brings forward the other
side, as in ver. 4.—**Do the same things.** Have the same
spirit; act in the same fear of Christ, according to the general
rule (5:21).—**Forbear threatening.** This habitual fault, with
which such vices as cruelty and oppression begin, is to
cease entirely.—**Their Master and yours.** Christ as Judge is
referred to. From ver. 5–7 it might look as if St. Paul really
made the demands of slavery more severe, just as if the Lord

were on the side of the master, whether he was just or unjust. But here Christ appears on the side of the servant, as the vindicator of his rights and the avenger of his wrongs. If the slave is to serve with fear and trembling (ver. 5), the earthly master also has his Master, before whom he must live in fear and trembling.—**No respect of persons.** The righteous Judge will consider the case, not the person. "Think not, he would say, that what is done towards a servant, he will therefore forgive, because done to a servant" (Chrysostomos). (See on Col. 4:1.)

Final Exhortation to Valiant Warfare. 6:10–20

Summary. The Church has a conflict to sustain with evil spirits, in which it must use the might of God (10). The panoply of God is needed in this warfare, for it is a battle against the devil, very different from warfare against feeble men (11–13). The various parts of the armor of God are the girdle, breastplate, sandals, shield, helmet, and sword, consisting respectively of truth, righteousness, Gospel-preparation, faith, salvation, and the word of God (14–17). The use of this armor is to be accompanied with prayer for the whole host of the Church, and in particular for Paul himself, in order that he may do his part successfully by boldly proclaiming the Gospel as an ambassador in chains (18–20).

10. Finally, be strong in the Lord, and in the strength of his might.

Be strong. At first sight a strange imperative. The command is not to become strong, but to be strong. Can we be stronger than we are? No, but we can be weaker than we really are by failing to use the power which God gives us.

(Cf. 1:19.) When we avail ourselves of the strength which
God has given through Christ, we are strong. The apostle is
not speaking of our own strength, but the power which we
have "in the Lord."

"With might of ours can naught be done,
Soon were our loss effected;
But for us fights the Valiant One
Whom God Himself elected."

11. Put on the whole armour of God, that ye may be able
to stand against the wiles of the devil.

The general conception of this entire paragraph is not
that of an individual conflict, but of the warfare of the
whole host of the Church against the kingdom of the devil.
But each individual in the army of God must put on his
armor.—**Armour of God.** That furnished by God.—**Stand.**
This verb is used three times in this connection. (Cf. ver.
13 and 14.) In the latter place the idea is clearly "to take
your stand, to be ready for the fight," and not "to stand your
ground," which is expressed by **withstand** in ver. 13. The
thought is the same here as in ver. 14. The believer is to be
fully armed and ready to take his place in the battle.—**The
wiles of the devil.** (Cf. "the wiles of error" in 4:14.) But
there the Greek word for "wiles" is in the singular, while here
it is in the plural, to indicate the separate "cunning assaults
of the devil," as Luther happily translates.

12. For our wrestling is not against flesh and blood, but
against the principalities, against the powers, against the
world-rulers of this darkness, against the spiritual *hosts* of
wickedness in the heavenly *places*.

Wrestling. The apostle is describing a battle; but this word
indicates an individual, hand-to-hand conflict. However, it

is doubtful whether the literal meaning of the word is to be pressed.—**Flesh and blood.** That is, men. But is not the Christian warfare against men and organizations of men? Yes; but the real enemy is invisible, fighting through men and their organizations.—**Principalities,** etc. (Cf. 1:21; 3:10.) These are general terms. They do not describe different orders of enemies. The particular class of beings referred to must be inferred from the context. There can be no doubt that evil spirits are meant here; but from the use of different terms to describe them no inference can be made as to different degrees or orders among them.—**This darkness.** The present spiritual and moral darkness. The times of the New Testament were times of great prevalence of evil in the world. (Cf. "the course of this world," ch. 2:2.) The apostle speaks here in the plural of "world-rulers," who dominated over this darkness. Elsewhere the N. T. represents the world as controlled by a single evil spirit. (Cf. John 16:11; 14:30; 2 Cor. 4:4; 1 John 5:19.) The devil is the world-ruler, but doubtlessly has other evil spirits associated with him.—**Spiritual hosts.** The word "hosts" is not in the original. But the form of the word "spiritual" which is neuter plural, and the context show that some term of this kind must be supplied. The "spirituals," against which the Church has to contend are principalities, powers and world-rulers, who form a host.—**In the heavenly places.** The location, the domain of the spiritual hosts of wickedness. Our surprise that the apostle should locate evil spirits in the region of the heavenly will be removed by a proper understanding of his language. The "heavenly" in this epistle is not what is commonly understood by heaven, the abode of God and good spirits. It forms the contrast with the earthly, and hence designates the supernal. (Cf. 1:20; 2:2.) In the heavenly places there may be different regions. The sphere of the activity of evil spirits is not the same as the sphere of the good.

13. Wherefore take up the whole armour of God, that ye may be able to withstand in the evil day, and, having done all, to stand.

The evil day. The day of trial, of temptation. Not every day is the evil day, but any day may become so.—**Having done all.** Some refer this to the preparations for the conflict. But it is better to understand it of the work of the conflict itself; yet not in the special sense of vanquishing (which the word may indeed have), but with the general idea of leaving nothing undone to frustrate the wiles of the enemy.—**To stand.** (Cf. note on ver. 11.) This verb cannot have the meaning here of taking one's stand. Standing, after having accomplished all in the fight, is to stand as victor, safe and triumphant.

14. Stand therefore, having girded your loins with truth, and having put on the breastplate of righteousness,

Stand. As in ver. 11, ready for the conflict. The apostle may have had Isaiah 59:17 in mind when he wrote the description of the armor which follows.—**Girded.** For unimpeded action, the first necessity is preparing for conflict.—**Truth.** In defining the significance of this and the following terms, which make up the armor of the Christian, it is necessary to bear in mind that the panoply is of God. Hence the reference here is not to mere human sincerity or truthfulness, but to the truth of God as apprehended in the heart.—**Breastplate.** For protection.—**Righteousness.** Not mere moral rectitude, but the righteousness which God gives, the imputed righteousness of Christ. (Cf. Rom. 8:33.) The man who is filled with God's truth is ready for action; the man who is covered

114

with Christ's righteousness is secure against the thrusts of the adversary.

15. And having shod your feet with the preparation of the gospel of peace;

Shod. For free and active movement. A Christian soldier must not be annoyed by sharp stones, thorns, briers and other little obstacles in the path of duty.—**The preparation of the gospel of peace.** Possibly this means readiness to preach the Gospel which proclaims peace. Certainly this is a part of the Christian warfare. But it is not so easy to perceive how this readiness is a part of the warrior's outfit corresponding with the other parts mentioned. Hence it is better to understand the expression of the preparation, the readiness in movement, which the Gospel of peace imparts. The Gospel gives to the soldier peace, takes away his inward fears and fightings, and thus is the source of that strength which enables him to go to meet his foes, trampling difficulties under foot.

16. Withal taking up the shield of faith, wherewith ye shall be able to quench all the fiery darts of the evil *one.*

The shield of faith. "Faith is not a shield and defence of the soul in as far as it is a quality or virtue in us, but in as far as it apprehends God and His promises and acquiesces in them" (Calovius quoted in Harless).—**Fiery darts.** Missiles wrapped with combustible materials were used in ancient warfare. Satan's weapons are of the most dangerous kind; nevertheless they are powerless against the believing soul.

17. And take the helmet of salvation, and the sword of the Spirit, which is the word of God:

The helmet of salvation. (Cf. 1 Thess. 5:8.) There the apostle calls the hope of salvation a helmet. But in this place salvation must not be understood of the hope of a future deliverance. It is the present application of Christ's redemption to ourselves, with which we are to cover our heads against all perils.—**The sword of the Spirit.** Not the sword of which the Holy Spirit is the author; nor that with which the Spirit Himself fights; but the sword which is the Spirit Himself. In what sense the Spirit can be denominated a sword, is explained by the clause which the writer adds.—**The word of God.** The Spirit is so closely connected with the word of God that the same effects are ascribed to both in the Bible. The living and saving power which is in the word (Rom. 1:16; Hebr. 4:12) is nothing less than the Holy Spirit Himself. Hence it can be said that he who wields the word of God wields the Spirit of God. In this sense it is true that the word of God is that sword, which is the Spirit.

18. With all prayer and supplication praying at all seasons in the Spirit, and watching thereunto in all perseverance and supplication for all the saints,

The entire preperation for battle described in ver. 14–17 is to be accompanied with persevering prayer. The punctuation of the R. V. does not sufficiently indicate this, for it connects this verse with only the one preceding.—**All prayer.** The prayer of the Christian soldier is varied according to different needs. Prayer is not spoken of as a weapon or part of the armor, nor is it such, however important it is in Christian life, and especially in conflict. But the armor here described is God-given; whereas prayer is man's act, by which he calls in the aid of God.—**In the Spirit.** It is the consistent teaching of the New Testament that there can be no real prayer to God except by the Holy Spirit.—**Watching.** So that nothing fail for the lack of prayer. Our activity is all in vain, unless we obtain God's co-operation by prayer. Hence there must be

116

perseverance in supplication.—**For all saints.** There must not only be prayer all along the line, but each part must try to sustain every other part of God's host by its prayers. Here is communion of the saints.

19. And on my behalf, that utterance may be given unto me in opening my mouth, to make known with boldness the mystery of the gospel,

St. Paul, the wonderfully endowed, the divinely inspired, the apostle of Christ, feels himself dependent upon the help and support of the prayers of much weaker men than himself for success in his ministry. (Cf. Col. 4:3; Rom. 15:30; Phil. 1:19; 2 Thess. 3:1.) What an exalted idea he had of the intercession of those whom he calls saints; notwithstanding their many imperfections. If he had great power with God, so that he prayed for all churches, he trusted that others also had power with God to assist in furthering his work by their prayers. So should it be between pastor and people.—**Utterance may be given.** The apostle knew the part he had to perform. He described it in chap. 3. He knew he had obtained a revelation from God to perform his ministry. But he also knew that God had to give him what to say in every instance. For it is not the opportunity to speak which he here desires; it is the utterance itself which he asks for.—**In opening my mouth.** This phrase, frequently used in the Bible (e.g. Matt. 5:2; Acts 8:35; 10:34, simply designates the act of speaking, and not the quality of the speech, either as bold or full or solemn. But the apostle certainly does not intend to say merely, "When I speak, may I have utterance." He looks to God for opening of his mouth as he looks to Him for utterance.—**With boldness.** This confident joy follows from the assurance of receiving speech

from God. The minister who is assured that he has a message
from God to deliver can speak boldly.

20. For which I am an ambassador in chains; that in it I
may speak boldly, as I ought to speak.

In chains. The Greek word is singular; and hence it has
been thought that St. Paul was here alluding to the fact
that he was chained to a guard, although allowed to move
about. (Cf. Acts 28:20; 2 Tim. 1:16.) But this inference
is questionable.—**In it.** In proclaiming the mystery of the
Gospel.—**I may speak boldly.** It is unlikely that this is a
mere repetition of the thought of ver. 19. The sense of duty
is emphasized. The apostle knew that he ought to speak
boldly. By their prayers he trusts it will be so.

Conclusion of the Letter. 6:21–24

Summary. He sends Tychicus to bear information concerning his condition and to comfort them (21–22). He wishes
peace, love and grace to the brethren (23–24).

21. But that ye also may know my affairs, how I do,
Tychicus, the beloved brother and faithful minister in the
Lord, shall make known to you all things:

Ye also. Some think this implies a contract with the apostle.
He has been writing about them; they also may learn about
him from Tychicus. An explanation to be preferred to this is,
that St. Paul was informing others about his affairs as well
as them also. Who these others were is not clear. Possibly
he refers to the Church at Colossæ (cf. Col. 4:7), to which
he wrote a letter about the same time with this. It has been
attempted to derive an argument from this in favor of the
idea that the apostle first penned the epistle to the Colossians,
then this epistle. But the whole matter is too uncertain to
draw any satisfactory conclusion.—**Tychicus.** He was "of

Asia" (Acts 20:4), possibly an Ephesian, the bearer of this letter and of the one to Colossæ (Col. 4:7). Later he was sent to Ephesus (2 Tim. 4:12) and possibly to Crete (Titus 3:12).

22. Whom I have sent unto you for this very purpose, that ye may know our state, and that he may comfort your hearts.

Comfort your hearts. In whatever respect they needed comfort. The comfort may have reference to their sympathy with his afflictions. (Cf. 3:13.) At any rate some degree of personal friendship is implied in the personal messages alluded to here. Although the force of the fact, that there is a remarkable absence in this letter of any personal references to the intimacy existing between Paul and the Ephesians, cannot be underrated, nevertheless even the slight personal references here given at the end of the epistle accord better with the theory that it was addressed to a Church like that at Ephesus, where the apostle was known, than that it was a circular letter for Churches which had no personal acquaintance with the apostle.

23. Peace be to the brethren, and love with faith, from God the Father and the Lord Jesus Christ.

The absence of salutations such as are found in most of St. Paul's epistles is remarkable and inexplicable. For even a circular letter might have salutations, as is the case with 1 Peter.—The benediction is more comprehensive than is usual. The full meaning of its terms is best understood by referring back to the truths taught in the epistle. The **peace** is that described in chap. 2:14–18. The **love** is that spoken of in chap. 3:18. With this love is to be blended **faith,** as is the case in a harmonious Christian character. The faith is the underlying principle of their religious life, as was shown in chap. 2:8 and 3:17.

24. Grace be with all them that love our Lord Jesus Christ in uncorruptness.

A second and general benediction. The whole epistle is an exhibition of the **grace** of God. The pronouncing of this benediction is therefore an application of all the glorious blessings unfolded in the epistle to those who receive it.—**In uncorruptness.** This addition is most naturally connected with **love** and not with **grace.** It is not imperishable grace, but imperishable love, which the apostle speaks of. The idea of **uncorruptness** is not that of sincerity and moral purity, but of imperishableness, indestructibility. True love to Christ is immortal. True love to the Lord never ceases. The love that perishes is not genuine. The grace of Christ with its eternal blessings will remain only with those who have undying, unfading, imperishable, incorruptible love to the Saviour.

II

Philippians

ANNOTATIONS
ON THE
EPISTLE TO THE PHILIPPIANS

BY

EDWARD T. HORN, D. D.

8

Introduction

I.

In the 16th chapter of the Acts of the Apostles we have the story of the foundation of the Christian Church in Philippi. It was in the year 52 a.d. that Paul, Silas, Luke and Timothy came up from Neapolis into Philippi. They had come by a rapid voyage from Troas in Asia Minor. They probably walked from Neapolis on the Egnatian Way. Paul's missionary journeys in Asia Minor had been successful: though persecuted there and driven out of cities, he had succeeded in founding Christian congregations that survived persecution. But on this second tour he had felt himself withheld whenever he planned new routes, until he had come to the limit of Asia, and looked over towards Europe; and there a man of Macedonia, a European, came to him in a vision, and said, *Come over into Macedonia and help us.* This explained God's unwillingness to let him go northward or southward. And, without delay, he set out, impelled by these

two motives: the assurance that he was sent by God and
sustained by Him, and deep pity for the most civilized men
on earth, who needed his help because they did not know
Christ.

Paul is said to have been an odd-looking little man, with
close curling hair, quick, enthusiastic, irrepressible. Of Silas
we know little, save that his name indicates that he was either
a Greek or a Jew born and bred out of Palestine, and like
Paul he was a Roman citizen. Luke was an educated Greek
physician of cheerful temperament. He had joined Paul at
Troas; became a very son to him, having fully imbibed his
spirit; and, though separated from him at times in discharge
of duty, remained his companion, attendant and assistant
to the end of his life. The Gospel of St. Luke may also be
described as the Gospel of St. Paul. I would not be surprised
to be told that St. Luke had been a surgeon and physician on
the ships plying regularly between the Asiatic and Grecian
ports. He may have been God's instrument in first turning
Paul's mind to the need of the Gospel in Greece and the
kind reception that awaited him there. He may have been
acquainted in Philippi, and it may have been he who did not
let Paul linger in Neapolis. Timothy was a delicate young
man, like-minded with Paul, who soon would show that he
labored with him in the Gospel like a son with a father.

They remained in Philippi several days before they are
said to have preached to any one. There were not enough
Jews in Philippi to have a synagogue. Philippi was a Roman
colony; i.e. the city that stood there, near to the field of battle
where Brutus and Cassius were defeated after the death of
Julius Cæsar, had been adopted by Augustus and settled with
Roman soldiers, the adherents of his rival, Antony. Such a

colony made it a point to imitate Roman customs; it was more Latin than Greek in the fashion of its life; so that Paul's claim to *citizenship* and his subsequent reference to our *heavenly citizenship* get especial meaning.

On the Sabbath the four knew of a place of prayer where the very few who knew of the One True God were likely to resort. It was a mere enclosure by the side of a stream which, in summer, became but a river-bed, some distance beyond the gate. Here, unobserved and undisturbed, while the rest of their townsmen sought their pleasures or did their work, these few regularly assembled; and these few were *women* only, and, as the names would indicate, women not of Jewish birth, but attracted to the Jewish faith. To these Paul and his companions came, and sitting down like teachers told why they had come, and what had happened twenty years before at Jerusalem. Just so now in India missionaries accost persons in the market-place or join them on the roads, and in simple conversation tell the Gospel. God also was in that place, and He opened the heart of one of the women. A Lydian woman, perhaps named *Lydia,* a purple-seller of Thyatira in Asia, a city famed for its purple cloth, was then residing at Philippi in the way of her calling. She believed. Her household—whether her children or her work-people or both, we cannot say—yielded to her influence, and were baptized with her. Luke does not say all the women they spoke to believed. There may have been others besides Lydia, but she is mentioned because of her ability and readiness to help. She modestly put her house at their service. For the rest of their stay in Philippi they were her guests. Her place of business and home gave them room and prominence.

The mission of St. Paul and his companions made rapid

progress in Philippi. Other women were gathered in—such
were Euodia and Syntyche. But men also; for we are told that
before Paul left the city he met the *brethren* at the house of
Lydia. Such was Epaphroditus, whom he afterwards refers to
as his companion in labor and fellow-soldier; and Clement;
and there were others who passed to their reward before his
epistle was written; and one, unnamed in the letter, whose
assistance was so marked that Paul called him his true *yokefellow*. It is extraordinary that in a few days such zeal was
begotten. Not Paul and Silas and Luke and Timothy only, but
all, men and women, *labored in the Gospel*. It may be because of
this character of the Philippian Church as a *working* Church,
that, while other Christian Churches are said each to have had
a bishop by the end of the first century, there is no record that
the Philippian Church ever had any one person who could
be said to unite in himself the force and authority of the
congregation. Paul writes to the *bishops* and *deacons*, or, more
properly, the *overseers* and *servants*. This working Church
divided itself for organized service.

This active Church soon encountered the works of the
devil. There were men who led about a slave girl, who, under
alleged spiritual influence, told fortunes, and taking up a
mocking echo of their own words, followed Paul and his
friends day after day, crying, *These are the servants of the Most
High God, which shew unto us the way of salvation.* Paul cast the
evil spirit out of her; her masters accused him and Silas before
the magistrates of teaching wrongful customs, and especially
complained against them as Jews. The Jews had just been
expelled from the city of Rome, for making a disturbance
there. The magistrates yielded to the crowd, had Paul and
Silas whipped and threw them into the inner prison. We

cannot linger to tell of their prayers and songs in the prison, of the earthquake that liberated them, and of the apology of the magistrates; except to note that the jailor and his household were added to the little Church.

It continued to be a *helpful* Church. Those who had labored in the Gospel in their own town determined to become partners in Paul's mission. From Philippi he went to Amphipolis, thence to Apollonia, and came to Thessalonica. He was there about three weeks, and while there worked at his trade as a tentmaker so as to be independent; but more than once in that time messengers came to him from Philippi bringing gifts to him. Paul was a proud man; he gloried in being a burden to nobody; he made it a rule to take nothing for himself from the churches he planted, though he taught it as a principle that they who labored in the Gospel should live from the Gospel; but he was so touched by the prompt and insistent kindness of the Philippian Church, and so assured of the spirit in which they gave, that he accorded them the distinction of being the one Church from which he would receive what they offered to give for his own relief.

Not till the year 57 did he see them again, as he went down into Greece; and in the spring of the next year he came back, on his way to Jerusalem. He was then occupied in making up a great collection in all his churches in Greece and Asia to carry up to the relief of the poor in Jerusalem. It was to signalize the unity of spirit between the Christians who had been heathens and those who had been Jews. In this work the Philippians were helpers. He used their example to urge those of Corinth, for they had their gifts ready long before his coming and had given cheerfully far beyond their ability, because they first gave themselves to the Lord.

The Epistle to the Philippians affords the last picture in the New Testament of this earnest people. Ten years have elapsed (a.d. 62). They bear all the features of an ordered congregation. It is almost the only congregation St. Paul has written to, in which he finds no reason for blame. Only, he detects the danger that always hangs over an active congregation—the peril of dissension; and he urges them *to be of one mind.* He was at this time a prisoner at Rome. They had sent Epaphroditus to him with a generous gift. In his trials he professes himself sustained by their fellowship. And he grounds his hopes of release and further usefulness upon his assurance of their prayers.

This epistle is sweet because of its unreserved outpouring of the apostle's heart to those who, he knows, understand and love him. He gives thanks upon every remembrance of them; he is confident of their final salvation, because he has them in his heart; he acknowledges them as sharers in his calling, and in the defence and confirmation of the Gospel; he sets before them the master-motive of his life, the humiliation and crucifixion of our Lord; and in the third chapter pours out the earnest longing that filled him. Rejoice, he says, Rejoice. Rejoice in the Lord always: and again I say, Rejoice.

II.

King Agrippa said to Festus, after he had heard Paul's defence, If this man had not appealed unto Cæsar, he might have been set at liberty. But his appeal was not a device to escape the passing danger at the hands of clamorous adversaries and a judge who foresaw that inconvenience would arise to himself from strict justice; but Paul wished to be carried to Rome and brought into the presence of the master of the world and allowed to state there the Gospel for preaching which he had been arrested. God assured him that his life and mission could not end until he had borne witness at Rome. To some the book of the Acts of the Apostles may seem incomplete. It tells very little of what Paul did at Rome. It leaves us in the dark as to the issue of his testimony there. But inasmuch as in his coming to Rome the story of the Gospel had reached its climax, it is evident that Luke had brought it to the very point he had had in mind from the beginning. Here, at length, the story that began at Nazareth, the publication of the Gospel begun on Pentecost, had penetrated to the presence of Cæsar. That which had been whispered in seaport towns, which had been driven from synagogues, which Roman governors considered beneath their attention, having attained to the centre of the empire, demands the attention of the most august court on earth.

And yet, in what shape did the Gospel come to Rome? What dress did the ambassador of Eternal God wear; what state, when he drew near to Cæsar? Like Christ was before Pilate, so St. Paul came to Rome a poor prisoner. The impression he had made on his guards during his voyage was lost. His high thoughts and irrepressible purpose seemed to be overwhelmed. When our Lord was before Pilate, He met the hardness of Roman criminal law, and detected the flaw in the judge; when Paul was summoned before Cæsar, he met the absolutism of Rome, and met it in the man who has become the symbol of unbridled and frightful power, the Emperor Nero.

The Rome of that day was a city of 2,000,000 inhabitants. The stately edifices, of which relics are now being dug up,

belong to a later period. Only after the time of Julius Cæsar
did marbles begin to take the place of brick, and the wonders
of Nero's "Golden House" belong to the period succeeding
the great fire, which was after St. Paul's first captivity. There
were a few extensive buildings; the house of Cæsar occupied a
precinct; but the Rome St. Paul saw was a vast stretch of lofty
brick buildings, crowded on narrow and tortuous streets, and
filled with people from every part of the world. Maybe half of
the population were slaves; most of these spoke Greek; many
of them were of a high degree of intelligence, and most of the
mechanical work was in the hands, not of free artisans, but
of the servile households of great proprietors. There were
many Jews in Rome. Pompey had brought many of them, and
they dwelt in a district of their own. They were more or less
turbulent. Before his coming, in the time of the Emperor
Claudius, the Jews had been banished because of a tumult
excited, it is said, by one Chrestus: most probably it was a
tumult occasioned by the first preaching of Christ among the
Jews. At any rate, there were Christian communities whom
Paul had addressed in his letter to the Romans a few years
before, and these met him and welcomed him to the city.
Agrippa was well known at Rome. While Paul was a prisoner
there, the historian Josephus came as a petitioner to Cæsar;
and a solemn embassy headed by the high priest came also.
For the emperor, after divorcing and murdering his young
wife, married an infamous woman, who pretended to be very
religious and was reputed a proselyte to the Jewish faith.

When Paul was brought to Rome he was delivered to the
commander of the imperial guard. He was allowed to rent
a house for himself, most probably near the great fortified
camp of the guard, and here to see any one he pleased. But

130

he was always chained by the wrist to the wrist of a soldier, and perhaps at night had to sleep between two. That he made good use of this vexatious restraint is shown by his description of the Christian armor, and by the fact that "his bonds became manifest throughout the whole praetorian guard." We know how he won the centurion who had charge of him on shipboard. And here, as every day a different soldier was locked to him, to spy upon and guard him, he preached to him the Gospel. The man saw and heard in the apostle's manners and the intercourse between him and his friends, in their prayers and hymns and sacraments, a truth and hope and life he had not known before. Many came to Paul, and he taught them boldly. Timothy, Luke, Mark, Demas, Tychicus, Aristarchus, were with him, except when sent on errands, and acted as his messengers and servants. One day Epaphroditus came with a gift of money from Philippi. Then the faithful messenger fell sick and the whole house of Paul were deeply concerned until the good man was well enough to go back to the home he so longed to see. Then Epaphras of Colossæ arrived to bring a long story of new heresies, of false teachers, of weakness that might have been expected,—intelligence weighed and discussed in the little circle, and occasioning such letters as we have, which Paul composed and his friends wrote at his dictation and joined in after reading them. A runaway slave found refuge there, and was converted and readily went back to his master with Paul's letter and at his bidding. Thus the "hired house" of Paul was a council of the Church, a centre of evangelistic effort in the city of Rome, and a centre of correction, encouragement and leadership to all the churches which had known the apostle.

It is quite clear that the activity of that household made

a stir in Rome. Up to this time we know of but one
lady of prominence supposed to have become a Christian.
The philosopher Seneca was living then; he seems to have
been a fair-minded man, though too subservient; he was
a brother of that Gallio who refused to trouble himself
about the questions between the Jews and the Christians;
in his writings are many thoughts so like some sayings of
the Gospel that succeeding ages accounted him a Christian
and invented a correspondence between him and Paul; but it
is very strange indeed, and indicative of the hidden manner
in which the leaven worked, that Seneca himself does not
seem to have known or cared about Paul at all. Yet at this
time Paul could congratulate himself that the whole guard
was interested in him. In the city many brethren were
emboldened by his bonds to speak the word of God without
fear. Some even tried to stir up the flame in order to increase
his danger. Among "the saints" were numbered some of
Cæsar's household. It was not very long after this that Nero
endeavored to divert the hatred and vengeance of the people
by charging the Christians with having set fire to Rome, and
persecuting them for it. Soon afterwards we read of Christian
converts, confessors and martyrs, in the highest circles, even
in the family of the emperor.

During this captivity Paul wrote the letters to the Philippians, Ephesians, Colossians, and to Philemon. It has been
debated whether our letter preceded, or followed, the others.
On the one hand, in its general tone it is more like Paul's
earlier epistles than like these; on the other, it has been
thought to show a gloomier outlook than theirs. He spent his
enforced leisure in reflection on the peculiar dangers which
threatened the churches. He added to the eager joy with

which an evangelist tells the Gospel to the unconverted, the penetrating, careful sympathy of a pastor, who seeks to use opportunity and ward off perils from imperfect faith and character. His Christian friends passed under review; he prayed for all, he prayed for each; he studied the theories which were urged instead of, or beside, the Gospel; he tried to develop the truth from their standpoint and to express it in the language they thought in, instead of his native Jewish forms of thought. He fretted at being shut up so, longed to see them again, felt how necessary he was to them, and was cast down to think how much was left undone. Now he would commend his attentive friends. Then he would compare a faithful one with others who were lukewarm and double-faced. Life became a burden; but his work was unfinished. And under these temptations he learned more and more of the riches of Christ. The Epistle to the Philippians shows how he put before him Christ on the cross, and made the Passion and the Resurrection the motto, the master-thought, the be-all and the end-all of his life. It is his resource, his model; it is the talisman he commends to others; it is the criterion by which he tries everything. And if moved by the aspect of the greatness and complexity of the world of mankind, which must have been felt so near to the Imperial Court at Rome, it only led him to see how Christ is before all things, and in Him all things hold together.

This captivity continued for about two years. We have no certain account of the end of it. Some writers have believed that he continued a prisoner until executed under Nero. But it was the universal tradition of the ancient Church that he was set at liberty and was able to fulfil the promise of visiting him, which he makes to Philemon. He is said to have visited

Spain. The letters to Timothy and Titus deal with other
questions than those which occupied the imprisonment to
which Philippians and Colossians belong.

These epistles show the springs of the Christian piety of the
great apostle. They teach us the uses of a period of enforced
inaction. Such a period offers above all an opportunity for
reflection. We owe many of the deepest thoughts of our
religion to Paul's imprisonment. It gave him occasion and
opportunity to look at it from all sides, and then to penetrate
to the very centre of the Gospel he preached to others. He
tried himself; he analyzed his motives; he recognized the only
hope of any man; and he saw how strong, how immovable
that Hope is.

9

Philippians 1

1–2. Paul and Timothy, servants of Christ Jesus, to all the
saints in Christ Jesus which are at Philippi, with the bishops
and deacons: Grace to you and peace from God our Father
and the Lord Jesus Christ.

1. The Salutation. **Paul.** As in 1 and 2 Thess. and
Philemon, he writes here as *a friend,* not asserting his
apostolic authority.—**And Timothy.** Timothy was well
known in Philippi (Acts 16:1, 2; 19:22). Paul thus associates
with himself one whom he means to send to Philippi, in order
to accredit him (1 Cor. 1:1). Timothy also consented in this
letter, and was in so far a co-author.—**Bondsmen of Christ
Jesus.** Significant as written from Rome, a centre of human
slavery, where perhaps half of the inhabitants were bondsmen.
Paul and Timothy had been "bought with a price." A title of
dignity outweighing all earthly honors. (See also Numb. 12:7;
Josh. 1:2; 9:24; 1 Chron. 6:49.) Accordingly, early a technical
appellation in the Church (Col. 4:12; 2 Tim. 2:24; Tit. 1:1;
James 1:1; 1 Peter 2:16; 2 Peter 1:1; Jude 1; Rev 1:1, etc.).—**To
all.** He addresses *all* without distinction, in acknowledgment

of the kindness in which all had joined; in exhortation to
the unity which should be the aim of all.—**The saints** (1 Cor.
1:2). Not, as Ruskin says, the Church Invisible only. The
word *saints,* or *holy ones,* is here "used in its most inclusive
sense" (Ellicott). All were *consecrated* to Christ in baptism and
their faith (Col. 2:11, 12), as the Israelites were consecrated in
the Old Testament; a holy priesthood; a peculiar people. He
embraces them *all* in the New Covenant.—**In Christ Jesus.**
In contradistinction from the Old Covenant. The distinction
lay uppermost in Paul's mind, whether he was writing to
Jews or Gentiles. All in Christ are holy. "These alone are
holy, and those henceforward are profane" (Chrysostom).
"Those who are in Christ Jesus are holy indeed" (Theophylact).
See 1 Cor. 5:13.—**Which are at Philippi.** A Roman colony
in Macedonia, near the field where Augustus and Antony
defeated Brutus and Cassius. Settled by Augustus with
adherents of Antony. Imitating Rome, and more Latin
than Greek in its customs. The first place in Europe Paul
had visited (Acts 16). Here Lydia, Epaphroditus, Clement
and others "labored in the Gospel," with Paul. At least ten
years intervened between that first visit and this letter—a.d.
52–62. (See Introduction.)—**With bishops and deacons.**
See Bengel: "The Church is before the bishop. And the
apostolic scripture is sent more directly to the Church than
to those who have the leadership in it (Hebr. 13:24; Eph.
3:4; Col. 3:18 ss.; 4:17; Rev. 1:4, 11; 1 Thess. 5:12)."—He
addresses the Philippians, not as individual persons, but as
an organized community. The Church at Philippi had as its
officers *overseers* and *serving-men.* The word *bishop (episcopus)*
then had the general meaning of *one set to oversee.* In the
Septuagint the name is applied to public officers, religious

as well as civil; and thence the apostles took it (Acts 1:20; Ps. 109:8. See Numb. 4:16; 31:4; Judges 9:28; 2 Kings 12:21; 11:16; Neh. 11:9, 14; Isai. 60:17). The Syriac version renders the word here *elders.* The elders in the early Christian Church were such overseers. Both words are used of the same office, Acts 20:17, 28; Tit. 1:5; 1 Peter 5:1, 2. Among the Greeks, the name overseer (bishop) was given to the financial officer of burial clubs, confraternities, etc., and to the special officer sent by the Athenians to subject states. The synagogues of the Jews were ordered by a body of elders, of whom it is not by any means certain that one was chief. Christian communities naturally adopted the same order. So at Jerusalem, Acts 15:6. Sohm has suggested that the confusion of lists, and the short terms of "bishops" of Jerusalem and Rome, may be due to the fact that several were *overseers* at the same time there, as here in Philippi.—St. Paul began by appointing *elders* in his mission congregations in Asia Minor (Acts 14:23). These were not primarily the *teachers,* but the *leaders* of the community (1 Thess. 5:12; 1 Tim. 5:17; Rom. 12:8; Hebr. 13:7, 17, 24; Clement of Rome, 1:21).—The government of the congregation was not a monarchy, nor was it a democracy, nor was it even an aristocracy. That time was familiar with government by a *gerousia* or *senate,* as we are with monarchy or representative government, which they did not know at all. The *elders* were the governing college in a community where any one taught to whom the Holy Ghost came with the charism and the call. The decision was by the word of God, not by vote. (See Ramsay, The Church in the Roman Empire, p. 367: "The modern idea of a committee was unknown; any presbyter might become an *episcopos* for an occasion, yet the latter term conveyed

an idea of singleness and of executive authority which was
wanting to the former. Bodies of 3, 5, 10 or more officers
were frequent in Rome; but they were not committees. Each
individual possessed the full powers of the whole body. The
act of one was authoritative as the act of all; each could
thwart the power of his colleagues; no idea of acting by
vote of the majority existed.") *Elders* were called *bishops*
first in Greek communities, because they were overseers,
shepherds, pastors. How the *monarchical episcopate* grew out
of the earlier order still is a matter of dispute. Sohm declares
that those became bishops, in contradistinction from the
other presbyters and deacons, who had the administration of
the Holy Supper especially committed to them, originally as
surrogates for those specially designated by the Holy Ghost,
or for confessors. (See Teaching of the Twelve Apostles,
XII., XV.: "Now appoint for yourselves bishops and deacons
worthy of the Lord, men meek and not avaricious, and
upright and proved; for they, too, render you the service of
the prophets and teachers. Despise them not, therefore; for
they are the ones honored of you, together with the prophets
and teachers.") Hatch teaches that the one who received the
offerings in the Holy Supper and distributed them, having
in his power the list of those entitled to offer, and to receive,
and who could give or determine upon the recommendatory
letters of visiting brethren, became *the bishop par excellence.*
Ramsay, that the office developed under the system of
correspondence established by Paul—the representative of
the congregation *ad extra* became the bishop. Baur, that the
office developed in the opposition to Gnosticism, in the need
of a depository of traditional doctrine. At the beginning, the
elders were for the most part really the *older* members, with

whom were associated those of ripe piety, or distinguished by their gifts and service; first of all the earliest converts (Clem. Rom. 42). But these "clergy" did not at at once give up ordinary avocations (Hatch, 148). It was natural, therefore, that the actual oversight, the *leitourgia*, should be concentrated in the hands of one. This arrangement became general by the *opening of the Second Century;* and the leaders of the Church endeavored to confirm it as of divine appointment. At Philippi we see the earliest stage. There are several presbyters, and *all* are appointed overseers or pastors. This arrangement may have continued there, for Polycarp in his letter does not address *a* bishop. Only since the Council of Trent is the *divine institution of the episcopate,* and its *original distinction from the presbyterate,* a dogma of the Roman Church.—**Deacons.** Servants. With these cf. *the young men* (Acts 5:6, 10), and the *seven,* appointed to relieve the apostles from "serving tables" (Acts 6:1–6). *Diakonie* or *service* was the technical term for the offices of mutual love in the congregation. It is used of the *apostolic office* (Acts 1:17, 25; 20:24; 21:19; Rom. 11:13), and Eusebius (H. E. 5, 1) says, "The Diakonie of the episcopate." The diaconate of Archippus (Col. 4:17) and these deacons at Philippi are the first mention of the office outside Jerusalem. Hatch teaches that originally *bishops* and *deacons* were the same, but that, afterwards, while the former received and blessed the offerings of the people, the latter only distributed them; and they were then likened to *Levites.*—*Service* is the fundamental notion of the ministry and ministers of the New Testament.

2. See on Eph. 1:1; Rom. 1:7; 2 Cor. 1:2; Col. 1:2; 1 Thess. 1:1; 1 Peter 1:2.

3–7. I thank my God upon all my remembrance of you,

always in every supplication of mine on behalf of you all
making my supplication with joy, for your fellowship in
furtherance of the gospel from the first day until now; being
confident of this very thing, that he which began a good
work in you will perfect it until the day of Jesus Christ: even
as it is right for me to be thus minded on behalf of you all,
because I have you in my heart, inasmuch as, both in my
bonds and in the defence and confirmation of the gospel, ye
all are partakers with me of grace.

3–7. **Paul's thanksgiving and prayer for them.** (Eph.
1:15; John 17.)   He had them in mind continually, and
never thought of them without thanksgiving. "His whole
association with the Philippian Church prompted him to
devout acknowledgment" (Eadie). "To be loved of Paul so
earnestly is a proof of one's being great and admirable"
(Chrys.). The faithful friend, the faithful pastor, thinks of, and
prays for, and gives thanks for, all. He did not only preach,
but prayed for those entrusted to him. Mark the weapon and
means of a pastor (Rom. 1:8; 1 Cor. 1:4; Col. 1:3; 1 Thess.
1:2; 2 Thess. 1:3). His thanksgiving, supplication and joy are
based on their fellowship for the Gospel, his confidence in
the good work which has been begun in them, his own love
for them and theirs for him, and their actual share in all that
made his life. The passage abounds in technical Christian
terms. Thanksgiving, the *Eucharist,* became the name of the
Holy Supper.—**The gospel,** the good tidings. *The day of Jesus
Christ* marks the term for Christian preparedness.

Your fellowship in furtherance of the gospel. *Fellowship* means *partnership,* participation, sharing together, having
things in common. We have fellowship of the Body and Blood
of Christ (1 Cor. 10:16), of the Holy Ghost (2 Cor. 13:14), "the

140

apostle's fellowship" (Acts 2:42); "fellowship in ministering to the saints" (1 Cor. 8:4); "of the stewardship" (Eph. 3:9); "in giving and receiving" (Phil. 4:15); "with the Father and the Son" (1 John 1:3); and the contribution (Rom. 15:26) and "distribution" (2 Cor. 9:13) of the churches are called *a fellowship for the poor.* So Hebr. 13:16 and 1 Tim. 6:18. The idea runs all through this epistle. Here he calls them partners in his bonds (ver. 7); and he refers to their continued contributions to his relief and support as a fellowship with him. The first Christians looked upon their association as a *fellowship* with one another and with the Father and the Son and the Holy Ghost (1 John 1:6, 7). The Comforter had come, and abode in all of them. They were members of one another; washed the saints' feet; and their homes were the homes of travelling brethren. The contributions they made to their needy brethren were naturally called *fellowship* with them; and as from the very beginning it was the custom to make such offerings at the Holy Supper, the offering in the Sunday Service came to be called the *fellowship* (Acts 2:42). Under this one term are included, our communion with God, with the Body and Blood of the Lord, with the Spirit in the Apostolic Benediction, our regard for one another, our mutual duties, our works of charity and missions, and our Sunday collections. All this was in Paul's mind, as he acknowledged their gift and the motive that prompted it.—**From the first day.** (See 4:15.)

Being confident. Neander: "It is not God's way to do only half of a thing." The mere beginning of faith and repentance, a mere desire to know and do God's will, is a proof of His gracious operation and purpose.—**Even as it is right,** etc. (See 2 Cor. 3:2; 7:3.) We may read, *Even as you have me in your*

141

heart. Doubtless Paul was conscious of this double sense of his words, setting forth the reality of their fellowship; from which he as confidently argues to the reality of the fellowship between them and God.—**Both in my bonds,** etc. Even in bonds he asserted and proved the good tidings, and defended it against gainsayers and judges. They sustained him in this. He owns them as partners in his especial calling of the Spirit. Chrys.: "If he stands fighting and taking blows, and you wait on him when he returns from battle, take him in your arms, wipe off the sweat and restore him, and comfort, soothe and refresh his wearied soul, you shall be partakers of his reward" (4:14).

8. For God is my witness, how I long after you all in the tender mercies of Christ Jesus.

8. **Tender mercies.** Bowels—heart. Christ's heart beats in Paul. Mark the inner unity of the Church: they have one another in their hearts; they love one another in the bowels of Christ; they are conscious of all-inclusive fellowship; they have a common duty; they pray and give thanks for one another; they find in their own mutual love a witness and pledge of God's love and purpose.

9–11. And this I pray, that your love may abound yet more and more in knowledge and all discernment; so that ye may approve the things that are excellent; that ye may be sincere and void of offence unto the day of Christ; being filled with the fruits of righteousness, which are through Jesus Christ, unto the glory and praise of God.

9. **His prayer.** 1. Here, as in Col. 1:9; Eph. 1:18, he prays that they may increase in knowledge. The Christian love, which causes him such joy, is not of itself complete.—**May abound more and more** betokens a continued growth.—**In**

knowledge. More than knowledge: *accurate,* "complete, intelligent apprehension of an object," e.g. of revealed truth (Delitzsch). See Luke 9:45; Hebr. 5:14.—**And all discernment.** "Ethical tact" (Ellicott). Not vainly does Paul make love the starting-point. "Love imparts a sensitiveness of touch, gives a keen edge to the discriminating faculty, in things moral and spiritual" (Lightfoot). Wiclif has, *In kunnynge and al wit.* 2. This increase of knowledge renders possible the second thing Paul prays for: *That ye may try the things that differ,* and, having tried them, may approve the things that are better. Bengel: "In outward things we use great care in choosing; why should we not in things spiritual?" 3. This will render them clean and without offence unto the day of Christ.—**Sincere.** The word means *sifted;* "excludes all double-mindedness, the divided heart, the eye not single, all hypocrisies" (Trench). "Not for my sake, says he, do I say this, but that ye may be sincere, that is, that ye receive no spurious doctrine under the pretence of love" (Chrysostom). Wiclif has "clene." Luther, *lauter.* (See Luke 22:31.)—**Void of offence.** Causing no one to stumble, throughout their whole life. Such cleanness and harmlessness, so rendered possible, will cause them to be filled with all the fruits of righteousness. (See Acts 24:16.)

12–26. Now I would have you know, brethren, that the things *which happened* unto me have fallen out rather unto the progress of the gospel; so that my bonds became manifest in Christ throughout the whole prætorian guard, and to all the rest; and that most of the brethren in the Lord, being confident through my bonds, are more abundantly bold to speak the word of God without fear. Some indeed preach Christ even of envy and strife; and some also of good will:

the one *do it* of love, knowing that I am set for the defence
of the gospel: but the other proclaim Christ of faction, not
sincerely, thinking to raise up affliction for me in my bonds.
What then? only that in every way, whether in pretence or
in truth, Christ is proclaimed; and therein I rejoice, yea, and
will rejoice. For I know that this shall turn to my salvation,
through your supplication and the supply of the Spirit of Jesus
Christ, according to my earnest expectation and hope, that
in nothing shall I be put to shame, but *that* with all boldness,
as always, *so* now also Christ shall be magnified in my body,
whether by life, or by death. For to me to live is Christ, and
to die is gain. But if to live in the flesh,—*if* this is the fruit
of my work, then what I shall choose I wot not. But I am in
a strait betwixt the two, having the desire to depart and be
with Christ; for it is very far better: yet to abide in the flesh
is more needful for your sake. And having this confidence, I
know that I shall abide, yea, and abide with you all, for your
progress and joy in the faith; that your glorying may abound
in Christ Jesus in me through my presence with you again.

12–26. He tells them what has befallen at Rome, and of his
assurance that he will yet see them in the flesh.

I want you to know. They may have criticised or doubted
the providence of God; or the apostle may have feared
they would. Observe the process of debate in his mind.
He qualifies his own statements, and answers his own
words. Shows his boiling mind in the prison. And how
unpremeditated the letter is—a true picture of the inner
processes of his spirit.

13. **My bonds have become manifest in Christ** (Eph.
4:1; 3:1; 1 Peter 4:16). All saw he suffered not as an evil-
doer, but because he was a Christian.—**Throughout the**

144

whole prætorian guard, from which his watchers, chained to his wrist, were taken.—**And to all the rest.** Even some of Cæsar's household (4:22). 14. The brethren in Rome also were emboldened by his courage and willing submission. It is evident that there was courageous confession of Christ in that busy city. But even in the early Church there were conflicting motives; some preached Christ out of envy and strife, some of good will; some of love, assisting him; some with the self-seeking of a hireling, not purely, in order to add trouble to his bonds. It is impossible to avoid the conclusion that there were professed Christians at Rome, who were enemies of Paul, and made this enmity their master-motive; Judaizers, maybe. If they preached Christ to this end, it must have been to set up rival and separatist communities, or to draw the attention of the authorities to him as one that was turning the world upside down. Here is a peril among false brethren (2 Cor. 11:26). "Many of the unbelievers themselves also preached Christ, in order that the emperor's wrath might be increased at the spread of the Gospel, and all his anger might fall on the head of Paul. It is possible to do a good work from a motive which is not good" (Chrysostom). Paul answers his own bitter complaint, *In every way Christ is proclaimed* (Matt. 18:7; Phil. 4:14; Luke 22:42). "What is the force of this *nevertheless?* It wraps up (like the *therefore* of John 19:1) a whole train of thought" (Goulborn, The Collect for the Day, II. 96). Often since that day, strife and partisanship have been main factors in great movements in the Church; and while they are bitter enough to those who follow Christ meekly, He can make the wrath of man to praise Him.

19. Their **supplication** and the **supply** of the Spirit of Jesus Christ will transmute it, so that it shall turn to his

salvation. (A verbal quotation from Septuagint, Job 3:16.)
(See Eph. 4:16; 2 Cor. 1:11.) We have here the two forces
which sustain a preacher and a missionary—the prayers of
the Church and the Spirit of Christ.

20. **In my body.** (See Gal. 6:17; Col. 1:24.)

21. **To live is Christ.** (See Gal. 2:20.) The object of my
life is to attain to Christ. I seek those things which are above,
where Christ sitteth at the right hand of God. *Therefore* to
die is gain.

22. But if to live in the flesh, if this shall bring fruit from my
work (see American Revisers). *To live in the flesh* is contrasted
with attainment to Christ, for which he longs; and his *reward,*
with *fruit.*

22–25. He debates the matter with himself. "Both these
things lye harde upon me" (Coverdale.) "I am greatly in doubt"
(Geneva Version). He desires to break up camp and end his
pilgrimage and be at rest (epexegetical of ver. 21). This is
very far better (2 Cor. 5:1, 8). But to abide in the flesh,
in camp, or pilgrimage, *is more necessary for you.* Observe
the manner of Paul's intuition of the future: he balances
choice against his *vocation;* what is preferable against what
is more necessary to those committed to him; and thence
arises a conviction. There is not an immediate infusion of
knowledge. "The apostle had no revelations ordinarily as to
his own personal future" (Eadie). (Acts 20:22, 23; 16:6, 7.) He
also walked by faith. But he is confident that he shall abide
with them all. It is probable that he was set at liberty after
a captivity of about two years, and fulfilled his purpose of
visiting Philippi and Colossæ. The pastoral epistles belong
to a second captivity, which followed shortly afterwards,
and ended with his death under Nero, about a.d. 67. And,

doubtless, in that brief interval he was able to further their faith and to give them *matter for boasting* in Christ Jesus in him. In 21–25 we see the mind of one whose citizenship is in heaven. The dying Christian, the martyr, expects through death to be at once with Christ. There is no sleep of the soul, no Purgatory. But the longing of a heavenly mind to be with Christ must be postponed to the work to which Christ calls us. The advantage of those we can serve in Him, and not what seems most worthy, is the law of His disposition. Still, life in the flesh is only a pilgrimage, however full of fruit it may be. *With Christ* is the Promised Land.

27–30. Only let your manner of life be worthy of the gospel of Christ: that, whether I come and see you or be absent, I may hear of your state, that ye stand fast in one spirit, with one soul striving for the faith of the gospel; and in nothing affrighted by the adversaries: which is for them an evident token of perdition, but of your salvation, and that from God; because to you it hath been granted in the behalf of Christ, not only to believe on him, but also to suffer in his behalf: having the same conflict which ye saw in me, and now hear to be in me.

27–30. Moved by the hope of seeing them again, he exhorts them to unity of spirit.

27. **Only;** i.e. in any case.—**Walk worthily.** Behave as good citizens, fulfil your duty as citizens; i.e. your public and mutual duties as members of the Christian community. A remark having especial point in Philippi, a Roman colony, where Roman citizenship was of value, and had counted in the life of Paul; and as written from the centre of the world state. Refers (1) to such duties as Christians owe each other as members of one body; and (2) to such duties as belong

severally to each in his office in the one body.—**Whether I
come.** (See on ver. 25.) Shows that Paul received information
from his churches.—**Stand.** As soldiers.—**In one.** He exhorts
to *unity* above all, this evidently being the exhortation they
most needed. *Spirit* is the soul of the higher life, which is in
communion with the Spirit of God.—**Soul.** "The principle in
man which is affected by the world without, and is the centre
of perception and impulse" (Meyer).—**Striving together
with the faith** (1 Cor. 13:6; 2 Tim. 1:8; 3 John 8). The
faith is personified, because, like "the Gospel" and "the
Truth," it is recognized as an independent and active and
indefeasible power.—**And in nothing affrighted.** Shows
that the Philippians also had adversaries. These said, when
they saw the courage of Christians, *They are crazy.* " 'This
readiness to die,' writes M. Aurelius (XI. 3), 'should follow
from individual judgment, not from sheer obstinacy, as with
the Christians, but after due consideration,' etc." (in Lightfoot,
318). But their courage was the gift of God, and therefore an
earnest of all grace.

It hath been granted. To suffer for Christ is a charism
(Acts 5:41; Rom. 5:3).

Having the same conflict. 1. They had seen the persecution he endured with Silas. 2. They hear of the peril and
trial he is in at Rome. 3. They perceive *the conflict within
him,* which they had seen *in* him before. This debate, this
perpetual eager offering of himself for Christ and for them,
is to be compared only with the agony of our Lord before
His final passion. So they, both in actual suffering and in the
face of suffering, have an agony and a passion. "In ver. 5 he
mentions 'fellowship for the Gospel' as the prime distinction
of the Philippian Church, and in this last section he only

148

throws it into bold relief, by describing the united struggle it necessitated, the opposition it encountered, and the calm intrepidity which it ought ever maintain" (Eadie). (See Luke 13:24; 22:24; John 18:36; Rom. 15:30; 1 Cor. 9:25; Col. 1:29 (and note); 4:18; 1 Thess. 2:2; 1 Tim. 6:12; 2 Tim. 4:7; Hebr. 12:1.)

10

Philippians 2

1–4. *If there is therefore any comfort in Christ, if any consolation of love, if any fellowship of the Spirit, if any tender mercies and compassions, fulfil ye my joy, that ye be of the same mind, having the same love, being of one accord, of one mind; doing nothing through faction or through vainglory, but in lowliness of mind each counting other better than himself; not looking each of you to his own things, but each of you also to the things of others.*

1–4. Again an exhortation to unity, showing that in the lack of this lay the fault and danger of those in Philippi.

1. *If there be any encouragement in Christ, if any incentive in love.* So, practically, Conybeare, Howson, Lightfoot, Eadie and Meyer. (See Hatch, Biblical Greek, 82; 1 Thess. 2:17.) Here is a reference (1) to the gift of *prophecy*, so highly valued in the early Church and by Paul, an allusion which the Philippians would recognize at once (1 Cor. 14:3); and (2) to the brotherly *love*, which was the first and natural outcome of faith (Gal. 5:6), the bond of their fellowship, and the fundamental activity of the Church;

which moreover was celebrated in connection with their Eucharist (the *agape* or love-feast). If, he says, you have these and value them.—**In Christ** "defines the encouragement, etc., as specifically Christian, having in Christ its being and operation, so that it proceeds from the living fellowship with Him, is rooted in it, and by it is sustained and determined" (Meyer).—**If any fellowship of Spirit;** i.e. any fellowship with one another in the Holy Ghost, who pours out His gifts on you all (2 Cor. 13:14). *If any kindly feelings (hearty love,* Eadie) *and mutual pity,*—the natural feelings of those who are *in Christ.*—The fundamental motive to unity, therefore, was their assurance of the presence and continued operation of Christ among them by His Spirit (John 14:26; 15:26; 16:7–14), an assurance based on their own experience, on an encouragement and incitement they had received, and on a fellowship in which they were conscious of having part.—We see here how the belief in a holy Christian Church found its place in the Third Article of the creed.

2. *Then make my joy complete.* How? By thinking the same thing, having the same mutual love, your souls being accordant with each other, aiming at the one purpose, doing nothing out of factiousness or partisanship, nor of vainglory. Self-seeking, love of praise, party spirit, are inadmissible, and can bring only ruin to the Church (1:15, 16).

3. He says, in *the* lowliness of mind, indicating a distinctively Christian virtue, *manifested* by Christ. (See also Neander, Planting, etc., I. 483 ss. Ellicott: "With *due* lowliness of mind.")

4. *Not aiming each at his own ends* (not his own *profit* only, but his own *plans*). It is a lesson to those in the Church to postpone their own wisdom even, for love's sake and unity's.

5–11. Have this mind in you, which was also in Christ Jesus:
who, being in the form of God, counted it not a prize to be on
an equality with God, but emptied himself, taking the form of
a servant, being made in the likeness of men; and being found
in fashion as a man, he humbled himself, becoming obedient
even unto death, yea, the death of the cross. Wherefore also
God highly exalted him, and gave unto him the name which
is above every name; that in the name of Jesus every knee
should bow, of *things* in heaven and *things* on earth and *things*
under the earth, and that every tongue should confess that
Jesus Christ is Lord, to the glory of God the Father.

5–11. *Epistle for Palm Sunday.* The collect has grasped
St. Paul's argument: Who hast sent Thy Son, our Saviour
Jesus Christ, to take upon Him our flesh, and to suffer death
upon the cross, that all mankind should follow the example
of His great humility.—*Christian unity* is based upon the *self-
humiliation* of the members of the Christian body, after the
example of the patience of Christ. How immense the motive
urged here, in order to compose the disunion of a little band
of disciples! How immense the motive which always rests
on the conscience of Christian men!—St. Paul's reference to
the evident proofs of the presence of the Lord among them
suggests the use of His example (Matt. 11:29; 20:26–28; John
13:15; 1 Peter 2:21; 1 John 2:6).

5. **Have this mind in you.** Let this continually determine
your will.

6. Christ Jesus—existing in the form of God, i.e. being
essentially God, counted it not a prize to be snatched at, to be
equal with God. He might have asserted His Godhead in His
incarnate life, had He chosen to do so, and made the display
and use of His glorious power and Godhead the aim of His

life on earth (John 17:5; 2 Cor. 4:4; Col. 1:15; Hebr. 1:3; John 10:30, 38).

7. **But he emptied himself** of His glory, **having taken the form of a slave.**

"The Lord of all things made Himself
Naked of glory for His mortal change."
—Tennyson.

St. Paul wrote this in the centre of slavery; where intelligent and even lofty-minded men lived divested of all human right under the will of a master; and he had seen the lordly master who, without intrinsic worth, grasped at equality with God.—**Becoming in the likeness of men.** Exegetical of the form of a slave. Adam was made in the likeness of God; Jesus *grew up* like men in all things (yet without sin). Paul says not, In the likeness of *a* man, as if to suggest a docetic Christ, but, in the likeness of *men.*

8. Here a new sentence begins. There are three words: (1) *Form* signifies the specific character, the essence in which the essential attributes inhere; (2) *likeness;* and (3) *fashion* is the shape or appearance, that which strikes the eye. (See Mark 16:12; Matt. 17:25; Rom. 8:29; Phil. 3:10; 2 Cor. 3:18; Rom. 12:2; Gal. 4:19; Phil. 3:21; 1 Cor. 7:31; 1 Peter 1:14; 2 Cor. 11:13, 14, 15.) Therefore, *appearing to men simply as a man.* He further *humbled Himself,* **becoming obedient** (Rom. 5:19; Hebr. 5:8, *He learned obedience*), even to the extent of death.—**Of the cross;** i.e. a death of ignominy, rejection, which involved utter rejection by all, and, so far as their will went, extinction. The subject of this whole statement is Christ Jesus, not the Logos simply, but the Logos Incarnate. He retained the Form of God though Incarnate. He might have used this for His immediate

glorification, if He had pleased. This also He might have done
at any point in His ministry: He is the subject of the whole
sentence. His miracles—e.g. the stilling of the tempest, the
feeding of the multitude, the raising of the dead, and His
Transfiguration—show that He had not so divested Himself
of His Godhead as not to be able to use it as He pleased. He
did use it. He glorified the Father, manifested His Name, and
those whom His Father gave Him saw His glory, the glory as
of the only-begotten of the Father full of grace and truth. The
"form" of God, and "equality" with God are not only light and
glory, but grace and truth (John 1:14). Compare the collect
for 10th Sunday after Trinity: O God, who declarest Thine
almighty power chiefly in showing mercy and pity. However
inexplicable it may seem, the *form* of a *slave* which He *took*,
is as real as the *Form* of *God*, in which He exists. He *was*
subject to His parents; He increased in wisdom and stature;
He learned obedience by the things which He suffered; He
ran with patience the race that was set before Him, etc. He
was treated like a man. And *He* humbled *Himself* (John 10:17,
18). It must not be conceived that in His Incarnation He
took a step that shut Him up to this inextricably; but *He* took,
He emptied, *He* humbled Himself,—it was at every step His
choice, His conscious free self-determination, even to the
death of the cross; e.g. in Gethsemane, where He might have
asked for legions of angels (Matt. 26:53), but said, Not my
will but Thine be done. (See also the miracle of the Stater in
the Fish's Mouth, Matt. 17:24–27.)

9. **Him.** Christ Jesus, the Godman.—**And gave unto him.**
Gave to Him by grace, that which He might have taken as His
right.—**The name which is above every name** (Eph. 1:21;
Hebr. 1:4). The incommunicable Name of God. A reason for

prayer to Jesus, not in His Godhead only, but the Godman.

10. Isai. 45:23. Jesus is worshipped alike in heaven and on earth. The early Christians sung "hymns of Christ as God" (Letter of Pliny).

11. The acknowledgment of Jesus is to the glory of the Father. He is the express image of the Father (Hebr. 1:3); Eternal life is to know Him and Jesus Christ, whom He hath sent (John 17:3); No man hath seen God at any time. The Only begotten Son who is in the bosom of the Father, He hath declared Him (John 1:18).—It is a mistake to try to force the clauses of this passage into the categories of the Apostles' Creed and of later theology. And what we cannot reconcile, we still must state. The example set us is: 1. A surrender of one's rights. 2. A subordination of personal aims. 3. Self-humiliation. 4. Patience in it to the end. Such an imitation God will acknowledge, give to us a new name (Rev. 2:17), and will set us on His throne (Rev. 3:21).

12. So then, my beloved, even as ye have always obeyed, not as in my presence only, but now much more in my absence, work out your own salvation with fear and trembling;

12. **So then.** He takes up his exhortation again.—**As ye have always obeyed.** There may be an allusion to *the obedience unto death* of Christ. But it seems probable that he means they always have obeyed *Him.*—**Not in my presence,** etc. It is as if he said, You have been obedient when I was with you, and always have been obedient in my absence; and, as if I were present, and much more in my absence, **work out,** etc.; i.e. complete.—**Your own salvation.** 1. As the *obedience* of Christ suggested their unbroken obedience, so the exaltation of Christ suggests their *salvation,* which is to be the issue and reward of their obedience. 2. He commends their obedience

and devotion to Himself, but is mindful of their own supreme interest and need. The emphasis is on the verb.—**With fear and trembling.** Because of the incalculable importance of the matter. What shall a man give in exchange for his soul? and because of the perils which beset a soul that is being saved (Eph. 6:10–17).

Here is suggested the question, in what sense is the salvation of a Christian not yet complete? and in how far is the completion of it in his own power? We must hold fast … to the end. We must not grieve the Spirit of God, whereby we are sealed. We must let patience have her perfect work.

13 For it is God which worketh in you both to will and to work, for his good pleasure.

13. **Worketh.** Worketh *mightily,* effectively (Lightfoot).—**And to work.** The same word he has just used of God, the same from which our word *energy* comes.—**For his good pleasure.** For the fulfilment of His benevolent purpose (Lightfoot). This is an instance of the rush of Paul's thoughts and of the manner in which he immediately qualifies a statement, in order to secure a rounded truth. *We* must work out our salvation to the appointed end; but it is God who actually produces in us the desire and purpose to do so, and then enables us to carry that purpose to good effect (Hebr. 13:21). The Collect for Peace confesses the former of these thoughts: "O God, from whom all holy desires, good counsels and just works do proceed." The Easter Collect urges the other: "We humbly beseech Thee, that as Thou dost put into our minds good desires, so by Thy continual help we may bring the same to good effect." The text is not only a description of the methods of grace, and of amendment of character, but a promise. He who is conscious of a wish to

156

become what God would have him be, and to fulfill God's will, is thereby assured that God is working in him effectually and will perfect that which He hath begun (1:6; 1 Cor. 1:9).

14–16. Do all things without murmurings and disputings; that ye may be blameless and harmless, children of God without blemish in the midst of a crooked and perverse generation, among whom ye are seen as lights in the world, holding forth the word of life; that I may have whereof to glory in the day of Christ, that I did not run in vain neither labour in vain.

14. Those whom Christ saved may fail to work out their salvation. They may lag in their service, and, being brought to the very border of the Promised Land, may turn back to wandering and bondage.—**Murmurings.** Discontent with one's lot, fault finding with God. *Questionings*, not *disputings*,—in one's own mind, not dispute and debate with others. Some hesitate over duty, want to be convinced that it is theirs, weigh it against others' duty, suggest conflicting obligations, and so entangle conscience. Conscience and Christian service should be frank, simple and ready.

15. Rom. 16:19: Eph. 1:4; Col. 1:22; i.e. without faults which justly lay you open to the criticism of others; and *unmixed*, sincere and simple in your own heart and conscience, with nothing blameworthy before yourselves.—**Without blemish** (Deut. 32:5, Septuagint; Luke 9:41).—**In the midst,** etc. This is a quotation; but it describes the contrast between what it is God's good pleasure that His children should be, and the world in which they were. The contrast still holds. The world goes "on devious ways;" its life is perverse, distorted, confused; its aims manifold and contradictory; its motives will not bear the light. In the midst of this let Christians

be blameless and as harmless as doves.—**Among whom ye
appear as luminaries in a cosmos.** Christian men and
women, who live blamelessly and purely, nay, even those who
try to do so, and therefore give evidence that God is working
in them mightily to will and to do of His good pleasure, are
like the heavenly bodies that divide our day and night, and
order our seasons, and hold their places so that men can steer
by them. "As givers of light" (Wiclif). They are the proofs and
joints of the divine order of the universe before the eyes of the
world—the only certain things in its darkness and confusion.
Men who seek a word of life have recourse to them. To men
who seek a word of life they offer it. Their life points to the
word by which they live (Matt. 5:14).

16. **Run,** as in the race.—**Labour,** as one who disciplines
himself for the games (1 Cor. 9:24, 25). (See Gal. 2:2; 1 Thess.
3:5. Also Isai. 49:4; 65:23.)

17–18. Yea, and if I am offered upon the sacrifice and
service of your faith, I joy, and rejoice with you all: and in
the same manner do ye also joy, and rejoice with me.

17. **Yea, and if I am poured out as a drink-offering
upon,** etc. Here, in his characteristic manner, the apostle is
again overcome by the feeling of his actual peril. He looks forward hopefully to happiness in their completed salvation—an
issue of his self-discipline and strenuous endeavor after the
pattern of Christ, to an imitation of which he is encouraging
them; but will he live to see them again before "that day"? But
if not, how willingly will he pour out his blood for them; and if
he may, he will be glad, and they should be glad, and instead of
regrets for it there should be mutual congratulation. Here we
see a natural shrinking from execution, and a yearning of love,
striving with an heroical martyr spirit, which reproduces our

Lord's sorrow even unto death yet victorious resignation in Gethsmane. His description of his possible death as a *being poured forth as a drink-offering,* a *libation of his blood* (see 2 Tim. 4:6), refers to the fact that as a Roman citizen he could not be crucified (though intent to be obedient even unto death, after the example of Christ), but must be beheaded. The figure of the text is derived from the customs of heathen sacrifice and the usual phraseology of the early Church concerning its own worship. 1. It was customary to pour a libation of wine over the heathen sacrifices; and with this custom his readers were familiar. (See also Numb. 28:7.) 2. The word here translated *service* is *Leitourgia,* the original of our word *Liturgy.* (See Rom. 15:16.) It denoted primarily a public function rendered to the people as a state. Then it came to mean a public sacrifice; and consequently, "a sacerdotal ministration." It was applied to the religious services, sacrifices, of the Jews (Hebr. 8:6, 9:21, and commonly in the Septuagint). Then it began to denote the Chief Service, the Eucharistic Service of the Church; and became the common designation of them in early writings. (See Teaching of the XII. App. XV.) Doubtless Paul had this service in mind, and he adds *"Sacrifice"* (Hussia), to strengthen the illustration. (The Chief Service of the Christians, the Eucharist, consisted in a thank-offering of themselves and their possessions, especially of the fruits of the earth, and the reception of the blessed elements which, having been given to the Lord, He returned as the vehicles of His own Body and Blood in the Holy Communion. It was from offerings made at such a service, doubtless, that the contribution to the relief of St. Paul's necessities had been sent by the Philippian Church. Now St. Paul says, I will be glad and we should congratulate each other even if

my blood be poured out over this sacrifice and service of
yours, as a libation. The custom of the Church here alluded
to was familiar; the figures drawn from heathen customs,
obvious (1 Peter 2:5). "Paul represents his blood as a material
of sacrifice, yet as a constituent of a greater offering, with a
solemn service, in which the chief offering is the faith of the
Philippians, and Paul himself is the sacrificer and ministrant"
(Zockler).

19–24. But I hope in the Lord Jesus to send Timothy shortly
unto you, that I also may be of good comfort, when I know
your state. For I have no man like-minded, who will care
truly for your state. For they all seek their own, not the things
of Jesus Christ. But ye know the proof of him, that, as a child
serveth a father, *so* he served with me in furtherance of the
gospel. Him therefore I hope to send forthwith, so soon as I
shall see how it will go with me: but I trust in the Lord that I
myself also shall come shortly.

19. **I hope in the Lord Jesus.** Everything Paul does, and
especially all he does in relation to his fellow-Christians, he
does *in the Lord* (2 Thess. 3:4). This is not a mere phrase, but
it implies here, for instance, *if the Lord will,* resignation to
Him, recognition of His supreme wisdom.—**That I may be,**
etc. Shows his tender anxiety concerning them.

20. **Like-minded.** Allusion to Septuagint version of Ps.
55:13 Mine *equal;* whom I estimate to be worth as much
as mine own self (Gesenius). Vulgate: *Unanimis.* With a
spirit like his (Chrys.). Tyndale: "That is so like-minded to
me."—**Truly.** Genuinely, as being of the same blood and birth.
The relations between Timothy and the Philippians had been
intimate. (See 1 Cor. 16:10.)

21. A hard saying, showing how Paul was vexed by the

selfishness of even the professed brethren who surrounded him. The factiousness, enmity and selfishness that he complained of in that circle, were not strange in those newly converted to Christ who had not completely assimilated the Gospel nor more than begun to work out their salvation. So the missionaries of our day may expect to be vexed by the imperfections of the first generation of converts.

22. Acts 16. Also 1 Cor. 4:17; 1 Tim. 1; 2; 2 Tim. 1:2.

23, 24. He does not yet know what the outcome of his own case will be; but he hopes confidently to come to them. (See 1:25.) In that which seemed to be of the greatest importance for the work committed to him, he had to *trust in the Lord* (Philem. 22).

25–30. But I counted it necessary to send to you Epaphroditus, my brother and fellow-worker and fellow-soldier, and your messenger and minister to my need; since he longed after you all, and was sore troubled, because ye had heard that he was sick: for indeed he was sick nigh unto death: but God had mercy on him; and not on him only, but on me also, that I might not have sorrow upon sorrow. I have sent him therefore the more diligently, that, when ye see him again, ye may rejoice, and that I may be the less sorrowful. Receive him therefore in the Lord with all joy; and hold such in honour: because for the work of Christ he came nigh unto death, hazarding his life to supply that which was lacking in your service toward me.

25. **Epaphroditus.** A common name at that time. We know no more about him than this epistle tells us.—**My brother.** It is no condescension in the apostle to speak of this friend and messenger of his beloved Church as a *brother.*—**And fellow-worker.** He doubtless refers to work

for the Gospel which they had done together in Philippi in former days.—**And fellow-soldier** (Philem. 2). Their common labor had been a battle—against gainsayers, against persecution. Epaphroditus probably was an *"elder,"* one of the older members of the Church, a "booty" and associate of the earliest days of Paul's ministry among them. These names represented precious recollections of both.—**Your messenger.** Your "apostle," he says. An "apostle" was *one sent forth,* a missionary. There were many apostles. There came to be a recognized distinction between the apostles of the churches (2 Cor. 8:23), and the apostles of the Lord (Col. 1:1). In the second age it was a common designation of wandering evangelists, who probably enjoyed *the gift of teaching,* and like Paul claimed to be apostles not from men, nor through men, but through Jesus Christ (Gal. 1:1). Their immunities were abused by some of them, and in the Teaching of the XII. Apostles they evidently had become burdensome, and their rights were regulated.—**And minister to my need.** Paul says, *Leitourgos,* i.e. the one completing your liturgy, your churchly service, by bringing to me the "yield" of your offerings. It was the distinction of the *Liturgos* in the Christian Service, later the *Bishop,* to receive and distribute the offerings of the Church to their designated recipients, who, as, for instance, the poor, were accordingly called the altar (Hatch, Sohm). Evidently Paul was in need. As the Lord became poor for our sake, and was assisted by those women who followed and ministered to Him, so Paul had to accept the charity of the Church. (See 2 Cor. 11:9.)

26. Epaphroditus was homesick. Not homesick because sick; but the thought of their anxiety worried him. What an assurance of their affection he had! What tenderness of

sympathy! What simplicity of brotherly affection marked the infant Church! What delicacy does Paul show in describing the matter!

27. Imagine the delicate-minded stranger sick in Rome, and far from his dear ones, who had heard of his sickness, but were too far away quickly to hear of his convalescence.—**God pitied him.** Here we see Paul's fatherly and brotherly love. The continued illness, the death, of Epaphroditus would have overwhelmed him. Recovery from illness, the postponement of the death which would admit a Christian to the immediate presence of the Lord, is spoken of as *a mercy*. It is not wrong to pray for the recovery to health of those we love, and to rejoice in their recovery as a mercy of God.

28. He sends him back at once with this letter, for their sake, and, we may be sure, for Epaphroditus's too. It would be a pleasure to Paul too, to think of their happiness on being together again. He thinks of them, not of himself. But in spite of his exhortations to joy, and his joy in the Lord, he has sorrow, is sorrowful; and he will only be less sorrowful, not without care.

29. A solemn and, as it were, official commendation. He comes back not merely to his place in the family and among neighbors; receive him *in the Lord*.—**Hold such in honour.** Does this imply his presbyteral dignity?

30. **The work** is, like *apostle, liturgy, the way*, in Acts, and *the Gospel*, a technical expression (Acts 15:38; Ignatius, Eph. 14; Rom. 3). The early Christians spoke of "the Work," as now some speak of "the Cause." They were filled with inspiration for a great *work*, which Christ had done and was doing in the world, and to which they were enabled to contribute.—**Hazarding his life.** Epaphroditus then, like

Paul, like Christ, had been obedient unto death. In the discharge of ordinary duty, therefore, one can hazard his life for Christ, and may be a martyr dying of disease, as well as at the headsman's hands. Well might Paul accredit him to the place of honor in the Church, which in later times was readily accorded to Confessors. The phrase means that *he hazarded his life on the throw*, as when one plays with dice. That he did not die, was not because he was unwilling or afraid to be poured out. Though a delicate soul and homesick, he had been no weakling in zeal and faith.—**What was lacking in your service.** Their service is again called a *Leitourgia*, i.e. the public, common, sacred service of them all, sanctified in their Eucharist. It would have been ineffectual without Epaphroditus's service of love. It lacked only his bringing. He completed it at the hazard of his life. (See 1 Cor. 16:17.)

11

Philippians 3

1. Finally, my brethren, rejoice in the Lord. To write the same things to you, to me indeed is not irksome, but for you it is safe.

1. **Finally.** *For the rest;* in conclusion. It is evident that at the end of ch. 2, or perhaps at the end of this salutation, the epistle was interrupted.—**Rejoice in the Lord.** A parting salutation. But he begins anew, taking up the line of thought he has maintained throughout, having in mind the divisions and dangers of division among them. He seems, upon beginning the epistle again, after a short interval, excited perhaps by some new exhibition of meanness of the Judaizers among the Christians at Rome, perhaps by the thought of the necessity of warning his Philippians against a probable attack on their faith. He has determined to be more plain-spoken and personal in this part of the letter. He apologizes for recurring to the one theme of the letter—the correction of a personal or factious spirit in the Philippian Church, by the example of Christ. It has been suggested that new intelligence from Philippi had been received after the second chapter

had been written. The supposition is unnecessary.—**The
same things** has awakened the question whether St. Paul
had written other letters to the Philippians, which have not
come down to us. Polycarp refers to *the letters* which Paul
had written them; but Lightfoot holds that the plural might
have been used of a single letter. Commentators have been
unwilling to admit that letters of an inspired apostle may
have been lost. To us it seems probable that Paul wrote many
more letters than those we have; while we are not encouraged
to believe that they would have added any essential to our
faith. But, whatever answer may be given, there is nothing in
our passage that refers to another letter.

2. Beware of the dogs, beware of the evil workers, beware
of the concision:

2. **Beware.** He has warned them of his strenuous temper.
"*Look at* the dogs," he says. The *dogs,* the *evil workers,* the
concision, here referred to, are not three classes, but the
same class of teachers. While he would warn against them,
he rather points at them. They are before his eyes—at
work in the Roman Church; before *their* eyes—creeping
into every church; the Judaizers, who, while Christian in
profession, misconceive and misstate the Gospel, seeking
to lead all back to the Law and make the Gospel of none
effect. The Philippian Church was predominantly a Gentile
Church, yet not without Jews and proselytes in it, and near
to Thessalonica and Berœa, where the Jews were hostile
from the first, and where the temptation to conciliate them
might strengthen the opponents of Paul. Paul calls such
"*dogs*" (Ps. 59:14, 15). He was severe in controversy (Gal.
5:12). So was Christ sometimes (Matt. 23). The Jews
called the Gentiles *dogs;* their principal notion in the name

being that the Gentiles were *outside* the Covenant, went in and out of the house and got only the crumbs. St. Paul turns the name upon them. *They* now are outside the New Covenant. And he thinks of the homeless, snarling curs of an Eastern village. Such were these wandering enemies of the Gospel and the Church of Christ (Isai. 56:10, 11; Gal. 5:15; Rev. 22:15).—**Concision.** He will not even call them the circumcision, but puns on the word: "The circumcision, which they vaunt, is in Christ only as the gashings and mutilations of the idolatrous heathen" (Lightfoot). (See the story of Elijah on Carmel.) *Paronomasia* or *punning* is not unusual in Paul's style. Lightfoot alleges 2 Thess. 3:11; Rom. 12:3. Winer, LXVIII. 793 sq. There is a monograph on the subject by Boettcher. On puns in the Old Testament, see Lightfoot, p. 144, who also gives examples from profane Greek authors and from English. Meyer (p. 128) gives from Luther, *Decret* and *Decretal,* turned to *Drecket* and *Drecketal, Jurisperitos* into *Jurisperditos, Schwenkfeld* into *Stenkfeld.* So Fairbairn (Christ in Modern Theology, 144): "Controversies begotten of disputations, hate and unreasoning love are things the judicious, who love to pass for judicial men, do not care to touch." (See Horace, Odes, I. 33, 2.) So *Shakespeare:* "Old John of Gaunt, and gaunt in being old;" and *Tennyson:* "His honor rooted in dishonor stood, and faith unfaithful kept him falsely true."

3. For we are the circumcision, who worship by the Spirit of God, and glory in Christ Jesus, and have no confidence in the flesh:

3. **We are the circumcision;** i.e. you and I. St. Paul here asserts that those who are in Christ are the heirs of the promises, the true Israel, the continuation of the people

and "Church" of the Old Testament—even though he was
writing to those of whom a majority had been Gentiles
(Deut. 10:16; 30:6; Rom. 2:28 s.; 4:11, 12; Col. 2:11). But
note how familiar these already were with the customs and
themes of the Old Testament. The Old Testament, far from
being abrogated, already had been laid at the foundation
of the Gentile Church by the apostle to the Gentiles and
his fellow-workers.—**Who worship by the Spirit of God.**
The correct reading. Our worship is the spiritual worship
desired of God and to which He moves us, in contrast with
the service of God (Rom. 9:4), founded on previous revelation,
which the Jews have and boast and wish to compel us to
conform to. The word *Latreia, latrenontes,* is the broadest
word used to describe religious worship (John 4:23, 24; Rom.
12:1). The "reasonable" or "spiritual" service of the latter
passage often was referred to by early Christian writers as
a description of Christian worship in contrast with Pagan
as well as Jewish rites. In it they gave the sacrifice of
prayer, praise and thanksgiving, and offered their bodies
in reasonable service instead of the bloody sacrifices of the
old cults.—**And glory in Christ Jesus** (Jer. 9:24; Gal. 6:14).
The Judaizers doubtless boasted of their temple, history,
service, and pointed with scorn at the lowliness and isolation
of the Christian communities. These words are full of
encouragement to little companies of men who know they
are in Christ, but are despised by the world.—**And have,** etc.
The emphasis is on *the flesh;* a scornful fling at those who
boasted they had been circumcised.

4–6. Though I myself might have confidence even in the
flesh: if any other man thinketh to have confidence in the
flesh, I yet more: circumcised the eighth day, of the stock

168

of Israel, of the tribe of Benjamin, a Hebrew of Hebrews; as touching the law, a Pharisee; as touching zeal, persecuting the church; as touching the righteousness which is in the law, found blameless.

4–5. Paul says they cannot say he takes the other side because he has not what they have. He was not a proselyte. No rite had been neglected in his case. He was of pure descent. His father and mother were Israelites, and not of one of those tribes which broke away from the service of the temple. In every sense of the word he was a Hebrew; not a Hellenist; brought up in all the traditions and customs; from childhood in sympathy with the heart of the history of the race; speaking the ancient tongue. (St. Paul quotes the Old Testament from the Hebrew, translating it for himself, not leaning on the Septuagint.)—**A Pharisee.** The Pharisees were the strictest of the Jews in their interpretation and observance of the Law and the traditions, a society of recognized devotion, the Puritans of the time of Christ.

6. He had given proof of his sincerity and narrow devotion by his severity and cruelty toward the Church. In the eyes of men also, he was so good after the pharisaic fashion, that no man found a flaw in him. It is a confession of the earnestness and completeness of Saul's endeavor to meet the requirements of the Law. In every good sense he had been a Pharisee of the Pharisees, not a failure and an outcast.

7–8. Howbeit what things were gain to me, these have I counted loss for Christ. Yea verily, and I count all things to be loss for the excellency of the knowledge of Christ Jesus my Lord: for whom I suffered the loss of all things, and do count them but dung,

7. In comparison with Christ these things I boast were

worthless; and, inasmuch as they were obstacles to entire recourse and surrender to Christ, they were worse than worthless—a loss.

8. **Yea verily.** St. Paul heaps up little words here, as if almost stuttering with his pen, in unutterable feeling.—**My Lord,** he says, in his assured possession of that knowledge. (See Small Catechism, 2d Art. of Creed.) He does not mean a knowledge of the *doctrine* of Christ, but such knowledge of Him and of His Gospel of grace and of His power, as is got only by actual experience (John 17:3).—**The loss of all things;** i.e. of all *these things,* and the fancied or worldly advantages to which they might lead. He certainly had given up all for Christ.—**Dung.** Refuse, rubbish. The English word originally means that which is cast away (Skeat). "Expresses utter contempt" (Zockler). That which is fit neither to be touched nor to be looked on (Bengel).

9. That I may gain Christ, and be found in him, not having a righteousness of mine own, *even* that which is of the law, but that which is through faith in Christ, the righteousness which is of God by faith:

9. **In him,** as the very atmosphere in which I live, move and have my being. Without any other name, place or relation. (See 1:1, 8, 13, 14, 26; 2:2, 19, 29; 3:3, 14; 4:7, 10.) Mark that Paul, though confident that Christ is his, still exhibits this strenuous determination, aspiration and energy of faith.—**A righteousness of mine own.** Got by me, by my own endeavors.—**Which is from law, but that which is through faith of Christ.** Faith in Christ takes hold of *His* righteousness.—**Which is from God upon faith.** Here *God* is set against *law* as the source of righteousness. God gives righteousness to faith *upon* faith. Law merely provides a

method of working out a mechanical righteousness. *Through faith*, indicates that faith is the means by which we take the righteousness God gives. This righteousness rests *on* faith,—faith is its foundation in us. "The use of various prepositions to express the different relations of an object, is one of the apostle's peculiarities of style" (Eadie. Rom. 5:1).

10. That I may know him, and the power of his resurrection, and the fellowship of his sufferings, becoming conformed unto his death;

10. **That I may know him.** The reason why he wishes above all things to gain Christ and to be found in Him. Now he knows but in part; he yearns to know as he is known (1 Cor. 13:12). "This knowledge is that of a deep and deepening experience" (Eadie). It is the knowledge of Christ possessed by one who is conscious that he is justified in Christ (Isai. 53:11; John 17:3).—**The power of his resurrection** (Eph. 1:19, 20; 2:5; Rom. 1:4; 4:24, 25; 5:10; 6:5; 8:11; 1 Cor. 15:22; 2 Cor. 4:10, 11; 13:4; Phil. 3:21; Col. 2:12, 13; 3:4; 1 Peter 1:3; 3:21).—1. There is a power of an endless, indissoluble life. It raised up Jesus from the dead. It will quicken our mortal bodies. 2. That power of the resurrection of our Lord Jesus Christ still is in the world, and manifests itself whenever a man dead in trespasses and sins is quickened to newness of life. He is quickened by the same power that raised Jesus from the dead and gives eternal life to us. 3. That power is connected with holy baptism. When a person is baptized, he becomes a partaker of the power of the resurrection of Christ. 4. Having received the power of the resurrection in baptism, we keep it and *know* it, i.e. receive and feel it, by faith, by believing in the Risen Lord, and putting our trust in Him. And this faith is wrought in us by the power of

His resurrection.—**The fellowship of his sufferings.** John and James wished to sit on the right hand and the left of the Messiah in His kingdom: a lofty expression of faith in the Christ in the midst of His humiliation; Paul wishes for the fellowship of His sufferings (to be baptized with His baptism and to drink of His cup): an irrepressible utterance of his sympathy with the inmost mind of the Lord. Mark that the thought of 2:5–11 is here in Paul's mind, as it was when he wrote of Epaphroditus, and will appear again. He, for his part, he says it consciously or unconsciously, has and seeks to have the same mind in him that was in Christ Jesus our Lord. (See 1 Peter 4:13.)—**Becoming conformed unto his death.** The word here used for *form* is the same as that used of the *form* of God and the *form* of a slave in 2:5, 7. It implies that Paul does not seek to suffer like Christ in the estimation of men, but really *in himself* to be conformed to the death of Christ. Our Lord in His death gave Himself to pain, ignominy, abandonment, total rejection, expiatory suffering for the sake of His enemies. St. Stephen was conformed to the death of Christ (Acts 7:59, 60).

11. If by any means I may attain unto the resurrection from the dead.

11. **The resurrection.** An unusual and emphatic term for the resurrection is used. He means not the general resurrection of all merely, wherein good and bad alike will rise, as if he would imply that some never shall rise again while some shall; but he seeks the *first resurrection*, the resurrection unto life. This is the *exaltation* he ever keeps in view, while he seeks the fellowship of the sufferings of Christ (Luke 20:35; Acts. 26:7).

12. Not that I have already obtained, or am already made

perfect: but I press on, if so be that I may apprehend that for which also I was apprehended by Christ Jesus.

12. **Not that I have already obtained.** "In the highest fervor the apostle does not lose his spiritual sobriety," says Bengel. An instance of the essential sanity of Paul's mind. And also of his oratorical powers. No doubt, in his speech, as here in his letter, he knew how to concentrate his auditors' attention on himself and carry them with him in emotion; but always was master of himself, and so of them. He is careful to guard against any possible exaggeration or one-sided misapprehension of his saying; and knows how, having awakened their throbbing sympathy, to teach and stamp a lesson. The difference of tense of the two verbs is intentional. He says, Not that I attained in the moment of my conversion; nor that I now already am perfected. (The former verb is an *aorist,* descriptive of a momentary action, complete in a past moment; the latter verb is a *perfect.*) He teaches: 1. That he does not consider himself to be a perfect man; his attainments are not all they ought to be, nor all that he wishes and expects them to become. 2. A Christian is not made perfect in the instant of conversion, nor in any moment. 3. But his life in Christ should be a progress; he must be perfected. 4. Even before he has reached the goal, he is in Christ. A man may be in Christ, and be able to speak of Him as "*My* Lord," though he has not yet "obtained," neither is "already perfected." He explodes the theory of a "sinless perfection" on earth and that of a "total immediate sanctification" of believers. The Christian life is a moral progress. Salvation is given to those in whom dwelleth no good thing. Justification is the beginning, not the result, of holiness. "Indeed, so much will sinfulness still adhere to all his performances, that even the

most advanced Christian will come short of the requirements of duty; as Paul referring to himself acknowledges" (Neander, Planting, I. 474). "I have now been reading the Bible for thirty years with the greatest zeal and diligence, yet am I not so healed as to be able to acquiesce with complete trust in the remedies God offers. I wish to be stronger and more robust in faith, and to have more boldness in Christ, but am not able" (Luther, on Genesis 45).—**I press on.** A figure taken from the foot-race, with which the Philippians were familiar. Like a racer, hoping to get the prize.—**That for which also I was laid hold on by Christ Jesus.** The English translation seems to mean that the prize which Paul strives for is that which the Lord had in view for Paul when he first called him to the race. We prefer, *Because* I was laid hold on; with Meyer and Lightfoot. (See Rom. 5:12; 2 Cor. 5:4.) Paul runs this race because Christ has taken hold on him. He cannot do otherwise. His language may have been determined here by "the attraction" of the figure: and almost without Paul's intending it seems to imply that he tries to get the prize set before him, because he was the prize Christ ran for and got.

13–14. Brethren, I count not myself yet to have appre-hended: but one thing *I do,* forgetting the things which are behind, and stretching forward to the things which are before, I press on toward the goal unto the prize of the high calling of God in Christ Jesus.

13. He reiterates his sincere profession that he is not perfect: which implies a criticism of those in the Philippian Church who may have professed they were perfect. (See on Col. 1:28.)—**But one thing: forgetting.** It is not necessary to tell just what "things which are behind" are meant. Paul describes the eager straining forward of a runner. "Stretched

forward; the eye goes before the hand, the hand before the foot, and draws it after" (Bengel). The eager racer thinks not of the things he passes and leaves behind him. His eyes are on the goal (1 Cor. 9:24).

14. **I press on.** As in ver. 12. *In Christ* there was for Paul, there is for us, a calling (Col. 3:15; Eph. 1:18; 4:1, 4). It is God's call to us, *from above*, and *heavenward*, therefore *upward*.

15–16. Let us therefore, as many as be perfect, be thus minded: and if in anything ye are otherwise minded, even this shall God reveal unto you: only, whereunto we have already attained, by that same *rule* let us walk.

15. **Let us then, as many as be perfect.** He here insinuates a censure of those who claimed most faithfully to represent his own teaching; and, while in assenting to the name they gave themselves—the *perfect*, or grown up—there is inevitable irony, he mollifies it by charitably reckoning himself among them. Those who recognized that they were not under law, and perceived the newness and independence of the Gospel, were also tempted to hold themselves above law. They might be careless of the weak; and they might not hold the faith in a good conscience, and so would make shipwreck of their souls. Paul does not deny the maturity of their faith, conscience and spirit. But if they are "perfect," let them still with him recognize an upward calling of God in Christ Jesus, and with him press forward to the things which are before. "It belongs to him that is perfect, not to regard himself as perfect" (Chrysostom).

If in anything ye think *amiss.* It is possible that you differ in some things, and that some of you have some views that are wrong. Let us admit that we are not infallible. But if you keep your eye on the goal and press forward to it, if

the one consideration be the prize of your upward calling
in Christ Jesus, God will set you right whereinsoever you
now are wrong. Paul, while not undervaluing "orthodoxy,"
shows the method by which alone a Christian may attain to
a knowledge of the truth (John 7:17). And he indicates the
method by which a Church may attain and maintain unity in
a pure confession.

16. But he would not have them conclude that if only a
man tries to live a right life, it matters not what he thinks or
believes. They are to keep the foundation he has laid. They
are not to go back or away from that to which they have
already come. It is to be the starting point. In order to have a
right faith and live a right life, and obtain the prize of their
upward calling, they have not to unlearn all they have been
taught and undo all that has been done for them. But on the
basis of the faith they have been taught, let them run the race,
always keeping their eyes fixed "on the greater and higher
task which they see opening before them as they go forward
step by step" (Meyer). "This is a very necessary and firm rule,
not to accept any doctrine which is not revealed by God; and
that such doctrine must agree and accord with the doctrine
of faith in the Lord Jesus Christ. Where such a revelation
does not agree with the doctrine, it is not to be thought a
revelation of God, but a delusion of the evil one, it matters
not what miracles may accompany it" (Veit Dietrich).

17. Brethren, be ye imitators together of me, and mark
them which so walk even as ye have us for an ensample.

17. What a high consciousness of his exemplariness this
apostle of Christ had! Yet Paul would have them imitate
not himself, but his endeavor to be like Christ. No doubt
he wished them to be *imitators together with one another,* but

he refers them to those who in all the churches receive his instruction and mind his example. Association with others who are running the Christian race is a great help to the imperfect; and the thought of "the holy Church throughout all the world" is an inspiration. Our text is also a solemn admonition to the messengers of the Lord, whose disciples are likely to be imitators together of them and to walk so as they have them for an ensample.—**Mark them.** Look at them, to them, for instruction. St. Paul shrinks from pointing to himself only; he says, **us.**

18–19. For many walk, of whom I told you often, and now tell you even weeping, *that they are* the enemies of the cross of Christ: whose end is perdition, whose god is the belly, and *whose* glory is in their shame, who mind earthly things.

18. **Many walk.** Even so early in the Church, and in the days of persecution, there were in the Church *many* such as St. Paul now proceeds to describe. They were professed Christians; who easily could have left the Church; who, singularly enough, remained in it, when to be called a Christian was considered no honor; who had been baptized in ripe years with their own full consent and at their own desire. It is a mistake to speak of the apostolic age as necessarily the purest age of the Church. Those who were gathered into the churches were but partially dissevered from Judaism or from the errors and corruption of Paganism, and they had but imperfectly apprehended Christ. Here were Judaizers, puffed-up men who boasted they were full-grown men in Christ, belly-worshippers, selfish men and quarrelsome; there were roots of heresy, roots of bitterness, roots of perdition, at Rome and in the Church of Philippi (1 Thess. 5:14; 2 Thess. 3:11. Also Matt. 13:28–30, 42–50). See

177

Luther, on Gen. 37:20: "It is indeed miserable to see in that home and Church, which at that time was the one and holiest in the whole earth, such monstrous births. Isaac was the teacher, the Word of God and the promises concerning Christ flourished, the Holy Spirit reigned, and the most beautiful examples of piety, discipline and domestic life shone forth, yet from that home came forth horrible things. For Jacob and all his Church were under the devil and all his angels, so that not strangers, nor enemies, nor heretics, but his own sons, whom he himself had brought up and taught in the Word, were ready to slay their innocent brother." And so on ch. 44.

Of whom I told you often. When I was with you. Therefore he is not referring particularly to some in the Roman Church whose conduct just then offended him. And if he had often *told* the Philippians of such, there must have been numerous examples of such behavior in other churches and at an earlier period. Such behavior was not infrequent in apostolic churches. Missionaries may expect grave misbehavior among those lately won from heathenism. A faithful pastor is not to be discouraged if some of his flock are no better, and even urge his own teaching as their excuse. The truth and power of Christ may live in a church where some are whose end is destruction.—**Even weeping.** How grave must the cases have been! No doubt there were such before his eyes; and there must have been reason to remind the Philippians of what he had told them before.—**They are the enemies of the cross of Christ.** Instead of having in them the mind that was in Christ Jesus, or imitating him who wished to be conformable to His death. He refers not to those who were urging the righteousness of the Law and found the cross a stumbling-block, but to those who refused to take up

178

their cross and follow Christ. (See Gal. 6:14.) "Nothing is so incongruous in a Christian, and so foreign to his character, as to seek ease and rest; and to be engrossed with the present life is foreign to our profession and enlistment.... The cross belongs to a soul at its post for the fight, longing to die, seeking nothing like ease.... Every one who is a friend of luxury, and of present safety, is an enemy of that cross, in which Paul makes his boast" (Chrysostom).

19. **Whose end is perdition** (Rom. 6:21; 2 Cor. 11:15; Hebr. 6:8). He does not qualify this at all. It certainly will be the issue of such a mind and conduct. There is no intimation of delayed and probationary punishment.—**Whose god is the belly** (Rom. 16:18). A figure not unknown to heathen ethics. (Seneca, Euripides, Cicero, Lightfoot *in loc.*, Meyer.) Yet literally true of many. How easy is it, in prosperity, to fall to worshipping the belly.—**Whose glory.** They boast of what is most disgraceful.—**Who mind earthly things.** Here he sums up the whole description. Instead of the mind of Christ, who emptied and humbled Himself, their whole life is set upon things on the earth.

20. For our citizenship is in heaven; from whence also we wait for a Saviour, the Lord Jesus Christ:

20. 17–21 are the Epistle for the 23d Sunday after Trinity, and are thus made to answer to the Gospel (Matt. 22:15–22). The Church thus compared the heavenly commonwealth to which we belong with the earthly state. The word *is* is not the simple copula, but is emphatic: our state, our commonwealth, actually exists in heaven. Over against the system of things which our eyes see, and which were so real to the Roman colony of Philippi, St. Paul asserts the existence of the heavenly republic, with its relations, duties, powers, stability

(1:27; Eph. 2:12, 19; Gal. 4:26; Acts 23:1).—**From whence
also.** We earnestly expect; we confidently and patiently await.
The Christians of that age looked for the Lord's coming in
their lifetime. He would come to save them from the earthly
things which seemed so hostile and powerful, and against
which the heavenly commonwealth seemed so shadowy. We
also look for a Saviour from heaven (1 Thess. 5:1; 2 Thess.
2:1).

21. Who shall fashion anew the body of our humiliation,
that it may be conformed to the body of his glory, according
to the working whereby he is able even to subject all things
unto himself.

21. *Our* humiliation is here laid beside *His.* If we have the
same mind in us, if we humble ourselves, there shall be for
us also an exaltation. There may even be a reference to the
Transfiguration; but certainly to our Lord's resurrection-
body. In our *bodies* we shall be fashioned anew.—**That
it may be conformed** (1 John 3:2). The body in which
our Lord rose is a hint of what we shall some day be like.
"Fashion," in the former clause, means that the outward
appearance of our bodies shall be changed; "conformed,"
that they shall be essentially and permanently changed, to
be like that of Christ. As to problems suggested by the
promise of the resurrection and glorification of the body,
it is enough to know "the Scriptures and the power of God"
(Matt. 22:29). "By His resurrection, Jesus, we are told, became
the 'first-fruits,'—the preluding sample of them that sleep:
their change, on emerging from death, is simply into the
likeness of their forerunner; and is described by the apostles
in terms which, on the one hand, negative all the properties
of mere flesh and soul, and, on the other, affirm those of

180

Spirit,—incorruptibility, immortality, and, as manifested, a brilliancy as of a glorious light" (Jas. Martineau, Seat of Authority, 368–9). (See Rev. 1:14, 15, 16.)—"Designated as He is, the Mediator between God and Man, He keeps in His own self the deposit of the flesh which has been committed to Him by both parties—the pledge and security of its entire perfection. For as 'He has given to us the earnest of the Spirit,' so has He received from us the earnest of the flesh, and has carried it with Him into heaven as a pledge of that complete entirety which is one day to be restored to it. Be not disquieted, O flesh and blood, with any care; in Christ you have acquired both heaven and the kingdom of God" (Tertullian, de Res. Carnis, LI.). So Paul completes another strophe on this wonderful self-humiliation and exaltation of Christ. He urges the example of the Lord; he interprets the service of Epaphroditus by it; he makes it the inspiration and rule of his own life; he shows how every Christ-like "Passion" shall be made to issue in the communion of His glory. *Via crucis, via lucis.*

> "'Tis not this fleshly robe alone
> Shall link us, Lord, with Thee;
> Not only in the tear and groan
> Shall the dear kindred be.
> "Thou to our woes who down didst come,
> Who one with us wouldst be,
> Wilt bring us to Thy heavenly home,
> Wilt make us one with Thee."

12

Philippians 4

1. Wherefore, my brethren beloved and longed for, my joy and crown, so stand fast in the Lord, my beloved.

1. **Wherefore.** Because of this which he has said (3:17–21).—**Longed for.** St. Paul loved his Philippians especially. *Longed for* occurs here only in the New Testament. He lingers on the thought of them,—he yearns to see them, to be with them.—**My joy and my crown** (1 Thess. 2:19; Sir. 1:9; 6:31; 15:6; Ez. 16:12; 23:42; Prov. 16:31; 17:6; Job 19:9). The crown here meant is not a diadem, but a chaplet or garland, the victor's wreath, or the garland worn at feasts by those who make holiday. One cannot repress the thought of the difference between *real* crowns and make-believe crowns. Here is Paul a prisoner and little thought of, whose crown are these saved from death and assured of everlasting life (Dan. 12:3); and there Nero, the ruler of the world, and the garlanded master of orgies.—**So stand.** *So,* as I have said. *Stand,* as soldiers (Eph. 6:13). *In the Lord:* the one element in which he and they live.—**My beloved.** Observe here, and in the following sentences, the tremulous iteration which tells

Paul's excitement of affection.

2–3. I exhort Euodia, and I exhort Syntyche, to be of the same mind in the Lord. Yea, I beseech thee also, true yokefellow, help these women, for they laboured with me in the gospel, with Clement also, and the rest of my fellow-workers, whose names are in the book of life.

2. By all this introduction he has prepared the way for personal appeal. If they have followed him thus far, these women cannot resist his exhortation now; and in the face of the motive he has urged, they will not resent this direct address. *Euodia* and *Syntyche* were two women in the Philippian Church. That Church most probably was preeminently a *women's church.* It began with Lydia the purple-seller and her household. The faults alluded to in this epistle, especially dissension, women are most prone to; and the readiness they always had shown to minister to Paul's wants betokens the sympathy and good sense of women. Between these two leaders of the women of the congregation a difference had begun. St. Paul says I *exhort* E., I *exhort* S.; repeating the word, in order to make a direct and separate appeal to each. (The names *Euodia* and *Syntyche* occur in inscriptions. (Muratori, Gruter.) (See Lightfoot.)—**To be of the same mind in the Lord.** Not *to think the same thing.* It is impossible at once to change one's opinion, even at the bidding of an apostle. The same language is used 2:5. There may be unity in disposition and purpose between Christians, even where opinions differ. They were to be of the same mind **in the Lord.** Well does Meyer say, "A union of minds *out of* Christ, Paul does not at all desire." When men compromise truth for the sake of unity, they do not fulfil this exhortation. But it is addressed to those whose *hearts* are divided.

3. **Beseech.** Rather *ask.* The word here used (the former *ask*
in John 16:23) "implies that he who asks stands on a certain
footing of equality with him of whom the boon is asked, or,
if not of equality, on such a footing of familiarity as lends
authority to the request" (Trench, Synonyms, 137).—**True
yokefellow.** Who was the "true yokefellow" here addressed?
Lightfoot says Epaphroditus, the bearer of this letter; and
with him agree Grotius, Calovius, Michaelis, Hengstenberg,
Baumgarten-Crusius, and others. Bengel says, Silas; Estius,
Timothy; Clement of Alex., Isidore, Erasmus, Musculus,
Cajetan, Flacius and others think it is the *wife* of the apostle,
who Renen thinks might have been Lydia. But the word
is masculine. Others, that he may have been the husband
or brother of either Euodia or Syntyche; so Chrysostom,
Theophylact, Camerarius, Beza. Howson suggests Luke,
who at this time was not with Paul, but certainly had
had close relations with the Philippian Church. St. Paul,
however, seems to address him as one who had not shared
the elementary labor at Philippi. Luther says, "The principal
bishop at Philippi." St. Paul nowhere else uses this term
in address. But it is not improbable that, even at so early
a time, among several bishops or presbyters one should be
president. Meyer prefers to consider it (although it occurs
nowhere else) as a proper name, Syzygus, as in the margin of
Westcott and Hort. The name means *yokefellow.* And as Paul
addresses him, moved by the tender recollection of labor they
had borne like oxen in one yoke, and by confidence in him,
he plays upon his name, O Syzyge, O yokefellow, who truly
art a yokefellow, true to thy name!—**Help.** The same word
used (Luke 5:7) when Peter and Andrew beckoned to John
and James to help them. While he hints to them a rebuke of

the difference between Euodia and Syntyche, he recognizes their zeal and discouragement and noble purpose. Many a dissension arises in a congregation, because those who have borne the burden and heat of the day become weary in well-doing and are tempted to think no one stands with them. St. Paul, who could make the same complaint, and even has written that besides Timothy he had no man like-minded, could sympathize with such.—**For they labored with me.** They were among the original believers and fellow-workers with Paul at the beginning of the Church at Philippi. How tenderly does he recur to those earnest, happy days. There is no special mention of Lydia. Perhaps she, in the course of her business, had returned to Thyatira. How much may one do *in the Lord* during even a temporary sojourn in a place.—**With Clement also.** Lightfoot would read, "I ask thee with Clement also to help." Meyer, on the other hand, "Who labored with me, with Clement also." A change of prepositions causes this uncertainty of rendering. Clement of Rome, whom ancient ecclesiastical tradition recognized here, belonged to the next generation. The name was a common one. Tradition has confounded two who bore the same name. Evidently St. Paul refers to one held in grateful remembrance at Philippi, who with those women and Epaphroditus had shared with him the initial labors and persecutions of the Philippian Church. A pastor will know how dear are the recollections which unite those who, in a former generation, strove and agonized for the well-being of a church. Paul speaks of these to awaken the old feeling of unity, the former disposition to postpone all personal aims to the common good.—**The book of life.** Clement was dead, I think; and so were many Paul here refers to. Whether in this world now

185

or not, and though he does not mention them severally by name, their names *are written* in a Book of Life. "The 'book of life,' in the figurative language of the Old Testament, is the register of the covenant people" (Lightfoot). (Isai. 4:3; Ez. 13:9; Dan. 12:1; Ps. 69:28; Ex. 32:32. See also Rev. 3:5; 13:8; 17:8; 20:12, 15; 21:27; 22:19. Also Luke 10:20; Hebr. 12:23.) St. Paul might have written thus of those still in the world. "It is clear from Rev. 3:5 that the image suggested no idea of absolute predestination" (Lightfoot). Ver. 1–3 are peculiarly the word of an affectionate pastor. By the highest motives and the tenderest recollections, by direct appeal and with sincere sympathy, he tries both to set those he speaks to on the right way, and to encourage and further them.

4. Rejoice in the Lord alway: again I will say, Rejoice.

4. A farewell But after his wont, the apostle dwells on the meaning of the word, suggested to him after it has been written. "I have bidden them *Rejoice*; yes, I will say it again, Rejoice." For he will show them how, under all possible trial, a Christian always should, and always can, rejoice.

5. Let your forbearance be known unto all men. The Lord is at hand.

5. **Forbearance.** Margin, *Gentleness.* A. V., Moderation. Wiclif, *Patience.* Tyndale and Cranmer, *Softness.* Geneva, *Your patient mind.* Rheims, *Modestie.* 2 Cor. 10:1, *Gentleness* of Christ. Lightfoot, The opposite, contentious and self-seeking spirit. M. Arnold, Sweet reasonableness. Making allowance. Eadie: "What is proper and fair, or what is kind and reasonable, especially in the form of considerateness and as opposed to the harshness of law.... It does not insist on what is its due; it does not stand on etiquette or right, but it descends and complies. It is opposed to that rigor

which never bends nor deviates, and which, as it gives the last farthing, uniformly exacts it.... That generous and indulgent feeling that knows what is right, but recedes from it; is conscious of what is merited, but does not contend for strict proportion. Slow to take offence, it is swift to forgive it. Let a misunderstanding arise, and no false delicacy will prevent it from taking the first step towards reconciliation or adjustment of opinion." (See Luther on Gen. 48:17.) In his sermon on 4th Sunday in Advent (8:118) he translates by the word *Lindigkeit*. "One makes not himself the aim and rule, nor wants every one to bend, go, and govern himself according to him. He divides all right into rigorous right and gentle right, and what is rigorous he softens; that is *equity, moderation, clemency* (1 Cor. 9:20–22; Matt. 12:1–13; Mark 2:1–13).... Nothing is necessary to a Christian but faith and love; all else should be left free to love, to hold or to refuse, as the interests of others may require.... There could be no better example than that of two good friends. As they are towards each other, so should we be to all men. Each does what pleases the other; and gives up, withdraws, suffers, does, yields, what he sees the other needs or wishes for. Neither uses any compulsion.... In short, here is no law, no right, no force, no need, but just freedom and favor. (See Eccl. 7:16.) By *all men* we are here to understand *all sorts of men*, friends and foes, great and small, masters and servants, rich and poor, our own and strangers." So Erasmus advises Melanchthon (C. R. I. 78) to show himself the superior of his opponents *in moderation as well as in argument.* This specific virtue of a Christian is explicated in the Sermon on the Mount (Matt. 5:37–48 and ch. 6). It was exhibited by our Lord when He girded Himself with a towel and washed the disciples'

feet; this, however, only because what He did then was of
a character with His whole life. A Christian should not set
his heart on his "rights"; should not urge his "claims." He
in every sense denies himself. This character should be so
real that men would perceive it. Thus, much more than by
busy activity, we would let our light shine. Luther (8:132):
"See how Paul teaches a Christian. First, let him be joyful in
God through faith, and then sweet and kind towards men.
If he answer, How can I? he answers, The Lord is at hand.
But if I be persecuted, and every one takes advantage of me?
He answers, Be not anxious; pray to God and let Him care.
Yes, but I become weary and heavy in prayer! No, the peace
of God will guard you."—**The Lord is at hand.** St. Paul's
watchword and the watchword of the early Church (1 Cor.
16:22; James 5:8). The thought of judgment and reward is
here. In view of the near coming of the Lord, why should
Christians insist on their "rights" over against each other in
earthly associations and in the estimation of men? A reason
for such "forbearance" as Christ set us an example of, and
a support of it. Luther: "This epistle teaches us in brief a
Christian life towards God and men; viz.: he lets God be all
things to him, and he is therefore all things to all men; he is
to men as God is to him; he receives from God and gives to
men; and the sum of all is Faith and Love."

6. In nothing be anxious; but in everything by prayer and
supplication with thanksgiving let your requests be made
known unto God.

6. **In nothing be anxious.** Bengel: "To be anxious and
to pray, are more contrary the one to the other than fire
and water are" (Matt. 6:25; 1 Peter 5:7).—**But.** This is the
reason a Christian never need be anxious.—**In everything.**

No care is too small to be shared with God.—**Prayer and supplication.** The former is a general term for address to God; the latter might be addressed to men. The latter seems to imply a deeper sense of need, while *prayer* might include ascriptions of praise and thankful vows. Prayers and supplications include particular *requests.* Our prayers should not be general only and formal, but we should ask of God the very things we wish for and think we need. If we do this in a filial spirit, He will sift our requests, giving us those things that be profitable for us, and not so granting our requests as to send leanness to our souls. Our prayer should be made **with thanksgiving** (Luke 17:18). From this word *Thanksgiving, Eucharistia,* was derived the name of the central and characteristic service of the Christian Church, the Eucharist. It was so called from earliest time. The *Preface* of our service represents the *thanksgiving* which characterized it, after the example of the Lord, who when He took the bread *blessed* it, *gave thanks.* In the early Church a thanksgiving was made at length rather for the gifts of God's providence than for redemption, as now; as was indeed natural in the first joy of those who were delivered from false gods to the knowledge of our Father in heaven (Acts 14:11–14; 17:23–31; Irenæus, Adv. Hær. IV. 18). And with this thanksgiving they joined a prayer for all estates of men in the Church. By prayer and supplication with thanksgiving they made their requests known unto God. In this passage St. Paul may have alluded to the Christian service of worship then in process of formation. At least, these words have had no little effect on that development.

7. And the peace of God, which passeth all understanding, shall guard your hearts and your thoughts in Christ Jesus.

7. **The peace of God.** "The rest and satisfaction of the
mind in God's wisdom and love, excluding all internal dissension, doubt and contradiction (Rom. 8:18, 28)" (Meyer. John
14:27).—**Which passeth all understanding.** "Surpassing
every device or counsel of man" (Lightfoot). Paul may here
allude to measures which some had been urging as absolutely
essential to the safety or well-being of the Philippian Church,
and in advocacy or criticism of which a danger of division had
risen. He suggests a better protection than the plans of the
wisest.—**Shall guard.** *In Christ Jesus.* All our works should
be begun, continued and ended in Him. The *heart* is the seat
of life and thought; *thoughts* issue thence. This is not merely a
wish, but a promise and a prophecy (see ver. 9); and it is fitly
incorporated in the Christian service of worship in which we
fulfil the injunction of the preceding verse. (Compare Numb.
6:24–26.)

Verses 4–7 are the Epistle for the Fourth Sunday in Advent.
The watchword of the apostle is there joined with the cry of
John Baptist.

8. Finally, brethren, whatsoever things are true, whatsoever
things are honourable, whatsoever things are just, whatsoever
things are pure, whatsoever things are lovely, whatsoever
things are of good report; if there be any virtue, and if there
be any praise, think on these things.

8. **Finally.** The apostle begins to sum up his thought
again, so as to conclude.—**Whatsoever things are true.** He
does not propose to separate virtues, but analyzes the one
Christian character. *True* is here not *veracious* merely, but *real,*
agreeing with reality, with the Gospel. Not theoretical truth,
but *fact.*—**Honourable.** Worthy of reverence, reverend. The
word *honest,* in the Authorized Version, bears the same

sense. "Opposed to what is mean, frivolous, indecorous and unworthy" (Eadie).—**Pure.** Stainless.—**Lovely.** Amiable, love-worthy.—**Of good report.** The word has not a passive sense, but should be rendered as in the margin—*gracious,* i.e. winning. Observe that we always are tempted to look away from what is true, to appearances; from that which is right, to that which is expedient; from that which is pure, to that which is amusing; from that which is amiable, to that which excites and is admired; from that which is winning, to that which asserts itself. How necessary is it to urge these particulars of the forbearance, moderation, gentleness of Christ.—**If there be any virtue.** A word used nowhere else in the New Testament, except 1 Peter 2:9; 2 Peter 1:3, 5; and there in a special sense. Meyer calls attention to the fact that instead of *virtue,* the Old Testament suggested another line of ideas such as *righteousness, holiness, sanctity, sanctification.* The heathen moralists who exalted virtue moved in another sphere. The word is too mean, Beza says (quoted in Trench), when compared with the gifts of the Spirit. Here, I think, is an instance of St. Paul's irony. *Virtue* and *praise* may have been urged as motives or ends in the dissensions at Philippi, to which he would make an end. He sums up his appeal in an *argumentum ad hominem.*—**Think on these things.** "First meditation; then practice" (Calvin). A rule for Christians in the selection of books to read, and in meditation on life and history.

9. The things which ye both learned and received and heard and saw in me, these things do: and the God of peace shall be with you.

9. **Which ye both learned.** From me and other teachers of the Gospel.—**Received.** Took them in, accepted, ap-

proved them.—**And heard and saw in me.** The matter
of St. Paul's instruction and example.—**These things do;**
i.e. practise.—**And the God of peace shall be with you**
(4:7). Here again a promise and a prophecy. Certainly this
seems to indicate a consequence, as in the former case. A
requisite of the presence with us of the God of peace, and of
His protection of our minds and hearts, is not only prayer,
praise and thanksgiving, and participation in the worship of
His Church, but also attention to the things which are true,
etc., and obedient practice of the things we have been taught
and have received.

10–20. But I rejoice in the Lord greatly, that now at length
ye have revived your thought for me; wherein ye did indeed
take thought, but ye lacked opportunity. Not that I speak
in respect of want: for I have learned, in whatsoever state
I am, therein to be content. I know how to be abased, and
I know also how to abound: in everything and in all things
have I learned the secret both to be filled and to be hungry,
both to abound and to be in want. I can do all things in
him that strengtheneth me. Howbeit ye did well, that ye had
fellowship with my affliction. And ye yourselves also know,
ye Philippians, that in the beginning of the gospel, when I
departed from Macedonia, no church had fellowship with me
in the matter of giving and receiving, but ye only; for even in
Thessalonica ye sent once and again unto my need. Not that
I seek for the gift; but I seek for the fruit that increaseth to
your account. But I have all things, and abound: I am filled,
having received from Epaphroditus the things *that came* from
you, an odour of a sweet smell, a sacrifice acceptable, well-
pleasing to God. And my God shall fulfil every need of yours
according to his riches in glory in Christ Jesus. Now unto

our God and Father *be* the glory for ever and ever. Amen.

10. Again *"in the Lord."* *Greatly* is made emphatic. He says, *I rejoiced;* i.e. on the reception of your gift.—**Ye have revived your thought for me.** The figure is derived from the putting forth of fresh shoots in the spring; as if they had been dormant for a winter, but now showed life again.—**Lacked opportunity;** i.e. it was not the season. He pursues the figure.—**Take thought.** He seems to pause on the meaning of the word, and after his fashion hastens to correct an inference they may draw from what he has said, which he had not intended.

11. I do not mean to imply that I have been or am in want. **I** is emphatic: I, for my part.—**Have learned.** By experience.—**To be content.** Sufficient in myself. "Self-supporting, independent" (Ellicott). St. Paul disciplined himself to want little, to be superior to wants. And he labored with his own hands (1 Thess. 2:9; 2 Thess. 3:7–9; 2 Cor. 11:7–9; Acts 18:2, 3).

12. **I know how to be abased.** I know humiliation. The same word he had used of our Lord: He *humbled* Himself.—**To abound.** To have more than enough. He had had personal experience of both conditions.—**I have learned the secret.** I have been *initiated,* as in the heathen mysteries, the allusion to which his hearers would at once perceive. (Initiation into the mysteries was very general.) Meyer calls attention to the climax: I have learned, I know, I have been initiated. The word is used of the initiation into the successive degrees of the heathen mysteries, and expresses a knowledge which Paul has, and not every one possesses, a knowledge got "by preparatory toil and discipline" (Eadie). (See Col. 1:26.)

13. **Both to be filled—that strengthened me.** These are

the degrees of the fraternity in which St. Paul was initiated.
He is equal to all things in Him, who infuses strength into
him (2 Cor. 12:9).

14. **Ye had fellowship with my affliction.** The verb has
an active sense. (See on 1:3–7.) It was good for them to have
assisted him, whether he absolutely needed their gift or not.

15. Acts 17:14, 15; 2 Cor. 11:8, 9.—**Fellowship.** In both
verses, the communion signalized in the prayers and offerings
of the Eucharist.—**No church—but ye only.** The relation
between him and this Church was unusually affectionate. Aid,
which he would shrink from taking from others, he received
from them from the first. This could only be because they
and he from the first were conscious that they understood
each other. He knew that they gave out of fellowship, not
in order to pay him; and they knew that he took to admit
them to fellowship, not out of a mercenary spirit.—**Once
and again.** Once and twice.

16. Paul was not maintained by the Philippians while he
was at Thessalonica, for while there he labored with his own
hands (2 Thess. 3:8); but he gratefully remembers the gifts
they sent him. It is a pleasing proof of their simplicity that
they continued to send to him their ineffectual gifts at the
very beginning of their life as Christians, at once entering into
admiring fellowship with the sailmaking missionary. A lesson
to "mission-churches." An instance of genuine Christian zeal,
the utterance of Christian faith.

17. **Not that I seek for the gift.** He does not say all
this, that by the exuberance of his thanksgiving he may
compel them to give him more.—**But I seek.** Emphatic: *I do
seek.*—**The fruit.** It is not necessary to define this *fruit* and
account. Whether he refers to the reward which will be laid up

194

for them and will be given them at the day of Christ, or to the blessedness he quickly knows who freely gives. Paul means both. He acknowledges their gifts courteously, and by all this circumlocution preserves his self-respect. He indicates the spirit in which a minister of Christ may accept gifts, and in which Christians should support the ministry. Like Christ, pastors dare not refuse to be ministered unto. They should admit others into fellowship with them. But they should be initiated both to abound and to be in want. They should be willing to receive, but not for their own sake, but for the sake of those who give. It needs grace, thus to receive, and yet to remain what Paul means when he calls himself *content;* i.e. superior to all gifts and all want.

18. *I have all things to the full,* I have more than enough, having received from Epaphroditus the things which came from you. What a gentleman Paul was! He shrank from seeming to be mean-spirited. But, having guarded his self-respect, he gives way to heartiest commendation of their thoughtfulness and generosity, and makes it very clear he is not asking for more.—**An odour—a sacrifice** (Rom. 12:1; 1 Peter 2:5; Hebr. 13:16; see on 1:3–7; 4:6). A figure from the Old Testament and from the usages of heathen worship, most familiar to them. Not only the calves of their lips, but the fruit of their works are appropriate sacrifices of Christians upon their altar. The support of the ministry and contributions to missions are properly called an offering to the Lord. And such sacrifices ought always continue in the Christian Church and have their place in Christian worship.

19. **And my God.** How confidently could Paul, in face of his need, and in acknowledgment of their kindness to him, declare that God would requite it.—**Shall supply every**

need of yours (Matt. 20:28). We should not infer that in
return for the kindness we do some one, God will give us just
so much in return. This would not be to give *in the Lord.* In
Christ we give, looking for nothing in return. Yet, Give, and
it shall be given unto you (Luke 6:38). Not in kind will God
repay those who devote all unto Him. Eye hath not seen nor
ear heard (1 Cor. 2:9).

20. All mutual thanksgiving, all sense of mutual obligation, merges in their sense of common obligation and joint
thanksgiving to *our* God and Father.

21–22. Salute every saint in Christ Jesus. The brethren
which are with me salute you. All the saints salute you,
especially they that are of Cæsar's household.

21. **The brethren which are with me.** He refers to those
who might be said to make up his household at the time.

22. **All the saints;** i.e. those of Rome, where the letter was written. Paul therefore was in communication
with the churches of the city and they knew his occupations.—**Cæsar's household.** Cæsar's household included a
vast number of persons, occupying various minutely-divided
offices. In the Catacombs many of their names and of
their offices have been recovered; and among them names
which occur among the salutations in the Epistle to the
Romans. The Gospel is not likely to have won many highly
distinguished persons, but those referred to here probably
were of the emperor's freedmen and slaves. Among these
were many Orientals and Jews. This probably was the
particular Christian congregation of Rome of whom Paul
saw most and with whom he may have worshipped regularly.

23. The grace of the Lord Jesus Christ be with your spirit.

23. **The grace of the Lord Jesus Christ be with your**

spirit. The salutation of Paul, which he was accustomed to write with his own hand, as a token (2 Thess. 3:17, 18; Rom. 16:24).

III

Colossians

ANNOTATIONS
ON THE
EPISTLE TO THE COLOSSIANS

BY
EDWARD T. HORN, D. D.

13

Introduction

Colossæ was a city of Asia Minor, on the river Lycus, within a few miles of the more important cities of Laodicea and Hierapolis, not more than a hundred and fifty miles from Ephesus, and on the great trade-route between that city and the East. The original inhabitants of the region were Phrygians; there were many Jews among them (Josephus, Antiq. 12:3, 4; 14:10, 20; Cicero. pro Flac. 28) and also Greeks and Romans. St. Paul had not visited these cities (2:1), but Colossæ, and perhaps Hierapolis and Laodicea, had received the Gospel from Epaphras (1:7), a disciple of Paul, who may have been converted during Paul's stay at Ephesus (a.d. 54–57). During Paul's first imprisonment at Rome, Epaphras came to him (1:8), and, while he reported that the Church of Colossæ was orderly and steadfast in the faith (2:5), he also told that its well-being was threatened by a false teacher or false teachers (2:4, 8), who pretended to lead into a higher knowledge than the Gospel furnished, which was to be attained by ascetic practices (2:16–23).

It was a period of great unrest. Christianity was not the

only religion that challenged the attention of the earnest.
Remnants of ancient religions, legends and rites, clustering
round prehistoric monuments, kept their hold in places under
the forms of the Roman worship. Ancient Asian Mysticism,
Persian Dualism, Buddhism also, the speculations of Greek
philosophy, "an idealized Mosaism" (Eadie), the symbolic
teachings of the Eleusinian, Egyptian and Mithraic Mysteries,
all were urged in the busy centres of trade and thought.
Travelling sophists commanded an audience; false brethren
hastened after St. Paul to disturb and undo his work; the
apostles John and Peter encountered a Simon Magus (Acts
8); Paul, a false prophet, who was a Jew, called Bar-Jesus, in
Cyprus (Acts 13:6), and vagabond Jewish exorcists who took
in vain the name of the Lord Jesus at Ephesus (Acts 19:13); and
St. John, in his letters to churches of this region, reproves
errors savoring of what was afterwards called *Gnosticism*
(Rev. 2:6, 14, 24). The *Essenes,* a fraternity of Jewish
anchorites, combined with rigid devotion to certain Jewish
tenets, elements derived from Zoroastrianism, and perhaps
from the Buddhism of India. Philo of Alexandria (b.c. 20–50
a.d.), a contemporary of St. Paul, tried by means of allegory to
subject the facts of the Old Testament to the forms of Greek
speculative philosophy. The mixture of these notions and
forms of thought with the Gospel issued, in the first and
second centuries, in what is known as *Gnosticism* (from the
Greek word *Gnosis,* meaning *knowledge*). There were many
systems—interesting as monuments of the struggle between
the Gospel and the Ethnic religions, and of a strange phase
in the history of the human mind,—but they may be divided
into groups, according as the Greek philosophy or Oriental
conceptions preponderated in them, or again, as they were

202

hostile or favorable to the Old Testament. It has been well said, "There was scarcely one of the Catholic determinations of doctrine in the second and third centuries, which was not affected by the conflict with Gnosticism" (Jacobi, in Herzog, 5:217). After that period it ceased to be a force, but influenced heretical sects during the Middle Ages, as, for instance, the Albigenses (see Lea's History of the Inquisition), was related to the Kabbala, or later mystical philosophy of the Jews, and survives in modern mystical and theosophic writings.

The subjects of Gnostic speculation are fairly stated in the Recognitions of Clement, I. 20: "First of all it ought to be inquired what is the origin of all things, or what is the immediate thing which may be called the cause of all things which are: then with respect to all things which exist, whether they have been made, and by whom, through whom, and for whom; whether they have received their subsistence from one, or from two, or from many; ... whether there is anything that is better than all, or anything which is inferior to all; whether those things which are seen, were always, and shall be always; whether they have come into existence without a creator, and shall pass away without a destroyer." It tried to explain creation as the result of a process in God. The Supreme God was said by it to be incapable of self-manifestation. One of the Gnostic systems identified Him with non-existence. The Creator of the world and the Saviour were assigned varying places in the series of emanations from the Most High. The problem of Creation started the problem of the *Origin of Evil.* The doctrine that matter is essentially evil led to a false asceticism, which, in turn, issued in license.

To meet such a danger St. Paul wrote this letter. Many of the words he uses play a great part in later Gnosticism. We

cannot decide whether the false teachers really derived them
from St. Paul, as they claimed to do; or whether he took them
up, to put a right meaning into words, which such already
had abused. The false teachers at Colossæ proposed to lead
the initiated into deeper mysteries than the Gospel opened
to the vulgar; they seem to have had doctrines about angelic
mediators; they did not accord to Christ His supremacy in
nature and in grace; and urged both a spurious asceticism
and a rigid observance of legal rites. It was the beginning of
the later Gnosticism, a first meeting of the mixed Judaism
and Oriental mysticism of the Essenes with Christianity and
the Alexandrian philosophy.

St. Paul shows us how Christianity in our own age
must meet Buddhism, Theosophy, Spiritism, the spurious
mysticism traditional in some secret organizations, and all
pantheistic speculation: it is by simple faith in the historical
Christ, God manifest in the flesh, offered for our sins, risen,
and ascended to the right hand of God.

The epistle was written at the same time as that to the
Ephesians. Opinions may differ as to which was written
before the other. Both were sent by Tychicus, about 62
a.d. With Tychicus was associated Onesimus, who brought a
special letter to Philemon.

14

Colossians 1

1–2. Paul, an apostle of Christ Jesus through the will of God, and Timothy our brother, to the saints and faithful brethren in Christ *which are* at Colossæ: Grace to you and peace from God our Father.

    1. **Paul, an apostle of Christ Jesus.** An assertion of his authority. An official letter, and in this respect different from the letters to the Philippians, to Philemon, and 1 and 2 Thessalonians. The former two were personal and familiar; the latter two are the earliest of his letters, written in conjunction with others, and before either his work had been so extended as to require and justify "the care of all the churches," or his apostleship had been impugned by Judaizers. We may add Melanchthon's note on this passage: "An *apostle* is a person immediately called by God to teach the Gospel, and having the divine witness that he does not err, but he is not sent to bear rule in an earthly kingdom. A *bishop* or *pastor* or *doctor* is a person called by God mediately, through the Church, or those to whom the Church commits this duty, to teach the Gospel as it has been written by prophets and

apostles, and having no witness to the truth of his teaching
except those very prophetic and apostolic Scriptures, and
when he dissents from these he errs.... This distinction
answers the question, why Paul is to be believed rather than
the bishops.... The Son of God is directly at work, whether it
be through prophets, or apostles, or pastors, that His Gospel
is preached."—**Through the will of God** (1 Cor. 1:1; 2 Cor.
1:1; Gal. 1:1; Eph. 1:1; 1 Tim. 1:1; 2 Tim. 1:1. See Phil.
2:25).—**And Timothy the brother.** So 2 Cor. 1:1; Philem. 1;
but in Hebr. 13:23 *our* brother. "The same designation is used
of Quartus (Rom. 16:23), of Sosthenes (1 Cor. 1:1), of Apollos
(1 Cor. 16:12. Cf. 2 Cor. 8:18; 9:3, 5; 12:18.)" (Lightfoot.)
Certainly an honorable appellation. The churches recognized
some as the constant companions, deacons, emissaries, of
St. Paul. Timothy may also have been the amanuensis, by
whose hand this letter was written. 2. **To the holy and
faithful brethren in Christ which are at Colossæ.** On
the import of *holy* or *saints,* see on Phil. 1:1. Observe that he
here addresses the *brethren,* not as a Church. (Cf. Phil. 1:1.)
Lightfoot calls attention to the fact that Paul uses this mode of
address in the Epistle to the Romans, and those which follow
it. The Christians at Colossæ do not seem to have been very
numerous. Though imperfect, they are addressed as brethren,
as holy, as faithful. Such they were **in Christ,** "the Head,
which is the centre of life and the mainspring of all energy
throughout the body" (Lightfoot). While the address to them
according to their ideal may have been an admonition, it was
not intended to separate some from the rest, and address such
as a Church within the Church.—**Christ** is the atmosphere
in which their spiritual life "lives and moves and has its being"
(3:3).—**Grace to you.** *Grace* is the generic word for all those

206

blessings which we receive from the favor of God through Christ (John 1:14, 16). *Peace* is a specific result of grace. It is the Hebrew salutation. "In this place it signifies, first joy in God, then the good estate of the Church, and then God's gift to each one of all that is required for his sanctification, life and calling" (Melanchthon. Ps. 122:7, 8).

3–8. We give thanks to God the Father of our Lord Jesus Christ, praying always for you, having heard of your faith in Christ Jesus, and of the love which ye have toward all the saints, because of the hope which is laid up for you in the heavens, whereof ye heard before in the word of the truth of the gospel, which is come unto you; even as it is also in all the world bearing fruit and increasing, as *it doth* in you also, since the day ye heard and knew the grace of God in truth; even as ye learned of Epaphras our beloved fellow-servant, who is a faithful minister of Christ on our behalf, who also declared unto us your love in the Spirit.

3. **We give thanks.** On hearing of the spiritual "progress of the Colossians, they did not congratulate one another, but both gave the glory to God" (Eadie).—**The Father of our Lord Jesus Christ.** *Herein* lies our relation to God.—**Praying always for you.** Indicates the apostle's unremitted intercession for the churches, and for the members of the churches.

4. **Having heard,** etc. The key of this epistle is to be found, on the one hand, in what St. Paul had heard of these Colossians, and secondly, in what he asked God to give them. It is not to be supposed that these words were an idle compliment. He had heard (1) of their faith; (2) of their love to all the saints (cf. Philem. 5, 7); (3) that the word of truth was bearing fruit and increasing in them; (4) of their love

for Him, ver. 8; (5) that there was a peril that they might be
moved from the hope of the Gospel (1:23), by one who might
delude them by persuasive speech, through philosophy and
vain deceit (2:4, 8), the particulars of which will appear; and
(6) they therefore needed to be admonished again concerning
the particulars of lowly duty. Philem. 7 would indicate that
their love to all the saints had shown itself in *hospitality*, a
characteristic and necessary virtue of the early churches.
Ramsay says (The Church in the Roman Empire, p. 364), "The
central idea in the development of the episcopal office lay in
the duty of each community to maintain communication
with other communities.... Such a vast organization of a
perfectly new kind, with no analogy in previously existing
institutions, was naturally of slow development. We regard
the ideas underlying it as originating with Paul. The first
step was taken when he crossed the Taurus; the next more
conscious step was the result of the trial in Corinth, after
which his thought developed from the stage of *Thessalonians*
to that of *Galatians, Corinthians* and *Romans.* The critical stage
was passed when the destruction of Jerusalem annihilated
all possibility of a localized centre for Christianity, and
made it clear that the centralization of the Church could
reside only in an idea, viz., a process of intercommunication,
union and brotherhood." Philemon showed distinguished
hospitality as a man, not as an officer; as many a family now
is representative in its congregation.

5. **Because of the hope.** Their love was founded on
their hope. Christian love must flow from Christian faith.
The proper way of cultivating Christian virtues, is the
establishment of *hope* based on *faith.* Here are faith, hope
and love, as in 1 Cor. 13, and 1 Thess. 1:3. It will be

found that, with all variety of expression, and upon all the various occasions of his letters, Paul holds certain definite principles and moves within a definite circle of ideas.—**Laid up for you in the heavens.** Stored up, as in a granary. The prime motive of a Christian is that which is laid up for him, which *shall be* revealed, which he *shall* have; not any earthly result.—**Whereof ye heard before,** etc. St. Paul is assured they had heard this. It must therefore have been of the substance of the ordinary instruction of the Church. See how much instruction these Gentiles must have received from those who first brought the good tidings to them. The whole conception of the other world which belongs to Christianity, must have been new to them (1 Thess. 3:4; 4:1, 11; 5:2; 2 Thess. 2:5, 15; 3:6, 10).

6. **Even as it is also in all the world.** Hyperbolical, indeed; but Paul's *all the world* meant the Roman Empire.—**Bearing fruit and increasing.** Like the leaven and the *grain of mustard-seed.*—**As it doth in you.** In spite of the imperfections and dangers at Colossæ, there was no check to the progress of the good tidings. Neither were they turned away from the truth, though Epaphras was so troubled about them. The word continued to extend the Church and do its work in the hearts of believers. "An unfruitful Gospel would be no Gospel, nor would one that did not continually strive to extend itself and conquer for itself new realms" (Rœntsch).

7. **Even as ye learned of Epaphras.** They had heard the Gospel of Epaphras, not of Paul (2:1). He was Paul's **fellow-slave of Christ.** (See on 3:22.) Like him, Epaphras realized that he was not his own, but had been bought with a price; and it was woe to him if he preached not the Gospel. He was a **minister,** i.e. a *deacon,* of Christ—not officially a deacon,

but really such as those, who were chosen afterwards by the
Church, should aim to be. He was a minister of Christ **for,**
or *on behalf of,* Paul. It is altogether likely that Epaphras
first visited Colossæ as a minister of Christ under Paul's
direction. When Paul resided at Ephesus, he not only gained
many converts from other places who then happened to
visit or reside in that metropolis (as Philemon, and perhaps
Epaphras), but he most probably sent out men, like our
catechists and *native helpers* in India and Japan, who visited the
cities and regions to which Paul could not go, especially their
own native places, and went back and forth between them
and him. These were Paul's churches; and there *his* Gospel
was preached, though they never saw his face in the flesh. A
like activity continued while he was in prison, as all these
epistles witness.

8. **Who also declared unto us your love;** i.e. their love
for Paul whom they had never seen, with whom they were
one *in the Spirit.* Here Epaphras has come to Paul in Rome, to
report to him; maybe sent by the Colossians; maybe driven
by his own anxiety concerning them.

9–12. For this cause we also, since the day we heard
it, do not cease to pray and make request for you, that ye
may be filled with the knowledge of his will in all spiritual
wisdom and understanding, to walk worthily of the Lord
unto all pleasing, bearing fruit in every good work, and
increasing in the knowledge of God; strengthened with all
power, according to the might of his glory, unto all patience
and longsuffering with joy; giving thanks unto the Father,
who made us meet to be partakers of the inheritance of the
saints in light;

9. **For this cause.** *Therefore:* On account of all he has told

us.—**We also.** Like Epaphras (4:12, 13).—**Since the day we heard it.** Paul's prayers for the churches were not a formal custom, but were prompted by their exigencies.—**Do not cease to pray and make request for you.** The churches were knit together by intercession for each other, as well as by mutual offices of love. The Church is blessed not only by the grace of God and the continual intercession of our Great High Priest, but also by the prayers and supplications and intercessions of all the Church for all the Church (2 Thess. 3:1). For what does Paul make request? (See on ver. 4.) (1) That they may be filled with the knowledge of God's will, (2) in all spiritual wisdom and (3) understanding. (4) That they may walk worthily of the Lord unto all pleasing, (5) bearing fruit in every good work, (6) increasing in the knowledge of God, (7) strengthened unto all patience and longsuffering with joy, (8) and giving thanks.—**That ye may be filled with the knowledge of his will.** (See the Collect for First Sunday after Epiphany: "Grant that Thy people may both perceive and know what things they ought to do.") The word means more than *knowledge,* a thorough and exact knowledge, a knowledge such as can come only of growth, experience. St. Paul lays much stress on this, and prays that his converts may have it (Phil. 1:19; Eph. 1:17; Philem. 6). This, not only in contrast with the sophistry and affectation which passed itself off as *gnosis* (knowledge), and because in this epistle and at this time he had especially to resist those who claimed to be *Gnostics,* or knowing ones, possessed of an esoteric knowledge confined to the few; but also because in the quiet of his prison, in his reflection on the dangers of his churches, he saw how much their knowledge of God and of the Gospel needed to be deepened and extended, in order

to withstand vain deceit. As the Gospel is now conceived
as a *faith,* or is urged as *a disposition of love,* so in earlier
time it was also conceived as a *philosophy,* as *wisdom,* and
this, without misconception of its purport (John 17:3; cf.
Collect 74: "In knowledge of whom standeth our eternal
life"). The antidote to falsehood is increase of knowledge.
Christian people should not be content with the elements
of Christ, but should press on unto perfection (Hebr. 6:1).
Not only should the formulas of faith be fixed in the memory
of all the children of the Church, but, as long as they live,
Christian people should give heed unto instruction and
search the Scriptures. But the knowledge we are to seek
is a thorough and accurate and growing knowledge of the
will of God. "It is indeed a marvellously great knowledge,
that the heart of a man, born in sin, should be able to ponder
and be assured of this, viz., that God, in the depths of His
majesty and of His divine heart, has finally and irrevocably
decreed, and would have every man know and believe, that
He will not impute sin to the sinner, but will forgive it and
be merciful, and will give eternal life for the sake of His dear
Son" (Luther). (See 1 Thess. 4:3.) "A wise man is a Christian
who is able to tell God's will towards us, and how we know it
by faith, and may grow in it, and may walk in it" (Ib.).—**In all
spiritual wisdom and understanding;** i.e. the *wisdom* and
understanding imparted by the Spirit of God. *Wisdom* is the
knowledge of things and their causes. It is a moral as well as a
mental quality. It conforms to the truth it recognizes. Luther
says: "Understanding makes use of wisdom, notes what
accords with it, puts it into practice, subtly tests what comes
with the name and appearance of wisdom, discriminates, and
therefore guards against anything that is not wise." "We need

in the Church not only the doctrine which gives wisdom, but the persistent admonition which gives understanding." See his discussion of these two words in sermon on this passage (24th Sunday after Trinity). *Understanding* marked the Boy Jesus in the temple (Luke 2:47). In the Parable of the Sower those who bare fruit *understand* the word (Matt. 13:23). In Phil. 1:9 St. Paul uses a term meaning *perception*. *Understanding* here is insight, discernment, spiritual sagacity; as we should say, the ability to put two and two together; and this in the realm of the Spirit. How desirable is it for Christian men not only to have a good disposition in general, but a faculty of spiritual discernment, a right judgment of things, motives and occasions; and also wisdom in the application of the heavenly rule to earthly details. These can be gained only by practice, by experience under the instruction of the Spirit of God. At this each should aim. And for this a pastor should pray.

10. **To walk worthily of the Lord unto all pleasing;** i.e. to please Him *in every way.*—**Bearing fruit in every good work.** The Church of Christ, united to the Vine, bears fruit in every kind of good work. So the Christian does not enough, in fulfilling a particular task. He should be fruitful in *every* good work, "works of our calling, done as unto the Lord, works belonging to our relations in life, the being good husbands, wives, parents, children, masters, servants, and so forth,—works of piety and philanthropy, and the use of every means in our power to spread the knowledge of Christ and His gospel" (Goulburn, The Collect for the Day, II. 137).—**And increasing in the knowledge of God.** The thorough knowledge, though it fills, ever increases, ever should grow.

11. **Unto all patience and longsuffering with joy.** *Patience* is a fundamental Christian virtue. Especially is patience *with joy* something more than resignation. It is endurance, courage, steadfastness, enduring to the end. *Longsuffering* is the same virtue in respect of those who treat us ill. "He distinguished longsuffering from patience as something greater and stronger. When the devil fails to overcome a heart with suffering and plagues, he tries to wear it out, so that patience seems too long tried and to have no end. That is knightly Christian strength that can withstand the devil's many, great and various attacks, and sustain them to the end" (Luther). Observe that, in order that we may endure thus and be patient to the end, we need the Almightiness of God. So great a basis—so great a need! who can be patient and longsuffering with joy, in his own strength?

12. **Giving thanks.** Always giving thanks.—**Who hath made us meet.** "Competent" (Lightfoot). Some read *you* for *us.*—**To be partakers,** etc. *For the part* or *share of the inheritance.* The apostle constantly keeps before the eyes of his converts the eternal reward of the Gospel.

13. Who delivered us out of the power of darkness, and translated us into the kingdom of the Son of his love;

13. **Who delivered us.** An act of God, done, once for all.—**Out of the power of darkness.** We were under the tyranny of darkness; we were its slaves. How pertinent here, in an epistle written to counteract the apostles of a false knowledge, is this contrast of their former with their present condition, as a contrast between *darkness* and light.—**And translated us.** *Transferred us.* As of old kings would bring whole nations from their native seats to colonize new regions. So Antiochus Epiphanes brought 2,000

214

Jewish families at once into a region of Asia Minor. So the Romans formed colonies throughout their empire.—**Into the kingdom.** The ordered kingdom of heaven is contrasted with the lawless tyranny of darkness.—**Of the Son of his love.** The equivalent of *"Beloved Son,"* in Matt. 3:17; 12:18; 17:5, and Eph. 1:6. Note the crises in the ministry of Christ, at which this was said to Him. Here Lightfoot has this instructive note: "In the preceding verses we have a striking illustration of St. Paul's teaching in two important respects. *First,* the reign of Christ has already begun. His kingdom is a present kingdom. Whatever therefore is *essential* in the kingdom of Christ must be capable of realization now. There may be some exceptional manifestation in the world to come, but this cannot alter its essential character. In other words, the sovereignty of Christ is essentially a moral and spiritual sovereignty, which has begun now and will only be perfected hereafter. *Secondly,* corresponding to this, and equally significant, is his language in speaking of individual Christians. He regards them as already rescued from the kingdom of darkness, as already put in possession of their inheritance as saints. They are *potentially* saved, because the knowledge of God is potentially salvation, and this knowledge is within their reach. Such is St. Paul's constant mode of speaking. He uses the language not of exclusion, but of comprehension He prefers to dwell on their potential advantages, rather than on their actual attainments. He hopes to make them saints, by dwelling on their calling as saints (Eph. 2:6)."

14. In whom we have our redemption, the forgiveness of our sins:

14. **In whom we have redemption.** The phrase, *through*

His blood, has been introduced here, from Eph. 1:7. Paul says,
the redemption, not *our* redemption. This is described as
a present possession, an accomplished fact. "I believe that
He has redeemed me." The work of Christ is described as
the payment of a ransom in order to free us. The price
was His *life, Himself.* This He gave for *all* (Matt. 20:28;
Mark 10:45; 1 Tim. 2:6). This is not a mere possibility, or
a figure, but the fundamental fact which the ministers of
the Gospel go forth to tell (Luke 24:47, 48). "The preaching
of the Gospel must show us both *sin* and *forgiveness,* wrath
and grace, death and life, how we lay in darkness, and how
we have been delivered therefrom. For it aims not first to
make sinners of us (like the Law), nor to lead us to deserve
and earn grace, but shows that, although condemned and
under the power of sin, death and the devil, we by faith
receive and know the redemption given to us, and should be
thankful for it" (Luther). This mention of *sin,* and assertion of
redemption, at the beginning of his letter, was aimed by Paul
at the fundamental fallacy of Gnosticism, "which, by virtually
denying the existence of sin, and consequently of redemption
from sin, took away the whole significance of the revelation
of Christ" (Mansel, Gnostic Heresies, 13). This *redemption*
is further defined as *the forgiveness of sins.* Goulburn says,
Forgiveness is of sins, *remission* is of a debt, and therefore
both are applied in the variants of the Lord's Prayer. Trench
(Synonyms of N. T.) says, "The image which underlies the
word here used is that of a releasing or letting-go. Probably
the year of jubilee, the year in which all debts were forgiven,
suggested the higher application of the word." In Eph. 1:7
Paul says *"trespasses";* here, *"sins." Sin* is "the word of largest
reach" (Trench). It is derived from a word meaning *to fail*

216

of, to miss, as to miss the mark. It is used 174 times in the New Testament, 71 of these by Paul. The word translated *trespasses* occurs 21 times in the N. T., 16 of these in Paul's writings. "There is such a thing as collective *sin,* but *trespasses* are individual, and save as single acts cannot be. Sin reigns, plays the lord, holds in bondage, has a sort of distinct being of its own, and is even independent of action, though action is not independent of it. But trespasses have no being save through choices, or as acts of will. Man may be a sinner without being a transgressor, but he cannot be a transgressor without sinning. Adam's act could be alternately described as sin, transgression, or a trespass, but the consequence to his posterity would be described as sin, but not by either of the other terms" (Fairbairn, Christ in Modern Thought, 312). All former English versions say *sins,* in both passages. The redemption of Christ frees us from our sin and our sins (John 1:19; 1 John 2:2; 3:5; see also the two versions of the *Gloria in Excelsis*). Because this verse is true, the Absolution holds so prominent a place in Christian worship. Our reformers held that "The sermon itself is properly and fundamentally an absolution, for the forgiveness of sins is in it proclaimed to many in common and publicly, or to one person alone either publicly or secretly" (Melanchthon to Senate of Nürnberg, C. R. II. 647. See Luther's concurrence, Ib. 650). So is the forgiveness of sins given in the Holy Sacraments. A minister can say with all confidence, "God *hath* had mercy on us, and forgiveth us." Paul here appeals to the Christian consciousness of the Colossians. "Our Christian experience is made the starting-point for Christian reflection" (Schnederman).

15–17. Who is the image of the invisible God, the firstborn

of all creation; for in him were all things created, in the
heavens and upon the earth, things visible and things invisible,
whether thrones or dominions or principalities or powers;
all things have been created through him, and unto him; and
he is before all things, and in him all things consist.

This passage contains words which are characteristic on
the one hand of the Alexandrian Græco-Judaic philosophy, an
attempt to construe the Old Testament Revelation according
to the forms of the Platonic philosophy; and on the other hand
of the Gnosticism of a later age. In some degree, the latter
may have derived these terms (as it professed to do) from St.
Paul's use of them. There is also allusion to doctrines which
were held by the Essenes among the Jews, and afterwards
received a fantastic development among the Gnostics. Some
of these terms were used in the Septuagint also. While it
is hard for us to appreciate the methods of thought of a
different and remote time—as the speculations of the later
Greek Fathers on the nature of the Godhead are not quite
intelligible to us—yet it is clear that it was not natural for Paul
either to think or express himself in the modes and terms of
Alexandrian philosophy. His method of reasoning was more
allied to that of the rabbins. He here accepts the cant of the
schools, of the would-be wise, and shows what the truth is.
There is a measure of irony in his use of these terms. In order
to explain them, we must compare their meaning, (1) in the
Septuagint, (2) in Philo and his like, and (3) in the later use of
the Gnostics.

15. **Who;** i.e. the Son of His love—Christ. St. Paul is
not wont to say one thing of Christ in His divine nature,
and another of Him in His human nature. He speaks of the
concrete Christ. He who was man is He who, before He was

218

man, was. And what is here said of Him is true of Christ exalted, "of the whole, full, divine-human Personality of the Lord" (Rœntsch).—**An image** (Wis. 7:26; 2 Cor. 4:4). The same thought as expressed by "the Word" in John 1:1, but not co-extensive with it. Lightfoot says the *Image* implies (1) Representation, but necessarily perfect representation; and (2) Manifestation. Philo says, "The image of the unseen nature." Trench says the word implies not merely *resemblance* but also *derivation.* The Alexandrian Jewish philosophy taught an incommunicable Godhead and a Logos, or Word, or Image, through whom He uttered Himself in Creation and Revelation. The Gnostics taught that there were many mediators, and had to be, each being finite and incomplete. St. Paul ascends in his ascription of completeness to Christ: he *begins,* Christ is an image of the invisible God (1 Tim. 6:16). In Christ, in His visible concrete manifestation, we have "the declaration of the unseen God, whom no man hath seen" (John 1:18): "the shining forth of His glory and the impress of His substance" (Hebr. 1:3). He who would know what God is may know Him in Christ (Matt. 11:27; John 1:14; 3:13; 14:9). "The Father is such as the Son proclaims Him; the Word is the Image of His mind" (Melanchthon). "The Father is eternal, immortal, powerful, light, king, sovereign, God, Lord, Creator and Maker. These attributes must be in the Image, to make it true that he 'that hath seen' the Son 'hath seen the Father.' If the Son be not all this, but, as the Arians consider, originate, and not eternal, this is not a true Image of the Father, unless indeed they give up shame, and go on to say, that the title of Image, given to the Son, is not a token of a similar essence, but His name only.... For what is the likeness of what is out of nothing to Him who

219

brought what was nothing into being? or how can that which is not be like Him that is, being short of Him in once not being, and in its having its place among things originate?" (Athanasius, Agt. the Arians, I. 21). "This Image of God has been sent to us, that through Him we may be made the image of God again" (Melanchthon). 2 Cor. 3:18.—**Firstborn.** It seems strange that he does not say *the* Firstborn. It implies His priority in *time* and *station* and His possession of the sovereignty over all derived from and created by God. It is Philo's designation of the Logos as the archetype of creation. It is the Old Testament designation of the chosen people, and was applied by the rabbins to the Messiah (Ps. 89:28; Ex. 4:22; 4 Esd. 6:58).—**Of all creation;** i.e. He is *before* all creation; He is *over* all creation. This may be translated *every* creation, and may cover other creations than that of which we are a part. Jesus Christ belongs to the creation of God. He has a created soul and body. Of this creation He is first in time (Eph. 1:4), and in dignity (Col. 1:18). "The Word also, when in grace towards us He became man, said, 'The Lord created me.' And in the next place, when He put on a created nature and became like us in body, reasonably was He therefore called both our Brother and 'Firstborn.' ... But if He is also called 'Firstborn of the creation,' still this is not as if He were levelled to the creatures, and only first of them in point of time (for how should that be, since He is 'only-begotten'), but it is because of the Word's condescension to the creatures, according to which He has become the 'Brother' of 'many' " (Athanasius, Agt. the Arians, II. 61, 62). "He says not, He is Firstborn above the rest of the creation, lest He be reckoned as one of the creatures, but it is written, of the whole creation, that He may appear other than the creation" (Ib. 63).

16. **For in him were all things created** "In Christ rested the act of creation. It took place not independently of Him, nor in a causal relation lying outside Him. It had in Him its essential conditioning basis. In Him lay the potency of life from which God let the work of creation proceed, inasmuch as He is the personal principle of the divine self-manifestation, and therefore the fulfiller of the divine idea of the world" (Meyer). In other words, Christ is the Principle of God's self-manifestation and of all His creation, essentially, from all eternity. In Him lay the idea of creation and of all created things; even as *through* Him they came into being. Observe that in this verse St. Paul denies that Christ is one of many co-ordinate Mediators, or one of a series. All things in the heavens and upon the earth ("all creatures, of whatever place, kind, or rank, without any exception whatever"), derive their being from Him. Our Lord here is said to have the same place in the physical as in the moral world.—**Things visible and things invisible,** or things seen and unseen. St. Paul may have thought of the series of emanations some teachers imagined. But his language will apply with equal truth to the unseen constituents of this visible world—to the forces, laws, media, relations, of which modern science speaks.—**Whether thrones, or dominions, or principalities, or powers.** (See Eph. 1:21.) *Dominions:* lordships. These names, in current Judaic theology, in subsequent Christian writings, and in Gnostic speculations, were applied to grades of angelic beings. Therefore, though they may be applied as truthfully to earthly dignities, they here refer to such a "worshipping of angels" as in 2:18 he rebukes. "It appears that St. Paul does not profess to describe objective realities, but contents himself with

repeating subjective opinions. He brushes away all these
speculations without inquiring how much or how little truth
there may be in them, because they are altogether beside the
question. His language shows impatience with this elaborate
angelology." (Lightfoot). He is asserting the *One* Principle of
the manifestation of God, over against those who taught that
Christ is but one of many.—**Have been created.** A change
of tense, intended to include *all* the works of God up to the
present time. Some Gnostics taught that God did not make
the world, but it was the work of an emanation from Him, a
"Demiurge"; and some taught that this Demiurge was hostile to
God, and His work, therefore, was essentially evil. They made
evil to reside in *matter* itself. And somewhat of this—allied to
Zoroastrian tenets and other doctrines of the East—may be
detected in the exaggerated asceticism censured in ch. 2. But
Paul says *all* things were made **by** "the Son of His love." And
they are made for, or **unto** Him. They tend to Him. They
are summed up in Him. As He is the Eternal Archetype and
Principle of creation, He is the Archetype of its processes,
and the end and summary of it. In Jesus we see God. No less
is Jesus Christ the fundamental principle, summary and key
of all the works of God. "We may observe that the mediate
creation, and final destination, of the world, here referred
to the Son, are in Rom. 11:36 referred to the Father. Such
permutations deserve our serious consideration; if the Son
had not been God, such an interchange of important relations
would never have seemed possible" (Ellicott).

17. **And he is before all things.** This teaches the pre-
existence of the Son of God. (Cf. John 8:24, 28, 58; 13:19; Ex.
3:14.)—**And in him all things consist;** i.e. *hold together.* (Cf.
1 Peter 3:5; Hebr. 1:3.) Philo also described the Logos as the

222

Bond of the Universe. Certainly St. Paul seems to assert of our Lord all that the Alexandrian philosophers taught of the Sole and Absolute Word of God. Jesus Christ is the Principle of Creation, and also of the preservation of all things—of *Providence.* Here ends Paul's description of the significance of Christ in reference to the natural creation.

18. And he is the head of the body, the church: who is the beginning, the firstborn from the dead; that in all things he might have the preeminence.

18. **He is the head of the body, the church.** (See Eph. 1:22, 23; 4:15, 16.) The Church is called the body of Christ, because it is the unity of many members. It is made a unity by its communion with the head. Christ is the head of the Church, not in the sense in which the pope assumes to be the head of the Church on earth—as an earthly ruler, speaking the mind of Christ; but in the sense of the head of the body of a man, the centre of sensation, motion, thought and will, having immediate relation to every part, and being the principle of the correlation and unity of all the parts. Lightfoot shows that the ancient physicians knew the significance of the head, as the centre of bodily life. At this time, Luke, the beloved physician, was Paul's intimate companion. Mark that here he speaks of the Church as a unity *in Christ.* (See on Eph. 1:22.)—**Who is the beginning.** *Who is Beginning,* Origin, Source of being and life. (See Gen. 49:3; Rev. 3:14; 1 Cor. 15:20.)—**Firstborn from the dead.** He seems to make the resurrection parallel with a new birth. It is natural to explain *firstborn* here and the same word in ver. 16 by each other. Lazarus, Jairus' daughter, the widow of Nain's son, had been awakened from the dead before our Lord's resurrection. He, however, was the principle, the source, of their resurrection.

Because He lived, they lived also. So Jesus was born in the
flesh only in the fulness of times: but in Him all things
were created. He is the Firstborn of all creation. (See Rom.
1:4.)—**He might have the pre-eminence.** That He who *is*
before all things (ver. 17), might *become* first in all things or
among all. The change of verbs suggests our Lord's historical
manifestation, His voluntary submission to human growth,
discipline, part in creation, moral development, and even
death. To the *essential* pre-eminence of Christ, is added the
historical pre-eminence, won by Him. Not in creation only,
not only in the physical world, but also in the realm of spirit,
of freedom, is He First.

19. For it was the good pleasure *of the Father* that in him
should all the fulness dwell;

19. This may be read, *For in Him all the Fulness was pleased
to dwell.* The words, *Of the Father,* have been supplied by the
translators. The word *Fulness* is, in the original, *Pleroma.* It
was used in the Old Testament to translate a word meaning
Contents or *Abundance* (Ps. 24:1; 96:11; 98:7). The Gnostics
used it for the complement or sum-total of the *æons,* as
they called the successive emanations from Deity; or for the
abode of the æons; or for the higher spiritual region from
which the manifestations of the divine powers issued forth.
Lightfoot says, "A recognized technical word in theology,
denoting the totality of the divine powers and attributes."
In 2:9 Paul further says, *The fulness of the Godhead*; Meyer,
Die ganze Gottheitsfülle. But in this place Meyer says, "The
whole charismatic wealth of God, the fulness of grace, of
spiritual blessing." So Beza: "The heaped-up store of all
divine things, which the scholastics call *habitual grace,* from
which, as from an inexhaustible fountain, all graces are

224

derived to us according to the measure of every part." This meaning the word bears in the Epistle to Ephesians. But, says Schnederman, "The meaning here does not coincide with its meaning in Eph. 1:10, 23; 3:19; 4:13. It is made clearer by its use there, and by the addition of the words 'of the Godhead' in 2:9. Everything in the world yearns for *completion,* which now it lacks. Wherever and howsoever such a completion takes place, it is a *'fulness,'* and in the highest and most comprehensive sense, according to the decree of God, it takes place in Christ." It does not appear why a distinction should be made between its meaning here and in 2:9. In the latter passage the declaration is made stronger, and in another relation.—**Dwell.** The word means, *take up its permanent habitation.*

20. And through him to reconcile all things unto himself, having made peace through the blood of his cross; through him, *I say,* whether things upon the earth, or things in the heavens.

20. **Unto himself;** i.e. unto God. Christ is the Mediator both in Creation and Redemption. (See on Eph. 2:16.)—**Having made peace through the blood of his cross.** Observe: 1. Peace has been made. 2. It has been made *through blood,* through the cross of Jesus Christ. Paul does not linger in speculations about cosmogonies, but hastens to that central historical fact, the death of Jesus on the cross. Religion depends on the One Mediator; and His mediation is not to be vaguely conceived. Blood, death, the cross,—these make the definite centre of faith.—**Whether things upon the earth, or things in the heavens.** As all things shared in the consequence of man's sin, so all have been reconciled to God by the blood of the cross (Rom. 8:20–23; James 1:18).

Jesus undid the fall.

21–22. **And you, being in time past alienated and enemies
in your mind in your evil works, yet now hath he reconciled
in the body of his flesh through death, to present you holy
and without blemish and unreproveable before him:**

21. **And you.** He concentrates the doctrine and applies
it.—**Being in time past alienated.** (See 2:13.)—**And enemies.** Hostile to God.—**In your mind, in your evil works.**
In your disposition and deeds. This is the actual condition of
those for whom Christ died, they yet being ungodly.

22. **Now hath he reconciled.** "Not through pacification
of men's hostile minds, but by taking away the relation of
guilt" (Schnederman). The work by which God saves men
has been done for every one of us. There remains no more
sacrifice for sin. It was and is a reconciliation of all things
to God—which it only needs that each should accept and
trust.—**In the body of his flesh through death.** If in the
preceding verses St. Paul has set forth the Godhead of our
Redeemer, how clearly does he here teach His incarnation,
humiliation and death. How clear does he make it, that
God does not mean to save us through Christ in any way
but through His death.—**To present you holy and without
blemish and unreproveable before him.** Before Him: in
His sight now; but also at the great day of judgment. Their
eyes must be directed to that account. And God has done all
this that we may then be found consecrated to Him, spotless
within, and faultless in our works. A contrast with our
alienated mind and our former condition and works.

23. If so be that ye continue in the faith, grounded and
stedfast, and not moved away from the hope of the gospel
which ye heard, which was preached in all creation under

heaven; whereof I Paul was made a minister.

23. We have seen what God has done through the blood of His Son. For us, for the Colossians, it remains necessary that we should accept this and remain firm in this faith until that great day. This passage emphasizes the necessity of a correct belief,—that we should believe *what is true.* He says, If so be that you continue in *the* faith. The faith is further defined as the Gospel *which ye have heard,* viz., under the instruction of Epaphras; *which was preached,* etc., i.e. by way of anticipation, *the Catholic faith;* and finally, whereof I, Paul, was made a minister—as he says elsewhere, *My* Gospel. There is no hope in any other Gospel than this of the One Mediator and of the Blood of His cross (2:8). (See Rom. 12:6; 1 Cor. 16:13; Gal. 1:24; 6:10; Phil. 1:27; Tit. 1:1, 4, 13; 1 Tim. 3:9; 4:6; 5:8; 6:10, 21; Jude 3; James 2:1; Rev. 2:13; 14:12.)

24. Now I rejoice in my sufferings for your sake, and fill up on my part that which is lacking of the afflictions of Christ in my flesh for his body's sake, which is the church;

24. **Now I rejoice in my sufferings for your sake.** *My* is not expressed in the original. *For your sake* is connected with *sufferings,* not with *rejoice. Now* refers to the glorious truth Paul has been telling, and to his joy in being a *servant* of it. The sense is, *Now I am glad to suffer for you.* Of course, the reference is to the sufferings they knew he was undergoing. "The patient sufferings of its confessors have always been the best defence of Christianity, because they thereby prove their conviction of its truth" (Rœntsch). 1 Peter 4:13.—**And I fill up on my part that which was lacking of the afflictions of Christ.** *Afflictions:* tribulations: not to be confounded with the sacrifice by which Christ redeemed us. "Many of the mediæval Catholic interpreters understood the clause

227

as referring to the atonement, and that its defects may be
supplied by the sufferings of the saints.... This inference
is in direct antagonism to the whole tenor of Scripture,
which represents the sacrifice of Jesus as perfect in obedience
and suffering, so perfect as to need neither supplement or
repetition" (Eadie; Hebr. 9:11, 12; 10:1–13). The apostle
rejoices to supplement Christ's tribulations by tribulations
endured with Him for His Church. He is glad if the Master
has left something for him to suffer. *Christ* suffers *in* and
with His Church (Acts 9:4, 5); and the sufferings which His
members endure for His sake, and in order to live godly, they
endure with Him (2 Tim. 2:10–13; 3:12; Matt. 20:22; 2 Cor.
1:5; Hebr. 13:13; 11:26; 2 Cor. 2:10). Christ suffers still in His
body, the Church, and He admits His chosen to a fellowship in
His sufferings (Phil. 3:10). They also suffer for the sake of the
world and of each other. "Because suffering for righteousness'
sake is the highest of all Christian sufferings, the Christian
must be careful not to confound his personal interests, or the
cause of his Church-party, with that of Christ, and imagine
himself a martyr. The sufferings we endure for God and
His kingdom's sake are likewise to be regarded as sufferings
for ourselves and our salvation" (Martensen, Ethics (tr.) II.
331).—**In my flesh,** etc. *Paul's* flesh is set over against the
Church, which is Christ's body, flesh of His flesh.

25. Whereof I was made a minister, according to the
dispensation of God which was given me to you-ward, to
fulfil the word of God.

25. **Whereof I was made a minister;** i.e. a *servant,* a
"deacon." Paul was a servant of the Gospel (1:23); of the
Church; and, like Epaphras, of Christ (1:7).—**The dispensation of God;** i.e. the *Stewardship.* He is a steward, with the

228

keys (Isai. 22:22; Eph. 3:2).—**Given me to you-ward.** The particular office of Paul, the apostleship to the Gentiles. The Colossians were for the most part a Gentile Church.—**To fulfil the word of God.** Paul, as apostle to the Gentiles, was called to carry out among them the purpose and promise of God's entire revelation—the unification and summing up of all things in Christ.

26–27. *Even* the mystery which hath been hid from all ages and generations: but now hath it been manifested to his saints, to whom God was pleased to make known what is the riches of the glory of this mystery among the Gentiles, which is Christ in you, the hope of glory:

26. **The mystery.** Here, and afterwards (1:28; Phil. 4:12; Eph. 1:14; cf. Ignatius, Eph. 12), there is an allusion to the Greek and other "mysteries." The word was used in the Old Testament Apocrypha for "the *secret* of a king" (Tob. 12:7; Judith 2:2), and "the secret counsels of God" (Wis. 2:22); and so in the New Testament (Matt. 13:11; Rom. 11:25; 16:25; 1 Cor. 15:51; Eph. 1:9; 3:3, 4, 9; 6:19. See also Col. 2:2; 4:3; 1 Tim. 3:9; 3:16; 2 Thess. 2:7). The "*mysteries*" were "scenic representations of mythical legends." They taught by means of symbols. "Such symbolical representations played a much more important part in the world in early times than they play now; the expression of ideas by means of pictures only passed by gradual and slow transitions into the use of written signs, in which the original picture was lost: and every written word was once a mystery" (Hatch, Essays in Biblical Greek, 61). The ancient "mysteries" professed to lead their adepts into a deeper knowledge of God than those outside could know, and perhaps did enshrine and hand down some central truths. It is probable that these mysteries threatened to be a temptation

229

to the lively-witted Colossians, whose conscience and spirit had been excited by the Gospel. Some of them may have been tempted to try whether in them they could not learn more and more truly about the nature of things and of God. The three allied perils at Colossæ were a false philosophy, the mysteries and a baseless asceticism. The earliest Gnostics (the Naassenes) are said to have borrowed some of their tenets from the ancient Mysteries (Hippolytus, Ref. of All Heresies, V. 2–5). Against the Mysteries, Paul opposes *the* Mystery, into which they have been initiated, and in which they may go on unto perfection. In explaining why He taught by parables, our Lord spoke of "the mysteries of the kingdom of heaven" (Matt. 13:11).—**Which hath been hid from the ages and the generations.** So in the Original. This Mystery God pleased to keep a secret, for ages and generations. The word for *ages* is *æons.* It signifies an indefinite stretch of time, including many generations. By the Gnostics it was adopted to be the designation of successive emanations from God, of whom the Valentinians fabled thirty.—**But now hath it been manifested to his saints.** This is a secret no longer to be enjoyed only by a few. Their consecration introduced them into this mystery.

27. The very substance of the secret of God is, its world-wide publication. The word **Gentiles** means *the nations,* and to the Colossians bore that meaning rather than suggested a contrast with *the Jews.* As they read it, it meant to them *all the world.*—**Which is Christ in you, the hope of glory.** There are two readings here. According to the one, the sentence means *the riches, etc., is Christ in you;* according to the other, *the mystery is Christ in you.* As Paul wrote it, he meant both. Commentators agree that the emphasis is on *in you:* it is

Christ in the Gentiles, not simply *Christ,* who is the *riches* and the *mystery*—a mark of the importance (almost impossible for us to appreciate), in the first age, of the truth that Christ died for *all* men. Meyer translates, Christ *among* you; Lightfoot, *in* you. (See John 14:23; 15:5; Rom. 8:10; 2 Cor. 13:5; Gal. 4:19; Eph. 3:17.) Christ in them is a pledge of their final and eternal salvation (1 Cor. 1:9; Phil. 1:6).

28. Whom we proclaim, admonishing every man and teaching every man in all wisdom, that we may present every man perfect in Christ;

28. **Admonishing:** to repentance.—**Teaching:** unto faith. Addressing both the *will* and the *understanding* (Schneder-man). "The one describes the means employed to arouse the soul and stimulate it to reflection, and the other the definite form of instruction which was communicated to the anxious and inquiring spirit" (Eadie). This writer quotes Clement: "Admonition is the prescribed diet of a diseased soul, advising it to take what is salutary, and warning it against what is pernicious." The apostles were not only "evangelists"; they *taught* (Matt. 28:19, 20). This whole epistle emphasizes the importance and necessity of instruction. In this admonition and teaching the apostle used *all possible wisdom:* indicating his deliberation, study and art.—**That we.** What he is saying, is a general description of the ideal and practice of preachers of the Gospel.—**May present every man perfect in Christ.** Observe: they admonish *every* man, teach *every* man, in order to present *every* man perfect. *Every* is repeated. The knowledge they offer is not to be confined to an esoteric few. The Gospel is for *every* man. It may also refer to the *personal* care of a pastor. He not only preaches to his congregation; he is to admonish and teach *each,* according to the measure

and need of each, in every way and upon every opportunity
that wisdom can suggest (Acts 20:20, 27; 1 Thess. 2:7, 8). In
the Greek mysteries "the perfect" were those who had gone
through all the "degrees." Probably those who were boasting
to the Colossians of a higher knowledge called themselves
"the perfect," as the Pharisees had looked down on "this people
who know not the law." Paul declares his endeavor and ability
to make *every* man perfect *in Christ.*

29. Whereunto I labour also, striving according to his
working, which worketh in me mightily.

29. It is difficult to reproduce the rugged energy of the
apostle's words. I labor, he says, agonizing, "like one who
contends in the lists," *according to the energy energizing in me
in power.* He has a conflict within him; he agonizes in prayers
and tears: a mighty self-consecration not unlike that of our
Lord in the Garden, a wrestling with spiritual wickedness
in high places; and out of that spiritual conflict he comes
to the contention with falsehood and imperfection in the
Church and the opposition of the world; and to this he is
brought and held by the inward operation of God working
in him.—A man's usefulness in the Church is built upon his
inward struggle. The agony we endure in spirit, under the
operation of the Spirit of God, is intended for the behoof of
the children of God. (See on Phil. 1:30.)

15

Colossians 2

1–5. For I would have you know how greatly I strive for you, and for them at Laodicea, and for as many as have not seen my face in the flesh; that their hearts may be comforted, they being knit together in love, and unto all riches of the full assurance of understanding, that they may know the mystery of God, *even* Christ, in whom are all the treasures of wisdom and knowledge hidden. This I say, that no one may delude you with persuasiveness of speech. For though I am absent in the flesh, yet am I with you in the spirit, joying and beholding your order, and the stedfastness of your faith in Christ.

1. **How greatly I strive.** How great an agony, or conflict, I have. The figure is taken from the Greek games. (See on 1:29 and Phil. 1:30.) Howson calls attention to the fact that Paul, who makes no allusion to scenery, draws many figures from the active life of men. He was a keen observer. Evidently he here means an *inward conflict.*—**Them at Laodicea.** Those of Laodicea and Hierapolis also belonged to Epaphras (4:13), and doubtless were exposed to the same dangers.—**And for as many,** etc. How different is Paul's feeling of responsibility

from the mind of a vulgar fanatic. Here is the proof that he was not personally acquainted with the members of those churches.

2. **That their hearts may be comforted.** The original meaning of the English word *comforted* is *strengthened.* (So Wiclif, in Luke 1:80, Tyndale in Luke 22:43.) Here the word means *encouraged.* It is the word from which is derived the designation of our Lord (1 John 2:1) and of His Spirit (John 14:16),—the *Paraclete,* the Comforter. The comfort, the encouragement, is real, not fictitious, being derived from the presence with our spirits of the Spirit of God.—**Being knit together in love.** *Compacted.* Septuagint and Vulgate, *Instructed.* Wiclif, *Taughte in charite.* A result of a process under the instruction of the Spirit. It is well to note that Christian comfort and strength are not infused as such, but result from instruction and unification in love. "In the peculiar condition of the Colossian Church, this virtual prayer was very necessary. The entrance of error naturally begets suspicion and alienation" (Eadie).—**Unto all riches of the full assurance of understanding.** Meyer: The complete certainty of Christian insight. A just confidence in one's own trustworthy Christian judgment.—**That they may known.** *Unto a thorough knowledege of.*—**The mystery of God.** "The mystery of redemption is the key to the knowledge of mankind; it opens to us the meaning of human life. By means of it we understand ourselves, and also the world" (Rœntsch).—**Of God, even Christ.** Here the MSS. vary. This seems the most probable reading, *Christ* being in apposition with *mystery.* Or it may be read "Of the God Christ," *Christ* being in apposition with God. Or it may be, "Of the God of Christ."

234

3. "While *knowledge* applies chiefly to the apprehension of truths, *wisdom* superadds the power of reasoning about them and tracing their relations" (Lightfoot). "The latter emphasizes the inner reasonableness of the thinking, the former its agreement with outer fact" (Schnederman). Knowledge apprehends things and truths; wisdom, their source and the ideas which underlie them. Knowledge is intellectual; wisdom, moral. Wisdom and *knowledge* were the good things which the false teachers at Colossæ were pretending to offer.—*In Christ,* Paul says, are not only what you now know; you have not exhausted this mystery. In Him all the treasures of wisdom and knowledge are *hidden,* stored away, to be searched for, found, enjoyed, inexhaustibly.

4. These verses testify Paul's nervous anxiety for the good estate of the churches. It may be that those who would have led them astray, said Paul cared no more for them and was indeed a thing of the past.

5. He explains how he comes to warn them of an instant peril.—**Your order.** Great as were the dangers which this epistle discloses, the Colossians had not yet yielded to them; and there is no hint of such dissension among them as there certainly was at Corinth and even at Philippi (Phil. 4:2).—**The stedfastness of your faith in Christ.** *Firmament:* a firm foundation built stably. They were *well-grounded in faith,* as we say, and had not moved therefrom. Epaphras had been a faithful builder.

6–7. As therefore ye received Christ Jesus the Lord, *so* walk in him, rooted and builded up in him, and stablished in your faith, even as ye were taught, abounding in thanksgiving.

6. (See 1 Thess. 4:1.) They had received Jesus as *the Christ,* and as their Lord. As we say in the Catechism: I believe

that Jesus Christ is my Lord, who has redeemed me (1 Cor.
12:3; Phil. 2:11). This involves faith in the historical Person
Jesus, and in the true explanation of Him. "The Gnostics
regarded the Christian revelation as having a similar relation
towards speculative philosophy to that in which the Jewish
religion was regarded by Christians as standing towards their
own belief. As the institutions of Judàism under type and
symbol prefigured in the Christian belief the fuller revelation
of Christ, so Christianity itself, in the estimation of the
Gnostics, was but a figurative and symbolical exposition
of truths, the fuller meaning of which was to be supplied
by philosophical speculation.... Christianity had furnished a
simple and universally intelligible solution of every enigma
which had occupied thinking minds—a practical answer to
all the questions which speculation had busied itself in vain
to answer. It established a temper of mind by which doubts
that could not be resolved by the efforts of speculative reason
were to be practically vanquished" (Mansel, *op. cit.* 9, 10).

7. They were in danger of being led astray from the faith,
the Christ, in whom they had begun. But in Jesus Christ
the Lord we are to walk; in Him are to be the roots of all
our life, which will wither and die if separated from Him;
in Him only can we be builded up. There is a constant
temptation to seek the continuation and growth of character
and knowledge outside the four Gospels and the Saviour
whom they tell of.—**Stablished in your faith.** *By the faith,*
in the original.—**Even as ye were taught**—by Epaphras.
This is directly connected with *as ye received.* He insists
on the vital importance of sound doctrine.—**Abounding in
thanksgiving.** Some MSS. add *in it.* (See 3:15; Eph. 5:4, 20.)

8. Take heed lest there shall be any one that maketh spoil

236

of you through his philosophy and vain deceit, after the tradition of men, after the rudiments of the world, and not after Christ:

8. **Take heed.** Christians have to be on guard not only against fleshly lusts, but also against teachings which "have a show of wisdom" (2:23).—**Lest there shall be any one.** The phraseology shows that there *was* some one, meant by Paul, who, however, does not mention his name, though the Colossians would know it well enough.—**That maketh spoil of you.** That carrieth you off as spoil. Inconceivable as it may appear to the simple, there are many who spread soul-destroying doctrines, of whose correctness they are by no means convinced, merely to win applause or get a following; and they take pleasure in unsettling men's minds.—**Through his philosophy and vain deceit.** St. Paul uses the word "philosophy" scornfully here. The false teacher boasted a "philosophy"; it *was* vain deceit. Paul does not precisely disparage all philosophy, but it is easy to know what he would have said of it if asked, who counted all things but rubbish for the excellency of the knowledge of Christ Jesus. Some of the Greek Fathers regarded philosophy as a divine training of the Greeks for the Gospel; Tertullian and others regarded it as "only the parent of all heretical teaching." Certainly the noblest speculation is flimsy rubbish in comparison of the life of Jesus and the Gospel of the Christ. "At a later time *philosophy* and the cognate words are found used almost technically for the anchorite life and principles. I do not know of a distinct instance before the Apologia Origenis of Pamphilus; but the usage is very common in Eusebius and in later Greek Fathers. This late usage, if not descended from an earlier mode of speech exemplified in

the Colossian 'philosophy,' is at least illustrative of it" (Hort,
Judaistic Christianity, 121).—**After the tradition of men.**
The Essenes, the Gnostics, the Scribes and Pharisees boast
an esoteric tradition. The later mystical theology of the Jews
was called *Kabbala*, or "tradition." The Greek philosophy was
a tradition; and, especially in the apostolic age, was rather a
threshing over of traditional ideas and profitless dialectics
than a discovery of truth. So Scholasticism was an unwinding
and reweaving of tradition. In our day German theological
and philosophical writers must trace a thought through its
successive digestions by Kantian, Schellingian and Hegelian
schools. Paul scorns a philosophy which came *by men* and
from men.—**After the rudiments of the world.** Lightfoot
says: "Do not submit yourselves again to a *rudimentary*
discipline fit only for children." "The A, B, C of religious
truth" (Rœntsch). The emphasis is rather on *world* than on
rudiments. Paul scorns a philosophy which pretended to an
explanation of God and of created things drawn from created
things, and not derived from Revelation.—**And not after
Christ.***He* is the only wisdom. Except in Him, no man can
know.

9–10. For in him dwelleth all the fulness of the Godhead
bodily, and in him ye are made full, who is the head of all
principality and power:

9. (Cf. 1:19.) There can be no question of the meaning here.
In Christ **all** that God is has His permanent habitation. He is
God, and is the manifestation of God. He manifests God not
by His teaching only—God dwells in *Him in a human body.*
The whole truth of the incarnation is taught here—true God
begotten of the Father from eternity, and also true man born
of the Virgin Mary.

10. In Him ye *are being* made full. (See quotation from Schnederman in 1:19.) In Him ye become partakers of that fulness that dwells in Him. But no otherwise than in Him. (See 2 Peter 1:4.)—**The head of all principality and power.** Of *every* principality and power: names applied by false teachers to fabled superhuman beings, which, they said, mediate between God and the world.

11–12. In whom ye were also circumcised with a circumcision not made with hands, in the putting off of the body of the flesh, in the circumcision of Christ; having been buried with him in baptism, wherein ye were also raised with him through faith in the working of God, who raised him from the dead.

11. It may be that Judaizers were found even at Colossæ; perhaps some of the Essenes took this line; or the thought may have been suggested to the apostle by what was going on around him at Rome and in other of his churches. Against the requirement of circumcision he alleges baptism as the circumcision instituted by Christ, in which the whole body of the flesh of sin is put off. Here baptism is paralleled with circumcision. The total putting-off of all sin is contrasted with the particular ascetic practices urged by false teachers.—"No hand imparts this circumcision, but the Spirit. It circumciseth not a part, but the whole man. When and where? In baptism" (Chrysostom).

12. (Rom. 6:4.) "In the burial of Christ all who confess Him are buried also, so far as their sinful flesh is concerned; but individually, the subjective appropriation of this by each is through his baptism, without which this communion of burial is not realized by the individual" (Meyer).—**Wherein;** i.e. in baptism.—**Ye were also raised with him.** We share

Christ's *eternal* life, which includes the *future* life.—**Through
faith,** etc. "The working of God in the resurrection of Christ
is the surety of our salvation" (Meyer). "Baptism confers
everlasting salvation on all who believe" (Catechism; Mark
16:16). The necessity of faith is taught here: but faith in
something, and guaranteed by an event, an event outside
ourselves and our experience.

13–15. And you, being dead through your trespasses and
the uncircumcision of your flesh, you, *I say,* did he quicken
together with him, having forgiven us all our trespasses;
having blotted out the bond written in ordinances that was
against us, which was contrary to us: and he hath taken it out
of the way, nailing it to the cross; having put off from himself
the principalities and the powers, he made a show of them
openly, triumphing over them in it.

13. **And you.** You Colossians.—**Being dead through
your trespasses.** They had been evil-doers.—**And the
uncircumcision of your flesh.** They were Gentiles. He
refers to the fact that before the Gospel they had been
outside the Covenant of God, without God and without
hope in the world.—**You did he quicken together with
him.** When God raised up Christ from the dead, He
raised up the Colossians also, and He raised up us, together
with Him. Should the Head rise, and leave His members
dead?"—**Having forgiven us all our trespasses.** How
natural for Paul to change the person and include himself
and us. And how courteous too. (See on Col. 1:14.)

14. **Having blotted out the bond,** etc. The *bond* is a note
or written obligation signed and therefore acknowledged
by ourselves. "The *ordinances* will include all forms of
positive decrees in which moral and social principles are

240

embodied or religious duties defined; and the 'bond' is the moral consent of the conscience, which (as it were) signs and seals the obligation" (Lightfoot). The laws men make are an acknowledgment of sin. And such are the "moral systems" they affect. So Luther says, "Nothing is so severe against us as our own conscience, whereby we are convicted as if by our own sign-manual, when the Law discovers our sin." Melanchthon calls the judgment of conscience "a valid practical syllogism drawn from the law."—**Having nailed it to the cross.**—Again the cross is indicated as the means of forgiveness. "By His blood, i.e. by His whole obedience, He destroyed the bond of the law" (Melanchthon). Christ is the sum-total of all law, and He made Himself the summary of our acknowledgment of guilt; and He thus died for us upon the cross.

15. The "principalities and powers" are most likely the object after "He made a show of." To interpret, "Having put off from Himself *His body*" like many of the fathers, is to change the subject. It is *God* who *quickened* and *nailed.* To read the word "despoiled," is to overlook the fact that it belongs to the middle voice, and should be rendered, "Having stripped Himself." Why not adopt the explanation (which Lightfoot dismisses as "an isolated metaphor which is not explained or suggested by anything in the context"), *Having stripped for mortal conflict, He made a show of principalities and powers, triumphing over them on the cross.* "He means that the devil held possession of the bond which God made for Adam, saying, In the day thou eatest of the tree, thou shalt die. This bond the devil held in his possession. And Christ did not give it to us, but Himself tore it in two, the action of one who remits joyfully" (Chrysostom).

241

16–17. Let no man therefore judge you in meat, or in drink, or in respect of a feast day or a new moon or a sabbath day: which are a shadow of the things to come; but the body is Christ's.

16. These are golden and prophetic words. The old legalistic conception has again and again threatened to get dominion in the Church—in Old Catholic time, in the Middle Ages, under the guise of Puritanism, and under the asceticism of the opposite theory. The supernaturalness of the revelation of Christ is visible in its dissent from the merely natural religion of earnest men. St. Paul here refers to the regulations of Jewish law. Schuerer shows that Jerome's statement that the Essenes abstained from flesh and wine is unfounded.—**Meats** refers to distinctions of meats made by the Jews, and may also include the difficulties with reference to meats offered to idols, which vexed the Corinthians and the Romans (Rom. 14; 1 Cor. 10).—**Feast-days** were the annual festivals, **new moons** the monthly, the **sabbath** the weekly. These, he says, were but *but a shadow cast by that which was to come.* It has come. The "body" that cast the "shadow" is Christ's (Hebr. 10:1). Now, says he, go on your way, and if any one judges or condemns you for your observance or non-observance of such particulars of Judaic law, I simply say, Do not be worried at all by doctrines of that kind. They have no reference to you at all. "Paul yields and gives way *to the weak* in the observance of food and times and days (Rom. 14:6). But *to the false prophets,* who wished to impose these on the conscience as *necessary things,* he will yield not even in those things which in themselves are indifferent" (Form, of Concord, 700). "The celebration of Christian festivals and Sundays was not yet elaborated. A one-sided passionate

opposition on religious grounds to this or that sort of food, or extravagance in keeping festivals, or the transference of the *Sabbath* to Sunday, is, accordingly, decidedly opposed to the Gospel" (Schnederman). There always will be a tendency to reduce religion to a system of rules. For the guidance of the young and uninstructed, rules are necessary. So Paul gave precepts to the Thessalonians when he was with them (1 Thess. 4:2); such, indeed, as follow in this letter. Luther urges this in his German Mass, while he begs that no one will make a law of it. An earnest man will make and adopt rules for his own discipline. But there is no system of rules of this sort which have necessary, because divine, authority. The one thing is for a man to be *in Christ* by faith, and to *walk in Him,* i.e. by His example, according to His teaching, as moved by His Spirit, in the system of relations into which union with Him places him, referring all to Him, and deriving all from Him. Observances, abstinences and compliances are a secondary matter. On the one hand, the false teachers at Colossæ would have made these rules the great matter, and Christ a matter by the way; on the other, to be in Christ is everything, and these rules are of no importance. We keep the *Lord's day* for devotion's sake and *love's;* and the *Church Year* for the sake of instruction in the Word of God. "If it be objected to us on this subject that we ourselves are accustomed to observe certain days, as for example the Lord's day, the Preparation, the Passover, or Pentecost, I have to answer, that to the perfect Christian, who is ever in his thoughts, words and deeds serving his natural Lord, God the Word, all his days are the Lord's, and he is always keeping the Lord's day. He also who is unceasingly preparing himself for the true life, and abstaining from the pleasures of this

life, which lead astray so many,—who is not indulging the
lust of the flesh, but keeping under his body and bringing it
into subjection,—such a one is always keeping Preparation-
day. Again, he who considers that Christ our Passover was
sacrificed for us, and that it is his duty to keep the feast by
eating of the flesh of the Word, never ceases to keep the
paschal feast; for *the pascha* means 'a passover,' and he is
ever striving in all his thoughts, words and deeds to pass
over from the things of this life to God, and is hastening
towards the city of God. And, finally, he who can say, We are
risen with Christ, and, He hath exalted us, and made us to
sit with Him in heavenly places in Christ, is always living in
the season of Pentecost; and most of all, when going up to
the upper chamber, like the apostles of Jesus, he gives himself
to supplication and prayer, that he may become worthy of
receiving the mighty wind rushing from heaven, which is
powerful to destroy sin and its fruits among men, and worthy
of having some share of the tongue of fire which God sends"
(Origen, Agt. Celsus, VIII. 22; see also 23). Incidentally,
Paul makes a pregnant remark on the Old Testament system
of worship, "That it was a shadow so designed, and not a
fortuitous and unmeaning system" (Eadie).

18–19. Let no man rob you of your prize by a voluntary
humility and worshipping of the angels, dwelling in the things
which he hath seen, vainly puffed up by his fleshly mind, and
not holding fast the Head, from whom all the body, being
supplied and knit together through the joints and bands,
increaseth with the increase of God.

18. **Let no man rob you of your prize;** i.e. you are
running a race, and running well. Let no one divert you
from the course. They were in danger of giving more

respect to the decision of others than to that of the true umpire. "What else is this but to divert us from faith, which is the only way to salvation, to *works,* as the monks and the popish teachings do?" (Luther). (See also 29, 376.)—**By a voluntary humility,** or, as in Margin, *Of his own mere will, by humility. Humility* is used in a bad sense. Such self-abasement, unlike the humility that submits to the calling of God, introducing at best an imitation of John Baptist, is characteristic of Ethnic religions, and doubtless was imported from the East. Neander (Planting, etc., I. 483) distinguishes between true Christian humility, based on the consciousness of dependence on God and faith in the Redeemer, and "a self-abhorrence with a denial of the dignity founded on the consciousness of redemption,—a sense of depression without that sense of exaltation which is blended with it in the consciousness of redemption." There is a Scotch sect that abstains from the Holy Supper, in such affected humility. How common is such affectation among sectaries! "Fanatical pride is often associated with this humility, as when, for show, the beggar's feet are washed, and the friar in his coarse rags walks barefooted and begs" (Eadie). "Humility, when it becomes self-conscious, ceases to have any value" (Lightfoot).—**And worshipping of the angels.** The word signifies *worship* in its outward aspect. For an exhaustive account of Jewish angelology, see Edersheim, Life and Times of Jesus the Messiah, Ap. XIII. He shows how many of the rabbinical notions about the angels were "brought from Babylon," as the Talmud indeed says; and adds, "The teaching of the New Testament on the subject of angels represents, as compared with that of the Rabbis, not only a return to the purity of Old Testament teaching, but, we might almost say, a new revelation." The Essene novices were sworn, on their admission to full membership, not to disclose *the names of the angels* (Josephus, Wars of the Jews, II. 8, 7). The Gnostics multiplied heavenly mediators, the Valentinians teaching that there were as many as thirty æons. We may gather from Irenæus (Against Heresies, II. 32, 5) and others, that they also used "invocations of angels, incantations and other curious wicked art." The early Church was profoundly affected by this tendency. It was thought a great thing to boast a knowledge of "the angelic orders, the distinctions between powers and dominions, the diversities between thrones and authorities, the mightiness of the æons, and the pre-eminence of the cherubim and seraphim" (Ignatius, ad Tral. 5). It is curious that the worship of angels seems to have persisted at Colossæ. At *Khonai* (Colossæ) there is a church dedicated to St. Michael, who is fabled to have descended and confounded the heathen there. "A remarkable example of the worship of angels is contained in an inscription of Miletos. In this strange instance of superstition, inscribed (necessarily by public permission) on the wall of the theatre, the seven archangels who preside over the seven planets are invoked to protect the city" (Ramsay, Ch. in the Rom. Empire, 468, 480). Among the canons of a Council of Laodicea, a.d. 364, occur the following: XX. It is not necessary for Christians to rest from labor on the Sabbath like the Jews. XVI. On the Sabbath the Gospels are to be read, as well as the Old Testament. XXXV. Christians ought not forsake the Church of God and go to meetings for paying reverence to angels. Another canon is directed against wandering magicians and the use of charms. (See Neander, Planting, etc., I. 326.) An indication of the particular heresy urged at Colossæ—a worship of lesser beings, as if it were virtuous for a man to think himself too mean to approach God through His Son. The same tendency afterwards encouraged the intrusion of saints as mediators. In the Roman Church the priest says, in confessing before the Mass, "Therefore I beseech blessed Mary ever Virgin, blessed Michael the Archangel, blessed John Baptist, the holy apostles Peter and Paul, and all the Saints, and you, father, to pray to the Lord our God for me."—**Dwelling in the things which he hath seen,** or *taking his stand upon,* or *invading.* Thus put, it means that these false teachers founded their teaching on visions and experiences of their own, instead of the revelation of Christ, common to the faith of the Church. Augustine notes (Confessions, 10:42) that many who had recourse to the angels, fell "into a longing for curious visions, and were held worthy of illusions." Even Gregory the Great tried to prove the existence of Purgatory from visions he had had of souls of the dead. It is characteristic of fanatics to put more confidence in visions of their own than in the written word. In order to relieve a difficulty here, a various reading was inserted, "Which he hath *not* seen;" and Lightfoot ingeniously conjectures an emendation, which would read, "*Walking on the air,*" like a tightrope dancer or a bird in flight; i.e. dealing with uncertain and perilous doctrines.—**Vainly puffed up by his fleshly mind:** *by the reason of his flesh.* The false teacher may have asserted that he was led by "reason." The apostle answers, By the "reason" of *his flesh,* his unregenerate and godless mind. "Their profession of humility was a cloke for excessive pride" (Lightfoot).

19. **And not holding fast the head.** The *sine qua non.*—**Supplied.** Nourished. (Eph. 4:16.)—**Knit together.** "Brought and held together in mutual adaptation"

247

(Eadie).—**Joints.** The relations between contiguous
limbs.—**Bands.** Nerves, muscles, ligaments. Although this
is said in pursuance of the figure, it reflects the fact that the
Body of Christ is not merely the Head and the members,
but is made and maintained by the mutual relations, the
arrangement, the offices, of all the parts.—**Increaseth with
the increase of God.** Perhaps this is an allusion to a demand
or promise of growth made by false teachers. Much that is
called *growth* and *progress* in the Church is not the *increase of
God.*

20–23. If ye died with Christ from the rudiments of the
world, why, as though living in the world, do ye subject
yourselves to ordinances, Handle not, nor taste, nor touch (all
which things are to perish with the using), after the precepts
and doctrines of men? Which things have indeed a show of
wisdom in will-worship, and humility, and severity to the
body; *but are* not of any value against the indulgence of the
flesh.

20. **If ye died with Christ from the rudiments of the
world** (2:8); i.e. from the principles which are not derived
from the revelation of God (Rom. 7:3, 4; Gal. 2:19).—**Why do
ye subject yourselves to ordinances;** such as those of the
Essenes, or of the Jews? It is common to regard will-worship
or legalism as higher than simple fidelity in the callings of
life, to which St. Paul in this epistle recalls the Colossians.
See Augsburg Confession, XXVI., XXVII., XXVIII. "This is
the grievous error which God sends upon those who love not
the truth, but believe a lie" (Luther, 26:188).

21. **Handle not, nor taste, nor touch.** He quotes a maxim
from the false teachers. How singular that this very maxim,
scorned by the apostle, should in aftertime have been adopted

and urged as an inspired commandment!

22. **All which things are to perish in the using** (Matt. 15:17; Mark 7:19).—**After the precepts and doctrines of men.** A warning against those teachers who affect an improvement on the morality of the Gospel. (See Matt. 15:9; Mark 7:7; Isai. 29:13.)

23. (See verse 18.) A condemnation of *will-worship.* Christ does not merely impart a sentiment, which can in turn construct a service better than His; but the utmost His disciple can aim at is, to be as his Master. In the Old Testament, vows made to God were to be fulfilled, but it was better not to vow (Deut. 23:22–24). In vowing, a man takes upon himself "an obligation which goes beyond ordinary duty. This comes near to being a God-tempting challenge: a sinful man should remember that he cannot come up to the measure of his ordinary duty. An Israelite should remember that as a member of the Covenant people of God he may rely upon God's goodness without a corresponding promise of special services; and if he has made a vow, he has a little distorted the relation in which he stands to God. The vow itself is a condition of guilt, which must be taken away by an atoning sacrifice" (Kliefoth). So Martensen (Ethics, II. 419): "There is no duty whatever to which we are not already bound; there is only one vow God requires of us, namely, our *baptismal vow.* No doubt it may be useful to renew a good purpose in the presence of God. But solemnly to vow to God that to combat a particular sin or temptation, we will apply this or that *means,* a means not at all expressly prescribed in God's word, but prescribed by ourselves or other men,—pedagogic, perhaps even merely experimental means, e.g. a sacrifice that God does not require, an abstaining from certain in themselves

permitted enjoyments,—is a folly. The whole doctrine of
special vows to God, so far as they should have an ascetic
import, is to be reduced to this, that in all our discipline we
constantly renew our baptismal vow, and especially should
remind ourselves that we have once for all renounced the
devil, all his works and all his ways, and apply this to the
special case, the special requirement." The austerities of early
"saints" are recorded as a warning. "Hermits hid themselves
in the wilderness, even their families having been forsaken.
Monks instituted celibacy and other rites" (Melanchthon).
Olympias, the friend of Chrysostom, was praised because she
did not bathe when she should. Among the most singular of
these ascetics were the Stylites or *pillar-saints.* Of Symeon
it is said: "He lived ten years in a narrow pen; after which
he built a pillar, and took his position on the top of it, which
was only about a yard in diameter. He removed successively
from one pillar to another, always increasing the height,
which in the last of them was forty cubits; and in this way
he spent thirty-seven years. His life is compared to that
of angels—offering up prayers for men from his elevated
position, and bringing down graces on them. His neck was
loaded with an iron chain. In praying he bent his body so
that his forehead almost touched his feet. A spectator once
counted twelve hundred and forty-four repetitions of this
movement, and then lost his reckoning." It is hard to see
wherein this differs from the extravagance of East Indian
devotees. (Cf. also the *Flagellants,* and Luther's experience in
the Erfurt Monastery.) Eadie states that in 1854 a new saint
was added to the Popish calendar, as a proof of whose holiness
it was alleged that "he was a model of humility, abstinence
and mortification, taking only for food remains of cabbage,

lemon-peel or lettuce leaves, which he picked up in the streets. He even ate, once, some spoiled soup which he found on a dunghill, where it had been thrown." Other detailed proofs of his filthiness were shown. But it must not be overlooked that the same spirit may be shown in a cleanlier way.

16

Colossians 3

1–4. If then ye were raised together with Christ, seek the things that are above, where Christ is, seated on the right hand of God. Set your mind on the things that are above, not on the things that are upon the earth. For ye died, and your life is hid with Christ in God. When Christ, *who is* our life, shall be manifested, then shall ye also with him be manifested in glory.

1. Accordingly, Paul now proceeds to give his prescription against will-worship. (See 2:12, 13.) Our ascension with Christ is guaranteed in our resurrection with Him. Christ's session on God's right hand is His reward, and is a promise that if we overcome we shall sit with Him in His throne (Rev. 3:21). That "virtue is its own reward," is not the doctrine of the Christian. He expects a reward.

2. "Mind the things above, for your life is hidden with Christ: when He is manifested, so shall ye be also" (Ellicott). This is the first particular of Christian morality. A Christian goes through the world, conscious that his citizenship is in heaven, and seeking the things that are there, and laying up

treasures there. He neither regards, seeks nor values what the world can give or take away.

3. Christ's death was ours. "Like His, our death is not the end to our life, but a being hid in God" (Schnederman). In Baptism we died and were buried, with Christ. We are to regard ourselves as dead, so far as this world is concerned, and alive only in Christ (Gal. 6:14; Rom. 6:11). Bengel: "The world knows neither Christ nor Christians; and, indeed, *Christians* do not yet clearly know themselves." It doth not yet appear what we shall be, St. John says (1 John 3:2). Neither doth it yet appear what we *are.* So was it with Christ (Acts 3:17; 4:11), but He was declared to be the Son of God with power by the resurrection from the dead (Rom. 1:4).

4. (Rom. 8:18–21; 1 John 3:2.) Christ is here identified with *our life* (1 John 5:12).

5–7. Mortify therefore your members which are upon the earth; fornication, uncleanness, passion, evil desire, and covetousness, the which is idolatry; for which things' sake cometh the wrath of God upon the sons of disobedience; in the which ye also walked aforetime, when ye lived in these things.

5. **Mortify.** *Put to death.* They will be put to death "if you acknowledge them in repentance and earnestly turn from them and accept forgiveness from Christ by faith, and resist sinful desire so that it come not to actual sin and get no dominion over you" (Luther). Matt. 5:29.—**Your members which are upon the earth.** Paul shows that Christian freedom is not license, but a very definite character.—**Fornication, uncleanness, passion, evil desire** (1 Thess. 4:5; Eph. 4:19). Unchastity of mind and body was a characteristic sin of the old heathen world; it still is the vice of heathendom; and,

in Christendom, of the *world.*—**And covetousness, which
is idolatry.** (See 1 Thess. 4:6.) Lightfoot: "Impurity and
covetousness may be said to divide between them nearly
the whole domain of human selfishness and vice. 'Man out
of God,' says Bengel on Rom. 1:29, 'seeks his gratification
in the creature, either through pleasure or through luxury.'
" Chrysostom (on John, LXV.) says, "The love of money
says, Sacrifice thy soul to me: and thou obeyest." Luther:
"Whatsoever a man hangs his heart upon, that is his god." (See
on First Commandment in Large Catechism.) How timely is
this warning now!

6. **Cometh the wrath of God.** *Upon the sons of disobedience*
was inserted here from Eph. 5:6. 1. The wrath of God is
coming on those who do these things. 2. The wrath of God
always is coming on such sin and vice, but all things hasten
to the great day of His wrath.

7. There are who live *in these things,* and no otherwise;
while Christians live *in Christ.* And such *were* the Colossians.
The moral condition of the heathen world at the advent of the
Gospel is almost inconceivable now (Rom. 1:18–32). Yet it
has been paralleled by those who have trampled Christ under
foot. The injunctions which follow indicate the former life
and the present environment of the Colossian Christians.

8. But now put ye also away all these; anger, wrath, malice,
railing, shameful speaking out of your mouth:

8. Paul now goes on to a new class of vices which are
members of ourselves *upon the earth.* Compare the 8th
Commandment.—**Anger.** Deep settled hatred.—**Wrath.**
The breaking forth of angry passion.—**Malice.** We have no
better word for it: the disposition that seeks to do evil to
others.—**Railing.** Evil speaking of others, slander, injurious

gossip. The original is *blasphemy.*—**Shameful speaking out of your mouth.** Abusive speech.

9. Lie not one to another; seeing that ye have put off the old man with his doings,

9. **Lie not one to another.** This does not imply that they were to be truthful to each other, though not to others; but reflects the fact that a lie is a breach of the charity which should be between Christians. A Christian should have nothing to conceal from his fellow; no motive to misrepresentation. Burger (in Herzog, 9:2) calls attention to the frequency of falsehood in our modern life, in the tone of society, in common conversation, in the public prints, in political and party life, in parliamentary debate and in diplomacy, in trade and on the exchange; falsehood with which we are so familiar that we do not call it *lying,* but invent softer names and ready excuses. It is evident that such falsehood betokens an absence of Christian love and a denial of Christian fellowship. *Lying* is any intentional deception of our neighbor. (See John 8:44; Eph. 4:25; 1 Peter 2:22; Rev. 21:8; 22:15.) The cases cited from the Old Testament (Gen. 12:11; 20:2; 1 Sam. 21:2, 13; 27:10, etc.) suggest the question whether it is ever allowable to deceive. "The greatest authorities are here opposed to each other. So even the most esteemed Church Fathers. Basil the Great rejects every lie of exigency, while Chrysostom defends it. Augustine condemns it most decidedly, and says that even if the whole human race could be saved by one lie, one must rather let it perish; Jerome again finds the lie of exigency permissible. Calvin will on no account hear of it; Luther calls it not good indeed, but yet excuses it in certain cases as admissible. Kant and Fichte reject it; Jacobi defends it" (Martensen, II. 216).

Among English moralists, Jeremy Taylor, Milton and Paley have been quoted as admitting it. But Martensen goes on to say: "The inevitableness of the lie of exigency will disappear in proportion as a person develops into a true personality, a true character; the more he grows in faith, in courage, in willingness to suffer and make sacrifices for the truth's sake, in right wisdom; in the measure in which a man grows in moral power and energy, he will be able to dispense with the application of craft." Burger urges the example of Christ (1 Peter 2:22). As a wilful lie is a violation of Christian love, and betokens its absence or imperfection; so what is called the *lie of necessity* or of *exigency* seems to be occasioned by distrust of God.—**Seeing that ye have put off.** *Put off* and *put on* are the words used for *putting clothes off* and *on,* as in 2:15. This intimates that aforetime the Colossians might have allowed such shameful sins. And indeed, are there not who now excuse themselves in them on the plea that they do not *profess* to be Christians? But they are totally incompatible with the new life hid with Christ in God.

10–11. And have put on the new man, which is being renewed unto knowledge after the image of him that created him: where there cannot be Greek and Jew, circumcision and uncircumcision, barbarian, Scythian, bondman, freeman: but Christ is all, and in all.

10. Our Christianity is: 1. A death and resurrection with Christ, complete in idea, appropriated and imputed in Baptism (2:12, 20; 3:1–4). 2. It commits us to the death of our old nature with all its dispositions and propensities, and to the birth and completion unto perfect knowledge of the new nature,—a restoration of the divine image which Adam lost. 3. Our Christian life is a continual slaying of these

256

evil propensities, even those which the world allows, and a continual renewal in the image of God. (See the last question on Baptism in the Catechism.)—**Which is being renewed.** The *renewal* is spoken of as present and continuous.

11. Here every possible distinction of nationality, religious training, culture and condition is considered. As the Jews divided all men into Jews and Gentiles, so the Greeks called all but themselves Barbarians. In Christianity all these distinctions ceased; and even the Scythian, the lowest of Barbarians, and perhaps looked upon with utmost disgust in this region, is made one with the rest in Christ. It was especially fitting that in sending this epistle by Onesimus, a converted slave returning to his master and now become a brother beloved, Paul should say, There cannot be freeman and bondman—Christ is all in all. The verb has the force of *cannot be.* All distinctions are lost in the primal unity of men *in Christ.* "The idea of mankind as one family, as the children of one God, is an idea of Christian growth.... The common origin of mankind, the differences of race and language, the susceptibility of all nations of the highest mental culture, these become in the new world in which we live problems of scientific, because of more than scientific interest" (F. Max Muller, Science of Language, I. 118).

12–13. Put on therefore, as God's elect, holy and beloved, a heart of compassion, kindness, humility, meekness, long-suffering; forbearing one another, and forgiving each other, if any man have a complaint against any; even as the Lord forgave you, so also do ye:

12. **God's elect.** Those *chosen* out of the world. (See 1 Thess. 1:1, 4.)—**Holy.** Saints—consecrated ones (Phil. 1:1).—**Beloved.** Sharers in God's love for His Son (1:13).—**A**

heart of compassion. (Cf. Luke 1:78.) The *bowels* included
all the nobler viscera.—**Kindness** (Gal. 5:22; Eph. 2:7; 4:32).
Friendliness, "sweetness of disposition" (Ellicott). "The lovely
character of a man who is friendly to every one, repels no
one with sour looks or harsh words or rude gestures, but of
whom every one says, Oh, he is so friendly! It denotes not one
sort of doing, but the whole life. On the other hand, there are
men who never are pleased unless others do what they wish
and accord with their opinion" (Luther).—**Humility** (Phil.
2:3). Lowliness of mind in our disposition towards others;
excluding all secret pride (2:18). "Where one holds himself
to be the least, and others to be above him, and, as Christ
says, takes the lowest place at the feast" (Luther).—**Meekness**
(Gal. 5:23). Opposed to rudeness, harshness. "Is not angry,
swears not, strikes not, hates not, nor does nor wishes any one
evil, not even an enemy" (Ib.).—**Longsuffering** (Gal. 5:22).
Slow to resent the unkindness of others. "You may find
those who bear much and are patient yet comfort themselves
with the thought that in due time they will be revenged. But
longsuffering does not wish to be revenged, but wishes the
amendment of the sinner" (Ib.).

13. **Forbearing one another.** Showing your meekness
and longsuffering thus *towards each other.* The virtues
of a Christian are to find their sphere in the close circle
of every-day life.—**And forgiving each other.** Paul says,
Forgiving *yourselves,* to indicate that they are members one
of another.—**If any man have a complaint against any.**
Evidently, against any one of the congregation. It is not to be
presumed that our life will be such that one will never have
any reason to complain of others. "Here all *rights* between
Christians are abolished, and no one of them is allowed to

258

demand anything of the other as a right, but we are to forgive and yield to one another. Christ is set as our example. He forgave not only the sin done and past, but St. John says, If any man sin, we have an Advocate with the Father, Jesus Christ the Righteous" (Luther).—**Even as the Lord forgave you.** The supreme motive, and the measure.

14. And above all these things *put on* love, which is the bond of perfectness.

14. **Above.** In addition to, upon, *over* all these; as one would put on a girdle over other garments to hold them together. "Since it is possible for one who forgives, not to love; yea, he saith, thou must love him too" (Chrysostom).—**The bond of perfectness.** Three related explanations are suggested. Luther says: "Love holds the hearts together, not partially, or only in some particulars, but through and through, over all and in all things. It makes us all to be of one mind, one heart, one purpose, and permits no one to set up a private separate opinion in doctrine and faith: all remains equal and in accord. It binds the hearts of rich and poor together, of the mighty and their subjects, of sick and strong, of high and low, of those honored and those despised, and withholds its blessing from no man; but on the other hand it takes up every man's burden as its own; so that everywhere there may be full and perfect unity and fellowship in prosperity and in adversity. That is the meaning of *the bond of perfectness.*" A little differently Melanchthon: "The word *perfection* here is not to be understood as the private perfection of some one person or the perfect fulfilment of the law; but means the unification of the body of the Church, or the conservation of its unity and concord. That is, so long as the teachers of the Church preserve mutual love for one

another, even though they may happen to differ in opinion,
the Church is not torn by that difference, but the learned bear
with the weak and try to heal them, and the weak heed the
more learned as modest children listen to their parents." But
again, Luther says: "Where love is not, hearts may be joined
and be of one mind, but only in certain points, while in others
they are far apart. Robbers are united in robbery and murder.
Worldly friends are of one mind, so far as their own profit
is concerned. Monks are at one in matters referring to their
order and their glory. Herod and Pilate were friends together,
but only in reference to Jesus Christ. But there scarcely is a
monk or priest or layman at one with the other; their bond
in worthless—as when one ties chaff together with a wisp
of straw." So Chrysostom: "What he wishes to say is this:
that there is no profit in those things, for all those things fall
asunder, except they be done with love. It is as in a ship, even
though her rigging be large, yet if there be no girding ropes,
it is of no service; and in a house, if there be no tie beams, it
is the same; and in a body, though the bones be large, if there
be no ligaments, they are of no service. For whatsoever good
deeds any may have, all do vanish away, if love be not there."
Love is the unity of all Christian virtues; the guaranty against
fault in our behavior. It is to be noted that the Gnostics taught
that *knowledge* was the bond of *completeness*.

15. And let the peace of Christ rule in your hearts, to the
which also ye were called in one body; and be ye thankful.

15. **The peace of Christ.** (John 14:27; Eph. 2:14; Phil. 4:7.)
"That calm of mind which is not ruffled by adversity, over-
clouded by sin or by a remorseful conscience, or disturbed
by the fear and the approach of death" (Eadie).—Let *the peace
of Christ* be arbiter, umpire, in your hearts. He had just told

260

them not to mind if any found fault, or would lead them to another race than that which the Captain of their salvation set before them (2:16). "He hath represented an arena within, in the thoughts, and a contest, and a wrestling, and an umpire. If two thoughts are fighting together, set not anger, set not spitefulness to hold the prize, but peace; for instance, suppose one to have been insulted unjustly; of the insult are born two thoughts, the one bidding him take revenge, the other to endure: if the Peace of God stand forward as umpire, it bestows the prize on that which bids endure, and puts the other to shame" (Theophylact). Meyer dissents, saying: The context goes deeper; and translates: Let the peace of Christ arrange and guide the conflict and give the reward. (See Wis. 10:12.)—**In one body.** (Eph. 4:4.)

16. Let the word of Christ dwell in you richly in all wisdom; teaching and admonishing one another with psalms *and* hymns *and* spiritual songs, singing with grace in your hearts unto God.

16. **Let the word of Christ dwell in you richly in all wisdom.** In *every kind of wisdom,* as in 1:28. The words of Christ may not yet have been written in the form of our Gospels. But each Church had received the tradition of His Word (Acts 20:35); and He spoke through the prophets. What Christ had said was normative; and they were (1) to keep it in mind and (2) learn to apply it on all occasions. "What is this word of God? The words of the holy Gospel and of the inspired apostles and of the prophets of God. How does the word of God dwell in us in all wisdom? Through the hearing and reading and observance of the Scriptures of God. When we attend to these constantly and carefully, our memory is stored, our mind is enriched, our heart over-

flows and streams of divine instruction pour from our lips"
(Nicephorus).—**Teaching and admonishing** (1:28; compare
the Third Commandment).—**One another.** *Yourselves.* "Here
St. Paul makes the teaching-office common to all Christians"
(Luther). The constant function of the Church within itself
is, mutual instruction and admonition *based on the word of
Christ.* It will appear that St. Paul is particularly bent on
excluding other "wisdom," by which false teachers and the
simple might seek to teach and admonish.—**With psalms.**
Doubtless the Psalter. The Psalms of David were sung by the
Jews in worship, and naturally formed a part of the service
of the early Church. (See Bingham, XIV.) The Psalms are the
Prayer-book of the fellowship of Christ—they are given of
God; they record the communion of the Old Testament saints
with Him; how dear they were to our Lord is evinced by His
words on the cross; and the experience of every generation
of His saints has been sung into them. "The Psalter is a
vast palimpsest, written over and over again, illuminated,
illustrated, by every conceivable emotion of men and nations;
battles, wanderings, dangers, escapes, deathbeds, obsequies,
of many ages and countries, rise, or may rise, to our view, as
we read it" (Stanley). "This is the peculiarity of the Psalter,
that every one can use its words as if they were peculiarly and
individually his own" (Ambrose). "The Psalms are interwoven
with the texture of the New Testament.... The fifth verse of
the 31st Psalm rises from saint after saint. It was spoken
by Jesus first; then it came from St. Stephen, St. Polycarp,
St. Basil, Epiphanius of Pavia, St. Bernard, St. Louis, Huss,
Columbus, Luther, Melanchthon, Silvio Pellico.... Many
portions of our Lord's teaching were addressed, through
an audience which could not receive or understand them,

to those far away in time and place. They presuppose such hearers and readers; they imply the kindling of a light in which they could be read, the existence of natures to which they should become intelligible. In the same way the Psalms presuppose an audience for which they were suited, and a tone of feeling and devotion which should answer to them. If these deep sighs and unutterable yearnings were intended to be used, they imply the knowledge of a character not yet perfected by the Holy Ghost; of souls, with finer gifts and higher susceptibilities, to be moulded out of our fallen humanity. They may well call themselves new songs. They are new songs for new men" (Bp. W. Alexander). The Church has assisted in the Christianization of the Psalter not only by its traditional interpretation, but by its arrangement of the Psalms in the service, in the special seasons of the Christian year, and as introits and responsories. These *inspired* songs are best fitted to be the perennial songs of the Church for the same reason that the Lord's Prayer fits all times and seasons. An earnest Christian *grows* in his appreciation of the Psalms.—**Hymns;** i.e. sacred songs of Christian composition. Luther makes it to refer to other songs taken out of Scripture, besides the Psalms, such as the songs of Moses, Deborah, Habakkuk, Hezekiah, and the *Magnificat, Benedictus, Nunc dimittis*, and Song of the Three Children. Such were the *Gloria in Excelsis* and *Gloria Patri* and *Alleluia*. (See Acts 4:24; 16:25; 1 Cor. 14:15, 26; Eph. 5:14; 1 Cor. 13; 1 Tim. 3:16; and the songs in Revelation.) That from the beginning the Christians sang hymns to Christ as God, we learn from the celebrated letter of Pliny (X. 97; see Eusebius, Hist. V. 28, and Bingham, XIV. 2; my Liturgics, pp. 78 ff.).—**And spiritual songs.** "Songs not taken from the holy Scriptures,

263

such as might be made at any time" (Luther). That this does
not refer to singing in common worship only, we gather
from Tertullian. (See Acts 16:25.) Clement of Alexandria
enjoins the substitution of such songs in their feasts and
mirth, instead of the objectionable music and songs of the
Greeks. "St. Jerome tells us that the Psalms were to be heard
in the fields and vineyards of Psalestine. The ploughman,
as he held his plough, chanted Hallelujah; and the reaper,
the vinedresser and the shepherd sang the songs of David.
Sidonius Apollinaris represents boatmen, as they worked
their heavy barges up the waters, singing Psalms till the banks
echoed with Hallelujah, and applies it to the voyage of the
Christian life.

"Here the choir of them that drag the boat,
—While the banks give back responsive note—
Alleluia!—full and calm
Lifts and lets the friendly bidding float—
Lift the Psalm.
Christian pilgrim! Christian boatman! each beside his
rolling river,
Sing, O pilgrim! sing, O boatman! lift the Psalm in music
ever."
—Alexander.

We are to observe St. Paul's recognition of the use of
Christian song in *teaching*. The songs of the Church, their
selection and arrangement in the service, teach, as well as
the lections and sermon. Therefore should we be careful to
guard against all falsehood and all that is unworthy in "sacred"
song. And a warning of Erasmus (letter of Aug. 13, 1529)
is also to be heeded: "The singing of hymns was an ancient
and pious custom, but when music was introduced fitter for

264

weddings and banquets than for God's service, and the sacred words were lost in affected intonations, so that no word in the Litany was spoken plainly, away went another strand of the rope."—**With grace;** i.e. in God's grace. The reading is, in *the* grace. Paul does not insist that singing must be sweet or graceful. Luther: "Some songs have the choicest words, but are worldly and of the flesh; others have good matter, but words so unfit that they have neither favor nor grace."—**In your hearts unto God.** Chrysostom: "Though thou be in the market-place, thou mayest sing in thyself without any one hearing it." "Not that your mouth is to be silent, but that the words of your mouth shall express your heart's sentiment" (Luther).

17. And whatsoever ye do, in word or in deed, *do* all in the name of the Lord Jesus, giving thanks to God the Father through him.

17. "The work of a Christian has no special name, season or place, but what they do—that is good; and when they do it—it is right; and whenever they do it,—it is well. Therefore St. Paul here names no special work, makes no distinction, but takes all together, and makes all good, eating, drinking, sleeping, waking, going, staying, speaking, silence, work and rest, all are alike precious if in the name of the Lord Jesus. We go in the name of the Lord Jesus when we hold in firm faith that Christ is in us, and we are in Him; therefore we rest, and He works in us (Gal. 2:20). But if we do anything as of ourselves, it is in our name, and has no good in it" (Luther).

18–19. Wives, be in subjection to your husbands, as is fitting in the Lord. Husbands, love your wives, and be not bitter against them.

18. This is Marriage *in the Lord.* (See on 1 Thess. 4:1 ss.) It

is proper that wives should submit to their husbands. There must not be disunited households. Nor would it be fitting to bid husbands obey their wives. (See on Eph. 5:4; Philem. 8.)

19. On the other hand, husbands are to love their wives, and not be bitter, harsh, cross-grained, towards them. As one thinks how applicable this and ver. 18 are to households in the Church in the present day, he cannot but admire St. Paul's close observation. In that day there were unloving, fault-finding husbands, hard to please, and wives who asserted for themselves a sphere of interests outside the home. He defines their mutual duty *in the Lord;* and a later age cannot escape from it.

20–21. Children, obey your parents in all things, for this is well-pleasing in the Lord. Fathers, provoke not your children, that they be not discouraged.

20–21. This is the Fourth Commandment "in the Lord." Certainly, these injunctions rest on close observation and much reflection. An exacting parent irritates his children; a harsh one breaks their spirit.

22–24. Servants, obey in all things them that are your masters according to the flesh; not with eyeservice, as men-pleasers, but in singleness of heart, fearing the Lord: whatsoever ye do, work heartily, as unto the Lord, and not unto men; knowing that from the Lord ye shall receive the recompense of the inheritance: ye serve the Lord Christ.

22–24. **Servants;** i.e. *bondservants, slaves.* Paul here approaches a delicate subject. The letter was brought by Onesimus as well as Tychicus, and the former was a runaway slave of Philemon, a prominent member of the Colossian Church. He had fallen in with Paul at Rome, perhaps resorted to him in distress, and under his influence had been converted; and now, transformed into "a brother beloved," was demonstrating the reality of his conversion by coming back to his master at Paul's bidding. It is possible that many others of the Colossian Christians were bondmen, and it may have been because of this, and in reference to the triumphant mission of Onesimus, that St. Paul refers to himself and Timothy, and Epaphras and Tychicus, as *bondmen* of Christ (1:7; 4:8). It is noteworthy how many sorts of persons were already to be found in the Church. Probably there was a representative of every class mentioned in 3:11 in the Colossian congregation. Paul addresses *bondmen* as moral personalities. Though treated by the law as chattels, their masters having over them the power of life and death, and often making them the dumb instruments of their sins, there is for them a rule and life in Christ. Paul had seen their *eyeservice* (a word of his own coining); their double-dealing, their trifling, superficial performance of duty. He says, In all things obey (1 Peter 2:18–24); in singleness of heart; diligently work, from your hearts serving; *as unto the Lord,* and not unto men. And the Lord will requite you. You are treated as if you were not human here—only slaves; but *there* you shall have an *inheritance.* How great the wisdom and sympathy of this great man, writing from Rome, the centre of slavery, to slaves!

25. For he that doeth wrong shall receive again for the wrong that he hath done: and there is no respect of persons.

25. While this verse is closely connected with the preceding verses, and shows the penalty of the disregard of what is said in ver. 24, it is no less closely connected with what follows. Bondage begets vices. He whom the law does not protect comes to think himself free from the law. But punishment

awaits a bad slave as well as a bad master. And, on the other hand, those who are suffering injustice from which there is no appeal on earth, are reminded that with God there is no respect of persons.

17

Colossians 4

1. Masters, render unto your servants that which is just and equal; knowing that ye also have a Master in heaven.

1. Thus says the man who rejoiced to call himself *the slave of Jesus Christ*. He requires from all servants hearty service; from all masters justice and fairness; and reminds them that they also must give account.

Prisoners taken in war were sold as slaves in the ancient world. It is estimated that about the time of Paul there were in the Roman world three times as many slaves as freemen. They were considered by the law as the absolute property of their owners. Revolting stories of cruelty are told. No doubt these were exceptional. And there are evidences of the gradual growth of a better sentiment, even outside the influence of Christianity. The *Essenes* forbade the ownership of slaves. Emancipation was urged by Gnostics, but not by the Church. Paul bade Onesimus return to his master, but introduced him as the dear brother of Philemon and himself, even as his own self (Philem. 16, 17). Early Christian authors (Tatian, Tertullian, Lactantius) take the same position,

accounting the outward condition of a man to be of small
moment in comparison of his *being in Christ.* The early
Church recognized no call to reform and reorganize the
state and worldly society. (See 1 Cor. 7:21.) It addressed
the individual heart and conscience, and transformed it, and
it was not until the Church became dominant in the world
that it recognized its duty in reference to social problems.
But by that time it had lost also somewhat of the singleness
of its eye. "The Christianity of the Roman Empire was not
a pure Christianity, but a mixture of Christian views with
those of the ancient world. It is the merit of Protestantism
to have finally delivered Christianity from the remnants of
the mixture of ancient life" (Uhlhorn). But the views and
practices of the Church contributed (1) to the mitigation
of slavery, and (2) to its final extinction. It recognized
the common manhood of slave and master, their equal
responsibility before God, their independent conscience. A
slave became a brother in the Church, and was eligible to
any, even its highest, offices. Pope Calixtus was a slave.
Slaves ate of the same blessed Bread and drank from the
same Cup. And slaves were honored among the martyrs and
confessors. *Slavery* came to an end in the Roman Empire by
gradually merging into *Villenage.* Christianity had the same
mitigating and solvent effect on this institution. (See Hallam,
Middle Ages.) "Slavery, for the first time in history, became
extinct in Europe somewhere about the fourteenth century....
The two doctrines which contributed most to producing the
extinction of slavery were the doctrine of salvation and the
doctrine of the equality of all men before the Deity" (Kidd,
Social Evolution, 151, 181). The same gradual effect is even
now being produced on the relations between employers and

their workmen, or capital and labor.

The method of Paul—wise in its simple truthfulness, and proved wise by the progress of centuries—doubtless sets a lesson and utters a prophecy in regard to other evil social institutions of the heathen world, with which our missionaries now come in contact, such as *caste* and *polygamy;* except that, because of increased means of communication and the preponderance of Christendom, the process will be much more rapid. The moral process of the Gospel in the social world is therefore rather that of resolution and reformation, than of revolution.

2–4. Continue stedfastly in prayer, watching therein with thanksgiving; withal praying for us also, that God may open unto us a door for the word, to speak the mystery of Christ, for which I am also in bonds; that I may make it manifest, as I ought to speak.

2. (Rom. 12:12.) **Watching therein.** Awake while you pray; not "lax and distracted."—**With thanksgiving.** (1 Thess. 5:17.)

3–4. Paul asks them to pray for his liberation. Now, he preached and wrote from behind a closed door. He longs that the door may be opened that he may go forth to fulfil his calling. (See 2 Thess. 3:1.)

5–6. Walk in wisdom toward them that are without, redeeming the time. Let your speech be always with grace, seasoned with salt, that ye may know how ye ought to answer each one.

5–6. A Christian must not be careless of the good opinion of those who are not in Christ. He must provide things honest in the sight of all men, that his light may shine and he may glorify God. Those without are not to be regarded as the Jews

271

regarded the Gentiles, but we should long to win to Christ
our brethren according to the flesh.—**Redeeming the time.**
Rather as the original, Buying up the opportunity. Valuing
and quick to acquire opportunity to do them benefit. "What
is really said is this, Buy out of the market what you may never
buy so cheap again; use the opportunity while you have it,
and use it thoroughly" (Howson, Metaphors of St. Paul, 69).

6. **Let your speech always be with grace;** i.e. animated
by kindliness towards every one, as God's grace is freely
given us, and therefore pleasant and attractive. In this sense,
we should bring sunshine wherever we go.—**Seasoned with
salt.** In the mouth of a Greek this would mean *witty*. Here
it means, Let it not be thoughtless, unconsidered; but, as
a cook makes a toothsome mess of that which savages eat
unseasoned, so let your speech always have flavor, taste,
worth. Salt makes food savory and also preserves it. Our
speech should be stimulating, and also pure. Conybeare and
Howson: "Free from insipidity." (See Matt. 12:36.)—**That ye
may know how to answer each one.** They had to answer
many questions and many gibes. Constant preparedness,
gravity, a kindly spirit, thorough sympathy with the Gospel,
would enable them to use each of these opportunities for the
benefit of the questioner. Upon *always,* Eadie transcribes this,
from Elton (1620): "Wouldest thou then be able to speak fitly,
and to good purpose on every occasion, as in one particular
case, in time of distress, in time of trouble, and vexation
of body or mind, wouldest thou be able to speak a word of
comfort, and as the prophet saith (Isai. 1:4), know to minister
a word in time to him that is weary? Oh, then let thy tongue
be ever powdered with the salt of grace, have in thy mouth at
all other times gracious speeches, and certainly thou shalt not

be to seek of sweet and comfortable words in time of need. Many come to their friends whom they love well, and wish well unto, in time of their trouble, haply lying on their sick-beds, and are not able to afford them one word of spiritual comfort, only they can use a common form of speech, ask them how they do, and say, they are sorry to see them so, and then they have done: here is one special cause of it, their mouths are not seasoned with gracious speeches at other times, and so it comes to pass that when they should, and (it may be) would, use gracious and comfortable words, they cannot frame themselves to them, but even then also they are out of season with them; learn thou therefore to acquaint thyself with holy and religious speeches, let thy mouth at other times be exercised in speaking graciously, and then (doubtless) though thou canst not speak so eloquently, as some that foam out nothing but goodly speeches, yet thou shalt be able to speak to better purpose, because (indeed) it is not man's wit, but God's grace, that seasons speech, and makes it profitable and comfortable."

7–9. All my affairs shall Tychicus make known unto you, the beloved brother and faithful minister and fellow-servant in the Lord: whom I have sent unto you for this very purpose, that ye may know our estate, and that he may comfort your hearts; together with Onesimus, the faithful and beloved brother, who is one of you. They shall make known unto you all things that *are done* here.

7. All my affairs shall Tychicus make known unto you. He was the bearer of this epistle, and also of an epistle to the Asian Churches, which we know as the Epistle to the Ephesians. They were at liberty to question him about the apostle and his manner of life and prospects of trial or liberation at Rome. Tychicus was a native of Asia (Acts 20:4). He probably had been one of the delegates of the churches appointed to accompany St. Paul when he carried up to Jerusalem their contributions for the relief of that Church, and certainly went at least part of the way with him. Again, he was Paul's messenger at this time. And later St. Paul sent him to Ephesus (2 Tim. 4:12), and proposed to send him to Crete (Titus 3:12). The name is found in inscriptions in Asia Minor, and once in connection with the name Onesimus.—**The beloved brother.** (See 1:1.)—**And faithful minister.** *Deacon, Servant.* Paul may have meant that he was a faithful servant of the Church. But probably this is an affectionate acknowledgment of the offices of love Tychicus did not fail to show him in his imprisonment.—**And fellow-servant in the Lord.** Fellow-slave (1:7). Tychicus was like-minded. Paul saw in him the same conviction of obligation.

8. The comfort Paul sends is exhortation and encouragement.

9. For **Onesimus,** see on 3:22, and Ep. to Philemon. He whom they had known as a slave, and not a reputable one, now returns as St. Paul's messenger, is recommended as *one of them,* and bears with Tychicus and Timothy the name of the faithful and beloved brother. He is signalized as one whose worth and service are well known.—**They shall make known unto you all things that are done here.** There seems to be an intimation that there is much to ask and to tell that St. Paul may not have thought it prudent to write.

10–11. Aristarchus my fellow-prisoner saluteth you, and Mark, the cousin of Barnabas (touching whom ye received commandments; if he come unto you, receive him), and Jesus,

274

which is called Justus, who are of the circumcision: these only *are my* fellow-workers unto the kingdom of God, men that have been a comfort unto me.

10. **Aristarchus my fellow-prisoner.** Aristarchus was a companion of St. Paul on the vessel from Cæsarea, and probably as far as Myra. He was a Thessalonian (Acts 19:29; 27:2). He was with Paul at the writing of this letter and of that to Philemon, but not when the letter to the Philippians was written. In Philemon Epaphras is called Paul's *fellow-prisoner,* as in Rom. 16:7 Andronicus and Junias are. Paul may thus have designated those who shared his hired house with him; or it may have been an affectionate reminiscence of their fellowship on the vessel at the beginning of his journey to Rome. Then Aristarchus, a passenger, may not have been ashamed of Paul's bonds, or he even may have taken passage in order to be with him, or afterwards joined him in Rome with the same mind. One who thus associated himself with the prisoner of the Lord deserved to be called Paul's fellow-prisoner.—**And Mark, the cousin of Barnabas.** Barnabas is mentioned as one in high repute. On *Mark,* see Acts 12:12, 25; 13:5, 13; 15:37–39. He was at this time with Paul. The recollection of his former disagreement and his departure from him had been effaced by commendable service (2 Tim. 4:11). A man who has made mistakes may recover himself on repentance. Mark's residence in Rome at this time is interesting in connection with the tradition that his gospel was written for that Church (Iren. III. 1, 1; Eus. Hist. III. 39), and contains Latin words and forms of speech.—**Touching whom,** etc. 1. There was a likelihood that Mark would visit them. In Peter's first letter (5:13), Mark, said to be his companion and amanuensis, salutes

these churches. 2. They had already received commandments concerning him. 3. There was especial reason for this very emphatic commendation. On **cousin,** see Numb. 36:11 in Septuagint.

11. **Jesus, which is called Justus.** Nothing more is known of this man.—**Who are of the circumcision.** All these were converts from Judaism. Aristarchus therefore was a Jew.—**These only,** etc.; i.e. these are the only *Jewish* Christians who have been fellow-workers and a comfort unto me (Phil. 1:15 ff.; 2:20). It is probable that after Paul's coming there was a division among the Christians of Rome, some associating themselves closely with Paul, others holding aloof. (See Lightfoot, on Galatians, p. 336.) "The last notice of the Roman Church in the apostolic writings seems to point to two separate communities, a Judaizing Church and a Pauline Church. The arrival of the Gentile apostle in the metropolis, it would appear, was the signal for the separation of the Judaizers who had hitherto associated with their Gentile brethren coldly and distrustfully. The presence of St. Paul must have vastly strengthened the numbers and influence of the more liberal and Catholic party; while the Judaizers, provoked by rivalry, redoubled their efforts, that in making converts to the Gospel they might also gain proselytes to the law." The word here rendered *comfort* occurs nowhere else in the New Testament. The two other words of like signification occur Phil. 2:1 and 1 Thess. 2:11. Lightfoot says that the word here used is *wider* in its import; Bengel, that while one of the others refers to comfort "in domestic sorrow," this refers to comfort and encouragement "in public peril." It is derived from a word meaning (1) to *address,* to *exhort;* (2) to *appease,* to *soothe.* It was used in medicine, of

"assuaging," "alleviating." It has in it also the sense of *advice, counsel.*

12–13. Epaphras, who is one of you, a servant of Christ Jesus, saluteth you, always striving for you in his prayers, that ye may stand perfect and fully assured in all the will of God. For I bear him witness, that he hath much labour for you, and for them in Laodicea, and for them in Hierapolis.

12. **Epaphras, a servant of Christ Jesus;** i.e. a *slave,* a *bondman* (1:7).—**Always striving for you in his prayers.** Agonizing and struggling like a wrestler in the arena (Rom. 15:30; Luke 22:44. See Col. 1:29). The *agony* or *conflict,* of which Paul speaks repeatedly, most likely was an *inward* conflict.—**That ye may stand perfect and fully assured in all the will of God.** Epaphras, parted from them, is always solicitous for them; and not, in the first place, for their outward well-being, but, like Paul, that they may stand firm, and be perfect (see 1:28), and may have the assurance of complete and unshaken conviction. Mark the first and chief object of a pastor's concern for his flock.

13. Laodicea and Hierapolis are neighboring places, and Epaphras most probably had been the evangelist, and practically was the pastor, of all. See how a pastor is married to his flock.

14. Luke, the beloved physician, and Demas salute you.

14. **Luke, the beloved physician** (Acts 16:10). Here we find two of the evangelists in Paul's company at once. (See 4:10; Philem. 24; 2 Tim. 4:11.)—**And Demas** (2 Tim. 4:10). He does not give Demas any special commendation. (See on Philem. 23, 24.)

15. Salute the brethren that are in Laodicea, and Nymphas, and the church that is in their house.

15. The Laodicean Church probably was a *filial,* or offshoot, of this at Colossæ, smaller and to some extent dependent on it, though, that being a larger field, it grew more rapidly (Rev. 3:14 ff.). It probably held its meetings in the house of Nymphas (or, if *her* be the right reading, of Nympha). *Their* might be intended to include all the brethren. The early Christians assembled in private dwellings. Separate buildings for Christian worship were not allowed before the third century. There might be several such groups, each having its own recognized place of assembly, as in Rome (Rom. 16:4, 10, 11, 14). But it is probable that the house of Nymphas was the centre of the only Church at Laodicea, as that of Philemon was the meeting-place at Colossæ (Philem. 2). For proof that regular assemblies of the Church were held, see 4:2, 5, 10, 15, 16; 3:11, 13, 16; 1:18, 24.

16. And when this epistle hath been read among you, cause that it be read also in the church of the Laodiceans; and that ye also read the epistle from Laodicea.

16. Here is a beginning of a canon of apostolic Scriptures. (See on 1 Thess. 5:27; 2 Thess. 3:17.) The apostle recognized the importance of a definite codex of apostolic explanation, exhortation and injunction, not to be read once only and then laid aside, but to be passed from one to another, to be preserved, to be read over, to be appealed to, as an authentic declaration of the word of Christ (1 Thess. 5:27; Rev. 1:3). Through their word, which is also His Word, the Spirit and the apostles witness to Jesus. The written word is the witness of the Holy Ghost and the Church (John 15:26, 27). There can be little doubt that the Old Testament Scriptures were read in the earliest assemblies of the Church, as was customary in the synagogues (Acts 15:21), and those of the New Testament

278

were soon ranged with them. Bingham says that at Rome only Gospel and Epistle were read, in earliest time. (See Bingham, Antiquities, etc., XIV. 3.; my Liturgies, 32 ff.)—**And that ye also read the epistle from Laodicea.** No epistle under this name has been preserved to us in our canon. It has been supposed that our Epistle to the Ephesians was a circular letter intended for several churches in that region, and is here referred to. From at least the sixth century a so-called epistle to the Laodiceans has been extant in Latin, and was generally acknowledged in the Middle Ages. It is nothing but a selection of texts from Philippians, without point. It is given by Lightfoot in his volume on Colossians, and by others.

17. And say to Archippus, Take heed to the ministry which thou hast received in the Lord, that thou fulfil it.

17. **And say to Archippus.** The only person of this name known to us is called by Paul his *fellow-soldier* (Philem. 2). He seems to have been the son of Philemon, and probably a young person.—**Take heed,** etc. This Archippus recently had received "a ministry"—been made *a deacon,* a recognized servant or minister in the Church. Here is a beginning of *offices* in the Church, in our modern meaning of the word,—in other words, of an organization of the congregation. It does not appear that he was the deacon *of a bishop,* as Sohm says always was the case. His ministry was in the Church, and under its direction. There seems to have been reason to fear he might be lax in his service. Archippus was of the second generation of believers, a son of those who had been converted to the faith from former darkness, and from childhood had been brought up in the Gospel. There always is danger of laxity in those to whom such service is rather

279

"a second nature" than distinctively an activity resulting
from the new birth. As a child of the Church, one known
by all from boyhood, an officer among elders who were
scarred by battle for the truth, he would be regarded by
all with especial interest. Finally, here is evidence that at
this time the offices in the Church and the proper discharge
of them were under the control of the Church itself. *They
were solemnly to admonish Archippus, See that thou fulfil
it.* "The assumption of a regular and continuous episcopate
in such a place as Colossæ at this date seems to involve an
anachronism" (Lightfoot on Philemon, 307. See on Phil. 1:1).

18.   The salutation of me Paul with mine own hand.
Remember my bonds. Grace be with you.

18. The customary autograph attesting the epistle (2 Thess.
3:17; 1 Cor. 16:21).—**Remember my bonds.** Remember
that I am a prisoner for you and for the Lord. A claim on
their love, confidence, attention, prayers.—**Grace be with
you.** *The* grace be with you. His blessing. (See 1:2.)

IV

1 Thessalonians

ANNOTATIONS
ON THE
FIRST EPISTLE
TO THE THESSALONIANS

BY

EDWARD T. HORN, D. D.

18

Introduction

Saloniki is the second city of European Turkey. It still is the residence of many thousands of Jews, the most recent estimate (1895) being, that of 120,000 inhabitants two-thirds are Jews. It is built on hills that rise like an amphitheatre from the Gulf, and commands a plain of great fertility. Its principal street is the old Egnatian Way, the great Roman road, which of old was the principal line of communication between Asia and Europe. In the Middle Ages a great fair was held there, to which came men of all nationalities and climes; and in much more remote ages it was such a mart, a place of liveliest intercourse, of enterprise and toleration, where every new thing was discussed, where the strangest contrasts jostled each other, and where one might meet and talk with other men from the ends of the earth.

As we walk its ancient streets, we are reminded of many things; of Philip of Macedon and his son the great Alexander, from whose sister the more ancient city derived its present name; of Cicero, who was an exile here; of the great Theodosius, who made this his virtual capital, and issued hence the edicts for the forcible extinction of ancient paganism, but chiefly marked it by his frightful massacre of its tumultuous and saucy people, for which the greater Ambrose exacted the public penance of the emperor; of the missions among the barbarians of Eastern Europe, which found their centre here; and of the unhappy days when Thessalonica was first a bulwark of the empire against the Goths, and a last stronghold of Europe against the Turks. But the greatest event in the history of Thessalonica was the foundation of its Church by the apostle Paul, 53 a.d., and the reception from his hand of the two letters to the Thessalonians, which were probably the first books of our New Testament that ever were written, 54 a.d.

Paul and Silas, having been whipped at Philippi and ex-pelled from that city, came directly to Thessalonica. On the way they passed through Amphipolis and the smaller town of Apollonia; but probably hastened to Thessalonica, because it was the metropolis of that district of Macedonia and then, as now, a great Jewish centre. There was the synagogue, which served all the Jews of the district. And besides the Jews, settled there for purposes of trade, there were many proselytes—persons of Greek extraction who had become adherents of the Jewish faith, either from conviction, or to escape military service, or under the influence of Jewish wives, or for the sake of profit,—and also many women of good estate who perhaps were Jewesses married to heathen men of distinction. Such always were Paul's congenial audience, having either on the one hand or the other broken with ancestral custom, having begun the habit of proving all things to hold fast that which was good, having their minds open to catch a further word of God to lead them into all truth. We are struck, as we read the story, by the unconquerable zeal of Paul and Silas. The pain of their wounds, the stiffness produced by a long and rapid journey on foot, and the apparent failure of their attempt at Philippi, caused no delay; but, as his custom was, Paul went at once to the synagogue and reasoned with those who gathered there, Three weeks at least they remained at Thessalonica, perhaps longer, for three weeks hardly would suffice for the work they did. Night and day they worked at their trades, to earn their living; staying in the house of Jason, perhaps a well-known lodging-house for Jews, but taking assistance from nobody, except that twice in that time their friends in Philippi sent aid to them; but on the Sabbath days work was laid aside and they became preachers. Adherents multiplied; besides Jason there were other Jews, and a great number of the proselytes, not a few of the chief women, and, as the epistles show, many who formerly had not been Jews in any sense, but worshippers of idols. The work of Paul is so important and so suggestive of the true principles of Christian missions, and the history and his letters tell us so much about it, that we may ask *how did Paul set about his work in Thessalonica, and what was it he said to win and to instruct these converts of a few eager weeks?*

It will be observed that he spoke to them first in the synagogue, and he took the Scriptures of the Old Testament read there as his text. Like Christ (Luke 24:26), he proved from them that the Christ promised in the Old Testament ought *to suffer* and *to rise again from the dead;* and having thus opened to them the sense of the Scriptures, he proved that *Jesus is the Christ.* The heathen further learned the meaning of Christ's coming, and all were stirred to a lively hope of

285

the second coming of our Lord Jesus Christ, and were called
to share in His kingdom and glory (2:13). The Gospel, as
yet unwritten, was told them by the word of Paul, and they
received it. as it was in truth, as the word of God, feeling its
power in themselves. The Holy Ghost came upon them, and
some were endued with prophetic gifts, enabling them to
further expound the Scriptures and admonish and instruct.
Paul did not hide from them that they were adopting a life of
trial, that Christians are called to suffer affliction (3:4). He
taught them how they ought to walk and please God, showing
the deep contrast between the carelessness of the heathen and
the conduct of those God had called to sanctification; and
admonished them to live as sons of light, whom the day of the
Lord would not overtake as thieves in the night (5:1–4). The
word of Paul came to them in power and in the Holy Ghost
(1:5); but this does not imply that without any effort on his
part he exerted a miraculous influence, which constrained
the minds of men. His boldness (1:5; 2:2) was heroic, and his
zeal was the outward flame of an inward agony. He did not
flatter. He did not try to please men. He lived in unbroken
consciousness of the presence of God. He impressed the
Thessalonians by his disinterestedness and his affection for
them. Without assumption, evidently eager to impart his
own soul to them, with tenderness like that with which a
mother presses her child to her bosom, he did not preach
only, but dealt with each, exhorting, encouraging, adjuring
them, like a father;—not only seeking to gain them to his
cause, but that they might walk worthily of God who called
them.

He was rewarded by the character of the Church he
founded. They became imitators of him, and ere long he

learned from the reports that reached him at Corinth that they had sent out the word of the Lord through all Greece, and that all Macedonia and Achaia rang with the story of their faith in God. The Jews of Thessalonica stirred up a tumult against his friends, and Paul had to be hurried away by night. The Thessalonians had to suffer the same things of their own countrymen as the churches of Judea suffered of the Jews. But they stood firm, and Paul could thank God for their work of faith, and labor of love and patience of hope.

When Paul had left Thessalonica, after brief service there of Silas and Timothy, the Church was presided over by certain men, who labored among them, and admonished them, as the apostle had done. There was some disposition to reject their authority (5:12), and perhaps on their part some want of respect for the opinion of others (5:27). As in the Corinthian Church, there were "prophesyings" in their assemblies; most necessary, we should think, for the further Christian exposition of the Old Testament, but, at the same time, alarming the more prudent by the peril of fanaticism; so that Paul afterwards had to admonish them, on the one hand, not to despise prophesyings nor quench the Spirit, and, on the other, to test what the prophets said and hold fast that which was good. To this end he had instructed them in the word of the Lord, and left them precepts and a tradition (2:13; 3:3, 4; 4:1, 2; 5:2; 2 Thess. 3:6). But some were disorderly (5:14; 2 Thess. 3:6). There might be danger of unfairness (5:19–22, 27). And, of course, old vices were not conquered all at once (4:1–8). But at the same time there grew up among the Thessalonians a dangerous error. These early believers seem to have been filled with an eager expectation of the coming of Christ, which threatened to border on fanaticism. Many of them gave up their daily work. They restlessly discussed the matter. And finally, when one and another of their number died, they were troubled for fear that these had passed away too soon, and would not share in the kingdom and glory which they fondly believed would come before many days. It is a lively picture of the lambent faith of the early Church, and of its necessary imperfection and immaturity.

In the Providence of God their danger became the occasion of a great blessing to us. To allay their excitement and lead them to the truth, Paul wrote them these letters. In the meantime he had been alone at Athens, his spirit stirred among those precious works of art to see that city wholly given to idolatry. Then he had come to Corinth, one of the busiest cities of the world, and one of the most corrupt. There he was at work now with Aquila and Priscilla, fugitives from Rome; probably Christians before Paul met them. And there Silas and Timothy returned to Paul and reported the prosperity and missionary activity of the Church of the Thessalonians, and also the peculiar questions and dangers which disturbed it. Paul, who once and again had wished to go back to Thessalonica, but found it impossible, wrote them a letter; and, on the return of the messenger by whom it had been sent, wrote them another. He had been in Thessalonica in the year 53; this was in 54.

In a sense, every book of the New Testament is a letter. The Gospel of Mark is the only possible exception. The Gospel of Matthew evidently was written to the Jews. Luke addresses his gospel and the Book of Acts to a friend; and John, by his "I" and "You" (21:25; 20:31), shows the same purpose. The Book of the Revelation is addressed to the Churches. And the other books are professedly nothing else than letters. Now

288

letters are written by men, to men; they betray the mind and situation of the writers and those they write to; and bear also the marks of the time and place in which they were written. To understand them, we must understand the writers and the recipients, and know much of their time and environment. It is very instructive, that God chose *letters* as the mode in which to give and preserve His living and effective truth to the end of time. The Holy Spirit, who spoke through apostle or evangelist, was the Holy Spirit who abode in his heart and in the hearts of those he wrote to, and bound them together in the One Body of Christ; and so the words which they have written are the Word of God who prompted them, and also the Word of Christ in His Church, out of whose heart they came, and into whose heart they came; they are the vital circulation of the life-blood of the Body of which He is the Head, and all Christians are members.

St. Paul did not write his letters (except that to Philemon) with his own hand. He dictated them, and added at the end of each a few words to attest his authorship. You can feel, as you read them, that he *said* them. They glow with personal affection; you can perceive the process and flood of his eager thought, and how he has had to struggle against the torrent of suggestion; he is led off by it sometimes; but he comes back again, and no more disdains to repeat than we do in a familiar letter. These letters also show us a good deal concerning the nature of the apostle's inspiration. He does not hesitate to say that he is telling the word of the Lord, and that they who despise it despise not man's word but God's, who has given His Holy Spirit to them. Yet the apostles of our Lord were not possessed of all possible wisdom and knowledge, so that they could give an infallible answer to any question on every

subject. Paul in the first letter to the Thessalonians, though
God enabled him to foretell the manner of the Resurrection
in answer to the peculiar difficulty of those he was writing to,
still expected to survive until Christ's coming and when he
wrote to the Philippians, years afterwards, did not foreknow
the circumstances of his own death. He was deceived in men
sometimes. So Peter made mistakes. They were not raised
above the necessity of using their judgment, of exercising
faith, of disciplining character. But God gave them wisdom
to decide perplexing questions; opened to them the sense of
the Scriptures; brought to mind what He had said and done;
granted them special revelations; and so provided them with
all they needed to tell for the guidance and continued well-
being of the Church.

God still gives His word to us through men; the word of
His Spirit is the testimony of His Church. He pleased to
save men by the foolishness of preaching. These holy books
come down to us by the hands of His faithful people through
many generations. In our customs, as well as through study,
we imbibe the explanation of them which these generations
have received and given. The Church has divided, selected
and translated them for us. And they are read and explained
again by preachers of the Gospel, come out of the bosom of
the Church, trained in her fellowship, and united with their
hearers in the one faith by the One Spirit.

19

1 Thessalonians 1

1. Paul, and Silvanus, and Timothy, unto the church of the Thessalonians in God the Father and the Lord Jesus Christ: Grace to you and peace.

1. **Paul.** This is the earliest of the extant letters of St. Paul, and probably was written in the year 54, while the apostle was at Corinth. (See Acts 18:5.) Paul uses his name only, not his official title (cf. Phil. 1:1; Col. 1:1), there being no occasion to assert his authority, which had not been questioned, and his relations with the Thessalonians having been recent, intimate and simple. "He drops his official title at the outset, not wishing to assert his apostolic authority when he could appeal to the higher motive of love" (Lightfoot, Biblical Essays, 249).—**Sylvanus.** So called by Paul (2 Cor. 1:19); the same as Silas. A chief man among the brethren of Jerusalem (Acts 15:22), himself a prophet (Acts 15:32), whom Paul chose to be the companion of his second missionary journey, after the parting from Barnabas (Acts 15:40). Acts 16:19 ff.; 17:4, 10, 18; 1 Cor. 1:19. Though a Jewish Christian, he was, like Paul, a Roman citizen. "He is

not mentioned as accompanying St. Paul, when the apostle
left Corinth at the close of this second missionary journey,
nor is his name found subsequently in St. Luke's narrative."
He afterwards appears as a messenger of St. Peter (1 Peter
5:12).—**Timothy** (Acts 16:1). Silas and Timothy had been
left at Berœa (Acts 17:14). The latter probably rejoined Paul
at Athens, and thence was sent by him to Thessalonica (1
Thess. 3:1), and with Silas rejoined Paul at Corinth (Acts 18:5).
These two had been Paul's fellow-workers in Thessalonica,
and now were working with him at Corinth (1 Cor. 1:19),
and therefore are associated with him in the salutation of
this epistle. One of them probably was his amanuensis at this
time. It will appear that in the letter he sometimes includes
them with himself, and sometimes uses the plural pronoun
of himself alone. ("A case for an epistolary plural in St. Paul's
epistle has not been made out."—Lightfoot.)—**Church of
the Thessalonians.** The word here translated *Church,* viz.,
ekklesia, was used by our Lord (Matt. 16:18; 18:17), and by
St. Stephen (Acts 7:38), and in this place first afterwards. As
it gradually became a technical term for the New Testament
people of God, it is well to inquire what its first meaning
was. It was the designation of "the lawful assembly in
a free Greek city of all those possessed of the rights of
citizenship, for the transaction of public affairs. They were
summoned out of the whole population, and were a select
portion of it" (Trench, N. T. Synonyms, 2). (Acts 19:32, 39,
41.) The Septuagint employed the word to translate the
Hebrew term for the *Assembly or Congregation of the people
of Israel, considered as a unity.* So St. Stephen speaks of
"the Church in the wilderness" (Acts 7:38). There can be
little doubt that St. Paul (and others) applied this term to

292

the Christian community in Thessalonica (and elsewhere) in express contrast with those who claimed to be the true "congregation" of God, or the real "assembly" of the city, and to cast them out (2:14–16; Acts 17:5–8, 13; Rom. 2:28, 29). They represented the true people of God the Father and the Lord Jesus Christ among the Thessalonians. It is noteworthy that in the later epistles (Rom., Eph., Phil., Col.) Paul addresses *the saints,* not the *Church;* but there the salutations of the *churches* are exchanged.—**Of the Thessalonians.** He does not say, At Thessalonica, as he afterwards says, At Philippi, etc. (Phil. 1:1); probably because the Church already had spread throughout the district of which Thessalonica was the metropolis, and of which the synagogue there was the Jewish centre (1:8). He did not know how far their boundaries extended, and did not wish to limit his greeting or his instruction.—**In God the Father and the Lord Jesus Christ.** This was the mark which proved them to be the true ecclesia in Thessalonica. The assembly of *God's people* in Thessalonica may be marked by these words in distinction—first, from their heathen compatriots, and, secondly, from their Jewish persecutors (2:14; Gal. 1:22).—**Grace, etc.** (See Col. 1:2.) The words, *From God,* etc., in the Authorized English Version, although found in several of the most ancient MSS., are supposed to have been supplied from other epistles, by copyists.

2–10. We give thanks to God always for you all, making mention *of you* in our prayers; remembering without ceasing your work of faith and labour of love and patience of hope in our Lord Jesus Christ, before our God and Father; knowing, brethren beloved of God, your election, how that our gospel came not unto you in word only, but also in power, and in the

Holy Ghost, and *in* much assurance; even as ye know what manner of men we shewed ourselves toward you for your sake. And ye became imitators of us, and of the Lord, having received the word in much affliction, with joy of the Holy Ghost; so that ye became an ensample to all that believe in Macedonia and in Achaia. For from you hath sounded forth the word of the Lord, not only in Macedonia and Achaia, but in every place your faith to God-ward is gone forth; so that we need not to speak anything. For they themselves report concerning us what manner of entering in we had unto you; and how ye turned unto God from idols, to serve a living and true God, and to wait for his Son from heaven, whom he raised from the dead, *even* Jesus, which delivereth us from the wrath to come.

2. (See Phil. 1:3.) There was an interval of ten years between this and the letter to the Philippians; and making allowance for the probability that there was a set form of salutation at the opening of letters, it still is instructive that Paul **always** gave thanks at the thought of his dear fellow-believers, who were his converts; and continued to give thanks for *all of them,* making mention of them in his prayers. His habit, thus stated, and abundantly illustrated in his letters, shows how he abode in communion with God, and prayed for each one committed to him. We are taught to pray for one another; for the members of our congregations; for those who require our especial care; and also to give thanks to God when we mention them in our prayers.—**Our prayers.** Paul observed regular seasons of prayer. Without doubt, Paul, Silvanus and Timothy prayed *together* for these Christians of Thessalonica, making mention of them before God, as well as discussing their faith, etc., and their dangers. Observe that

such a course contributes to both unity and wisdom in action. Ministers, missionaries, teachers of the word of God, should together give thanks to God and make mention of the objects of their care. (See Eph. 1:16; Philem. 4.)

3. **Remembering without ceasing before our God and Father.** In his prayers, but not while engaged in the act of prayer only (5:17), Paul always felt the presence of God; not that he simply kept in mind that God sees all, but in spirit he came before God and thought and did and said all before His Face. And, while in the very presence of God, he unremittingly thought of them (Rom. 1:9; 2 Tim. 1:3). Cf. 2:9, and think of Paul working night and day, preaching even while he worked, and praying meanwhile too.—**Faith, love, hope.** (5:8; 1 Cor. 13:13; Gal. 5:5, 6; Col. 1:4, 5; 2 Thess. 1:3, 4.) Mark the similarity of thought and expression at far different periods of Paul's life. Whatever progress he may have made in the truth, we see that he had the whole of it, from the beginning to the end. Their **faith** showed itself in active **work,** not in mere profession (Gal. 5:6); their **love** uttered itself in willing *toil* ("not only work, but fatiguing work," Lightfoot); their **hope** led them to patient, heroical endurance. (See Rev. 2:2; Tit. 2:2.) Beside the former picture of St. Paul working with his hands, praying and preaching, we must put this of the activity, that did not become weary in well-doing, and the endurance, of his Thessalonian converts. Lightfoot: "Here we have, *first,* faith, the source of all Christian virtues; *secondly,* love, the sustaining principle of Christian life; and *lastly,* hope, the beacon-star guiding us to the life to come."—**Hope.** Their hope was not a vague cheerfulness, but was *hope in our Lord Jesus Christ,* the hope of salvation in Him (5:8, 9); the hope of

His speedy coming to their deliverance (4:13–18).—**Before
our God and Father;** i.e. remembering this before God. (See
3:9.)

4. **Brethren beloved of God;** i.e. dear not to me only,
but also to God (2 Thess. 2:13). This is the ground of their
election (Eph. 1:4).—**Your election.** This word occurs also
Rom. 9:11; 11:5, 7, 28; 2 Peter 1:10; Acts 9:15. Paul says, I
know that you have been selected by God from among the
Thessalonians. He knows this, not by any special revelation,
but (1) from the manner in which his gospel came to them (ver.
5), and (2) the manner in which they received it, becoming
imitators of him in turn, and of the Lord (ver. 6). (See Bengel
on 1 Cor. 1:27: "Every one who is *called* is from the first
moment of faith *elect;* as long as he remains in the *calling* and
in faith, he continues to be elect; if ever he loses the calling
and faith, he ceases to be elect. When in faith he brings forth
fruit, he confirms his calling and election; if he returns to faith
and falls asleep believing he returns to the state of election
and dies one of the elect. And such are called both elect and
foreknown.")

5. Paul recalls the confidence (Rom. 14:5; Col. 2:2; 4:12;
Hebr. 10:22) with which he had addressed the Thessalonians
and worked among them, which was no less than miraculous
in view of the discouragement from which he had lately come
(2:2). The *power* of His Gospel was manifest in its speedy
success (Acts 17:5). And that this was the work of the Holy
Ghost was proved by the fruits of the Spirit immediately
manifest among them (1:3). They had also partaken of the
miraculous fruits of the Spirit (5:19, 20). And Paul and
they had felt, even while he spoke to them, the wonderful
power of the Spirit of Christ knitting together their hearts

in Him.—**Even as ye know.** Paul could confidently appeal to their recollection of his self-denying zeal for their sake (2:8).—**We showed ourselves.** We *became.* There was a great contrast between the former Saul, and the Paul they knew. The change was an evidence of the work of the Holy Ghost. It was wrought by God, and by the deep earnestness of Paul's longing for their salvation. We see here that *confidence* begotten of the Holy Ghost, and complete devotion, are requisites of a successful sermon.—**Our Gospel.** (See 2 Thess. 2:14; Rom. 2:16; 16:25; 2 Cor. 4:3; 2 Tim. 2:8.)

6. The second proof of their election is their reception of the word of the Gospel. To **receive** here means not to hear only, but to *heed,* to *accept* (Matt. 11:14). Though to accept the Gospel necessarily brought *affliction,* they received it *with joy of the Holy Ghost;* and they at once became imitators of Paul, and of the Lord Himself, *in self-sacrificing devotion to the spread of the Gospel of salvation* (1:8. See 1 Cor. 11:1. Also 1 Peter 4:13; Phil. 1:29).—**Joy of the Holy Ghost.** This is the joy which the Holy Ghost begets (Gal. 5:22); the exultant gladness of those who are in fellowship with one another in the Father and the Son; which goes forth in unresting and triumphant service of the Lord. "They have afflicted you and persecuted you, but the Spirit did not forsake you, even in those circumstances. As the Three Children in the fire were refreshed with dew, so also were you refreshed in affliction" (Chrysostom).

7–8. **For** shows that they became an ensample, etc., in that the word of the Lord sounded forth from them. They were an ensample, as a community, not simply as individual persons.—**Sounded forth:** "like the ringing peal of a trumpet" (Eadie). The Christians at Thessalonica sent

297

out preachers of the Gospel. Those who came to that busy centre of trade carried the story home with them. Their **faith to Godward** was contrasted with their former worship of idols. The story of the work among them of Paul and his companions, of the matter of their preaching, of the remarkable change in the Thessalonians, and of their hope of a second coming of the risen Jesus, was so spread, that Paul heard it told in every place, before he could begin to preach.—**To all who believe.** The obedience of a Christian man preaches to other Christians, not to unbelievers only. To imitate those who gave the Gospel to us, and Him who came to seek and to save the lost, is not only natural to a Christian, it is a test of the reality of his faith. "As a sweet-smelling ointment keeps not its fragrance shut up in itself, but diffuses it afar, so admirable men do not shut up their virtue within themselves, but by their good report benefit many, and render them better" (Chrysostom). We see also the wisdom of St. Paul in planting his missions in commercial centres, towns of great resort. For this reason, probably, he hurried past Apollonia and Amphipolis to Thessalonica. The country people coming to the synagogue there, and seamen and traders carried the Gospel everywhither. So, also, does this example lay an especial responsibility on Christians in towns. They should be centres of evangelization. So it was of old. The young should not come from country places to the towns to learn vice; but from towns the word of the Lord should sound forth in every place.—**Macedonia and Achaia;** i.e. all Greece.—**The word of the Lord.** The message of the Gospel (2:13).

9–10. **How ye turned unto God from idols.** Just before writing this Paul had come from Athens (Acts 17:16), "where

298

his spirit was provoked within him. when he saw the city full of idols." The Hebrew word for an *idol* means *nothingness;* for the Hebrew opinion of idols, see Ps. 115:4–8. These helpless "works of men's hands" the Thessalonians had turned from; to serve a **living God,** who is a **true** God; waiting with joyful expectation for His Son from heaven. (See Acts 14:15.) The majority of the Thessalonian Christians, accordingly, had been heathen. We see here some of the particulars of the faith in which St. Paul had instructed them during his brief ministry among them—a faith (1) in God the Father Almighty, Maker of heaven and earth; (2) in His only Son, our Lord; (3) who suffered, died, was buried; (4) and rose again from the dead; (5) ascended into heaven and sitteth on the right hand of God; (6) who shall come again to judge the quick and the dead.—**Which delivereth us.** An allusion to the meaning of the Name *Jesus.* (Septuagint, Isai. 59:20.) He says not, *who delivered* us, but *who delivereth.* Christ is even now delivering us from the wrath to come. The dispensation of the Spirit is the continuation of the Gospel. "Christ redeemed us once for all; He is delivering us always" (Bengel).—**From the wrath to come.** He speaks of it as *even now coming.* In spite of the Deliverer and the Deliverance He has accomplished, there still is **wrath;** the fulfilment of which is even now drawing nigh. "There is 'a wrath of God,' who would not love good, unless He hated evil, the two being inseparable, so that either He must do both or neither; a wrath also of the merciful Son of Man (Mark 3:5)" (Trench, Synonyms, 126). Evidently, Paul, in his preaching at Thessalonica, made very prominent the *Last Things,* death, resurrection, judgment, heaven, wrath (Rom. 1:18; 2:3–16; John 3:36; Rev. 6:16; Rom. 5:9).

20

1 Thessalonians 2

1–12. For yourselves, brethren, know our entering in unto you, that it hath not been found vain: but having suffered before, and been shamefully entreated, as ye know, at Philippi, we waxed bold in our God to speak unto you the gospel of God in much conflict. For our exhortation *is* not of error, nor of uncleanness, nor in guile: but even as we have been approved of God to be intrusted with the gospel, so we speak; not as pleasing men, but God which proveth our hearts. For neither at any time were we found using words of flattery, as ye know, nor a cloke of covetousness, God is witness; nor seeking glory of men, neither from you, nor from others, when we might have been burdensome, as apostles of Christ. But we were gentle in the midst of you, as when a nurse cherisheth her own children: even so being affectionately desirous of you, we were well pleased to impart unto you, not the gospel of God only, but also our own souls, because ye were become very dear to us. For ye remember, brethren, our labour and travail: working night and day, that we might not burden any of you, we preached unto you the gospel of God.

Ye are witnesses, and God *also,* how holily and righteously and unblameably we behaved ourselves toward you that believe: as ye know how we *dealt with* each one of you, as a father with his own children, exhorting you, and encouraging *you,* and testifying, to the end that ye should walk worthily of God, who calleth you into his own kingdom and glory.

1. **It hath not been found vain;** i.e. the event proves that I came *with power.*

2. **Having suffered before and been shamefully treated at Philippi** (Acts 16:22, 37). The Roman scourge was a whip, on whose leathern lash pieces of metal or bone were fastened. The prisoner was made to stoop and the lash tore his stretched back. Herein Paul and Silas were called to imitate the Lord. It involved great physical and mental suffering. To whip a Roman citizen, uncondemned, unheard, was, moreover, an outrage. Paul shows how keenly he still felt it.—**As ye know.** In all probability, it was very few days after their suffering at Philippi that Paul and Silas came to Thessalonica. and the Thessalonians could recall how they saw with their own eyes the marks of their pain.—**We waxed bold** (Col. 2:15; Eph. 3:12; 6:20). Paul looks back with wonder at the readiness with which God enabled them to begin again to preach His word.—**Our God** (Phil. 1:3; 4:19; Philem. 4). God was the source of his confidence. He was moved and sustained by his assurance that God directed and upheld him (1 Cor. 2:3–5).—**To speak unto you the gospel of God** (Acts 17:1–3). These men came to Jews and heathen with good tidings from God (Luke 2:10) which they never had heard before, and which cannot rest unspoken in the heart which believes it (3:2). It is the story of the fulfilment of God's eternal purpose in our Lord Jesus

Christ.—**In much conflict.** (See on Phil. 1:30; Col. 1:29;
2:1.) He sustained the sufferings that came upon him, not
without pain, and through a great battle and victory within
himself. The miraculous assistance given to the apostles
of our Lord gave them no exemption from trial and the
necessity of effort and sacrifice. The intensity of their self-
sacrifice is witnessed by this chapter. These words are as
true of Silas as of Paul.

3. **Our exhortation.** The Holy Ghost is the *Paraclete,* the
Comforter. The word used here is derived from the same
root, and is rendered *comfort, consolation, entreaty, appeal,*
as well as *exhortation* (Rom. 15:4; Phil. 2:1; 2 Cor. 8:4;
Lightfoot). His address to them was not simply *teaching,*
but appealed to their feelings as well as their understanding.
It included *summons, encouragement, incitement,* as well as
instruction. (See on 2:11.) It was an exhortation informed
with the quickening power of the Holy Ghost.—**Is not of
error.** Paul refers to his teaching while among them. But he
has in mind not a past address, but the contents of it, which
abide forever. Therefore the translators supply the word "is."
It was not grounded on error. He knew that what he told
them was true.—**Nor of uncleanness.** He may be defending
himself against insinuations which he and they may have
heard even while he was among them. There were not a few
women among his first converts (Acts 17:4), and some may
have slightingly said of Paul and Silas what he afterwards
had occasion to say of others (2 Tim. 3:6). "St. Paul was at
this very time living in the midst of the worship of Aphrodite
at Corinth, and had but lately witnessed that of the Cabiri
at Thessalonica.... How naturally prone the early converts
were to sensualize even the religion of Christ may be inferred

302

from many passages in St. Paul's epistles, and is seen in the monstrous aberrations of some forms of Gnosticism; i.e. of Simon Magus" (Lightfoot). Or they may have been accused of seeking their own profit, i.e. of impure motives (1 Tim. 3:8; Titus 1:7).—**Nor in guile.** They used no trickery. So should all preachers of the Gospel, without selfish aims, or uncandid methods, speak forth the convictions of the heart.

4. **So we speak.** This is contrasted with the wrong manner described in the preceding verse. Paul says, We do not speak error for our own ends, etc., but we speak as those to whom it has pleased God to entrust His Gospel; and therefore we aim to approve ourselves to *Him.*—**Even as we have been approved of God** (Gal. 1:1). This does not mean that God has given them this stewardship as a mark of His approval of their past conduct. It is equivalent to: *God has chosen to entrust this to us.*—**To be intrusted with the gospel.** The Gospel is a trust (1 Cor. 9:16; 2 Cor. 5:18). It is a talent, of which the Church of every age will have to give account. It is not enough to keep the faith in a pure confession; we must give an account of our stewardship of that Gospel which is the power of God (Rom. 1:16; Matt. 25:27).—**Not as pleasing men.** This is not our purpose at all, or at any time (2 Cor. 5:9). "They had none of that mixed motive, astute self-adaptation and versatility of address, discovered in menpleasing" (Eadie).—**Who trieth the hearts** (Jer. 11:20).

5. He proceeds to the proof of this, calling them to witness. He says, We were not found *in speech of flattery.* We did not cringe to you, trying to humor and wheedle you into consent with us.—**Nor in a cloke of covetousness;** i.e. we did not make pretences, to cover up covetousness; we evidently sought not our own profit at all. "Neither was our

conversacioun in cloked covetousness" (Tyndale).—**God is witness** (2:10). "Of an open thing He calls men to witness; of a thing hidden in the heart, God; of a thing partly hidden and partly open, God and men" (Bengel).

6. How common is it for those who care not for money to be greedy of praise!—**When we might have been burdensome.** The R. V. suggests three translations: (1) the one already given: (2) the Margin: *claimed honor;* and (3) the suggestion of the American Committee: *claimed authority.* For (1) the use of the same expression, in this sense, in verse 9, speaks. (See 2 Thess. 3:18; 2 Cor. 12:16.) So Wiclif: "Might be in charge to you," and Tyndale: "We might have been chargeable." For (2), the connection in this verse. For (3), Cranmer's Bible: "We might have been in auctorite." Paul hardly would have used the same expression twice, so nearly in the same place, yet with different meanings. It seems that he means, we might have exacted our support from you, inasmuch as we were messengers of Christ.—**Apostles.** Silas and Timothy are called apostles here. (See on Phil. 2:25; Col. 1:1; Gal. 1:1.)

7. We have in this verse an example of the manner in which "various readings" may occur. Some of the best MSS. read *Gentle,* and as many and as good read *Babes.* The decision hinges on the question whether St. Paul uttered a single consonant, or whether a reader or copyist prolonged or repeated the consonant which ended the former word. If Paul said, **We were babes among you,** he meant that they put themselves on a complete level with the Thessalonians. So the Vulgate has it, and accordingly Wiclif translates, "We weren made litil in the myddil of you;" and Rheims (1582), "We became children in the middes of you." But if Paul said,

we were **gentle,** it suits the rest of the figure, in which he likens his gentleness to that of a **nurse** cherishing her **own** children; i.e. to a mother pressing her own child to her breast. The words that follow, and the intense affectionateness of this whole letter, show that this is not an exaggerated figure. We cannot but wonder at the tenacious love Paul had for every one who received the Gospel from him. In it we learn to appreciate the Saviour's love for every soul of His (John 10:11, 15, 28; 13:1). "The inversion of the metaphor, the Christian teacher being first compared to the child and then to the mother, is quite in St. Paul's manner.... (2 Cor. 3:13–16; Rom. 7:1; 2 Cor. 2:14). His earnestness and rapidity of thought led him to work out his metaphor to the utmost, turning it about and reapplying it, as it suggested some new analogy.... Rhetorical rules were as nothing to him compared with what he had in view" (Lightfoot).

8. Paul, Silas and Timothy gladly gave themselves for and to the Thessalonians. This is the true method of "Church work." It is the history also of every real Christian pastorate. We greatly love the souls we toil for. The souls we are permitted to lead to God are bound to us by a tie stronger than that of blood. "From a friend we may both ask a favor and receive one without suspicion. When they enjoin anything upon us, then we feel indebted to them; but when they are slow to do this, then we are sorrowful. We have nothing which is not theirs" (Chrysostom).

9. **Labor and travail.** A good translation of these two words (used also 2 Thess. 3:8; 2 Cor. 11:27), which perhaps may differ in expressing (1) the actual labor and toil, and (2) the combination therewith of inward struggle and anxiety. "The teacher ought to do nothing that tends to the salvation

305

of his disciples with a feeling of being burdened. For if the
blessed Jacob was buffeted night and day in keeping his flocks,
much more ought he, to whom the care of souls is entrusted,
endure all toils, though the work be laborious and mean,
looking only to one thing, the salvation of his disciples, and
the glory thence arising to God" (Chrysostom).—**Working;**
i.e. with their hands, so as to earn their own bread (2 Thess.
3:8). "The other apostles in their youth had earned their
livelihood by a regular employment, but yet one which they
could not follow in every place; Paul, on the other hand,
though destined to be a Jewish theologian, yet according
to the maxims prevalent in the Jewish schools along with
the study of the law had learned the art of tentmaking, and
easily gained a maintenance by this handicraft wherever he
went, on account of the mode of travelling in the East and
the manifold occasions on which tents were used" (Neander,
Planting, I. 181).—**Night and day.** This shows how hard they
had to work.—**That we might not burden any of you** (2:6).
This was to maintain their independence, and to ward off
any imputation of selfish motive (Phil. 4:10–18). At their
first coming to Thessalonica it could not have been expected
that any would contribute to their support, inasmuch as
they and their mission were unknown. Afterwards, though
many of their converts were working people (4:11; 2 Thess.
3:12), there were not wanting some able to give much (Acts
17:4). But even then Paul and his friends were divinely led to
persist in independence (2 Thess. 3:8), and were thereby
enabled to set their converts a salutary example. In this
they were helped by repeated contributions from their loving
friends in Philippi. But even as it is said our Lord wrought
no miracles for His own behoof, these apostles could thus

maintain themselves only by labor and toil night and day. (See Acts 20:34. So he worked at Ephesus, as at Corinth, 18:3.) It is good to have one's feet on earth, while the heart is with Christ at the Right Hand of God, and not to be exempt from the cares and duties of our fellow-men.—**We preached unto you the gospel of God.** This, not their support, was their object. It is a pathetic picture. Even helped by the Philippians, it needed night and day work to make for them a mere subsistence; yet they found time and opportunity to see so many and so different people, to proclaim the Gospel, to tell them so much about it, and to pay especial attention to each one.—Several words are translated *preach.* The word here used means *to publish,* to *proclaim like a herald.* Paul proclaimed the good news of God.

10. **Ye are witnesses, and God** (2:5). How much God knows of a preacher's preaching, which his hearers cannot know.—**Holily:** before God.—**Righteously:** in all relations and dealings with men.—**Unblameably:** without any fault which those without could take hold of, if they knew it. Paul here utters the confident testimony of his own conscience. And he shows what the ideal and life of a Christian must be, in order that he may do the work of God.—**Toward you that believe.** Holiness, righteousness and blamelessness marked their behavior towards each other, *in the Church,* and were not merely a face they turned towards those without.

11. **As ye know.** He here appeals to the recollection of each one of them, calling to mind all that had passed between Paul, or his companions, and them.—**How we dealt with each one of you** (Col. 1:28). The work of Christ cannot be fulfilled in dealing with the congregation as a whole, but must be done with each member of it. A true pastor must adapt

his teaching to the want of each, and like the Good Shepherd must go after the *one* until he find it. Here is the example of Seelsorge, the responsibility for, and service of, each member of the flock. We are too much tempted to think the success of a pastor lies in the increase of the numbers and the corporate wellbeing of his congregation. The old Lutheran custom of personal confession of sin and private absolution afforded an opportunity which nothing else supplies.—**As a father with his own children.** Only after they had been won and instructed and arranged in a congregation, could the Thessalonians have recognized authority in Paul. But he did not lord it over God's heritage. The tie between them was that of affection. Without assumption, yearning over them, he admonished them as a father. "It is remarked by the commentators from St. Chrysostom downwards, that when the apostle wishes to dwell on his tenderness and affection for his converts he uses the figure of a mother; while here, where he is dwelling on his teaching and advice, he adopts that of a father as more appropriate. 'A nurse cherishes the little ones,' says Pelagius, 'but a father instructs those who are growing up' " (Lightfoot).—**Exhorting and encouraging.** (See 2:3; Phil. 2:1.)—**And testifying.** He also besought (Tyndale), adjured (Rheims), charged (Authorized Version) them (Eph. 4:17; John 3:11, 26, 28).

12. His exhortation and encouragement, and, finally, his solemn and urgent charge to them in the sight of God and in view of the Gospel, was **to the end,** etc. (See 4:1.)—**Who calleth you.** He speaks of God's call as present and continuous. God even now is calling us (Rom. 8:29, 30).

13. And for this cause we also thank God without ceasing, that, when ye received from us the word of the message, *even*

the word of God, ye accepted *it* not *as* the word of men, but, as it is in truth, the word of God, which also worketh in you that believe.

13. Perhaps Paul here means to resume the thought of 1:2.—**We thank God** (Phil. 1:3; Col. 1:12).—**Without ceasing.** Working, preaching, giving thanks, praying without ceasing, how busy must the heart of Paul have been.—**The word of the message.** The original is *the word of hearing.* (See Rom. 10:16; Hebr. 4:2.) It is not probable that at that early date the apostles brought a written gospel with them. Thus Mark is said to have written his gospel to preserve the stories of our Lord which he often had heard St. Peter tell. But this word, which Paul and his associates told, he expressly declares to have been a **word of God.—Which worketh,** etc. (Col. 1:29; Phil. 2:13; James 1:18, 21). This word of God is His Revelation in our Lord Jesus Christ. It is a seed; it is spirit; it is life. Paul states a fact here. He explains that which is going on in them and is being wrought through them: it is the natural operation of the word of God. He shows also the essential nature of that word: in those who believe, it *works.* "The word received into the ears, the word appropriated in the heart, the word fructifying in good works—these are the stages which the apostle here expresses" (Lightfoot).

14–16. For ye, brethren, became imitators of the churches of God which are in Judæa in Christ Jesus: for ye also suffered the same things of your own countrymen, even as they did of the Jews; who both killed the Lord Jesus and the prophets, and drave out us, and please not God, and are contrary to all men; forbidding us to speak to the Gentiles that they may be saved; to fill up their sins alway: but the wrath is come upon them to the uttermost.

14. **For.** He proceeds to give proof that the word of God works in them. These are, then, tests of the operation of the word of God, as well as of our election (1:5). Such a proof is found in their prompt imitation of the churches (1:6) in Judæa, viz.: in patiently enduring persecution for Christ's sake at the hands of their own countrymen.—**Of your own countrymen.** *Their* countrymen are contrasted with the *Jewish* persecutors of the churches in Judæa. The Christians of Thessalonica were some of Jewish and some of Gentile blood; and they were cast out by both Jew and Gentile. (See Acts 17.) Observe that *the Churches of God in Judæa* are spoken of in the plural. (See 1:1.) The several Christian congregations of one province, and of one race and tongue, are not spoken of as one organization.

15. **And drave out us** (Acts 8:1).—**Are contrary to all men.** Paul may here adopt the current criticism of the Jews (Tacitus, Hist. V. 3; Juvenal, XIV. 103, 104; Philostratus, Vit. Apoll. Tyan. V. 33; Diod. Sic. XXXIV. 1), but explains his meaning in the next verse.

16. Though they would not accept the Gospel, they still forbade the publication of it to others (Acts 17:13).—**To fill up.** (See Gen. 15:16.) **The wrath,** etc. As they always were filling up their sins, so the wrath of God, which broke upon them so often in the course of their history, is coming to the end. "The article, 'the' wrath, shows that it was long ago due and predetermined and predicted" (Chrysostom). "It had reached its extreme bound, and would at once pass into inflictive judgments" (Eadie). This is a prophecy of the destruction of Jerusalem and of the dispersion of the Jews. Doubtless Paul knew our Lord's prophecy of that event, and he could easily infer this issue of their final rejection of the

Messiah and of the violence they showed daily.

17–18. But we, brethren, being bereaved of you for a short season, in presence, not in heart, endeavoured the more exceedingly to see your face with great desire: because we would fain have come unto you, I Paul once and again; and Satan hindered us.

17. He speaks of his necessary separation from them as a **bereavement,** and declares that while he was at Athens, and even at Corinth, nevertheless his heart was with them at Thessalonica. This does not say, that he was not "in heart" at Corinth, too; though there can be no doubt that he felt a peculiar affection for his Macedonian converts.

18. He uses the singular here, because Silas and Timothy had been with them longer, while he had tried to come to them, and had not been able.—**Once and again; and Satan hindered us.** "What sayest thou? does Satan hinder? Yes, truly, for this was not the work of God. For in the Epistle to the Romans he says that God hindered him (Rom. 15:22); and elsewhere Luke says that 'the Spirit' hindered him from going into Asia (Acts 16:7). And in the Epistle to the Corinthians he says, that it is the work of the Spirit, but here only of Satan. But what hindrance of Satan is he speaking of? Some unexpected and violent temptations: for a plot, it says, being formed against him by the Jews, he was detained three months in Greece" (Chrysostom)—To **hinder** is *to throw obstacles in the way of.* It is idle to speculate as to the obstacles that prevented St. Paul's return to Thessalonica at that time. We observe that he does not hesitate to ascribe those hindrances to the operation of a personal devil (2 Cor. 4:4), and this literally. "Satan acts through bad men" (Bengel). F. D. Maurice says in a letter to Dr. Hort (Life, II. 21): "You

think you do not find a distinct recognition of the devil's personality in my books. I am sorry if it is so. I am afraid I have been corrupted by speaking to a polite congregation. I do agree with my very dear friend, Charles Kingsley, and admire him for the boldness with which he has said that the devil is shamming dead, but that he never was busier than now. I do not know what he is by theological arguments, but I know by what I feel. I am sure there is one near me accusing God and my brethren to me. He is not myself; I should go mad if I thought he was. He is near my neighbors; I am sure he is not identical with my neighbors. I must hate them if I believed he was. But, oh! most of all, I am horror-struck at the thought that we may confound him with God; the perfect darkness with the perfect light. I dare not deny that it is an evil will that tempts me; else I should begin to think evil is in God's creation, and is not the revolt from God resistance to Him? If he is an evil will, he must, I think, be a person. The Word upholds his existence, not his evil. That is in himself; that is the mysterious, awful possibility implied in his being a will. I need scarcely say that I do not mean by this acknowledgment of an evil spirit that I acknowledge a *material* devil. But does any one?"—Luther was not unlike Paul in ascribing hindrances to the evil one.

19–20. For what is our hope, or joy, or crown of glorying? Are not even ye, before our Lord Jesus at his coming? For ye are our glory and our joy.

19. Paul was at Corinth when he wrote this, near to the place where the Isthmian Games were celebrated. The victor in those games received a chaplet. So were the Thessalonians and others won by his Gospel, the reward of his conflict (2:2). The expression is found in the Septuagint (Prov. 16:31;

Ez. 16:17; 23:42).—**Even ye.** Also ye; for Paul is careful not to exclude his other converts (so Chrysostom).—**Before our Lord Jesus Christ at his coming.** If Paul looked at the Isthmian Games, or perhaps looked at a victor in those games, crowned, rejoicing and applauded, it must have been with deep wonder, and also with deep scorn in his heart (1 Cor. 9:25). With that award he compared the worth of the conflict in which he was a wrestler, the Great Judge who would award *his* prize, and the concourse of the Day of Judgment!

21

1 Thessalonians 3

1–2. Wherefore when we could no longer forbear, we thought it good to be left behind at Athens alone; and sent Timothy, our brother and God's minister in the gospel of Christ, to establish you, and to comfort *you* concerning your faith;

1. Unable to go to them, but unable to overcome his solicitude, he preferred to send Timothy to them, and to be left at Athens alone. Acts 17:14, we are told that Silas and Timothy remained at Berœa, when Paul was hurried to Athens; and from Athens he directed them to come to him with all speed. Acts 18:5, Silas and Timothy are said to have come to him from Macedonia after he had arrived at Corinth. As in Acts 17:16 he is said to have waited for them at Athens, it seems probable that Timothy alone joined him there, and Paul, because of his solicitude for the Thessalonians, at once sent him to Thessalonica. Then Silas and Timothy together came to him at Corinth. Paul's words show that at Athens he felt his loneliness.

2. **Timothy, our brother.** (See on Col. 1:1.) Phil. 2:20,

22. Timothy is not here called an apostle.—**God's minister;** i.e. *Servant;* the same word which is translated *deacon.* This passage has undergone much correction at the hands of copyists, many MSS. reading *Fellow-worker with God* (1 Cor. 3:9). Both terms indicate for Timothy a relation of direct service of God.—**In the gospel of Christ.** This shows the sphere of Timothy's service. The Gospel is conceived as including the whole work of *Missions,* by which the good news of salvation through Christ was being spread.—**To establish you,** etc. This was his object in sending Timothy, not merely to get word from them. He was solicitous lest their faith might prove not sufficiently instructed to bear affliction (3:3, 10)—**And comfort.** Timothy was sent to encourage their faith by the instruction of the Holy Ghost (2:3).

3–4. That no man be moved by these afflictions; for yourselves know that hereunto we are appointed. For verily, when we were with you, we told you beforehand that we are to suffer affliction; even as it came to pass, and ye know.

3. **Moved.** That no one be *disturbed* (Chrysostom and Theophylact); but Lightfoot: "Drawn aside and allured by the prospect of an easier life." He then translates, *In* these afflictions.)—**By these afflictions;** i.e. by the sufferings which come upon them because of their faith in Christ (2:14).—To this **we are appointed** (2 Tim. 3:12; Matt. 10:34–39).

4. **We told you before.** Paul had made plain to them that the confession of Christ would bring persecution. "The language employed had often been used to the Thessalonian converts; St. Paul had dwelt on this topic" (Lightfoot). Acts 14:22. They had counted the cost.

5. For this cause I also, when I could no longer forbear, sent

that I might know your faith, lest by any means the tempter
had tempted you, and our labour should be in vain.

5. Here we see the reason of his anxiety. Every convert
he won, thenceforth lay upon his heart.—**In vain.** Had they
yielded to persecution, his work among them would have
been fruitless (Gal. 2:2: Phil. 2:16; 2 Cor. 6:1; Septuagint:
Isai. 29:8; 65:23; 45:18; Jer. 6:29; 18:15; 51:35; Job 39:16;
Mic. 1:14; Hab. 2:3).

6–10. But when Timothy came even now unto us from you,
and brought us glad tidings of your faith and love, and that
ye have good remembrance of us always, longing to see us,
even as we also *to see* you; for this cause, brethren, we were
comforted over you in all our distress and affliction through
your faith: for now we live, if ye stand fast in the Lord. For
what thanksgiving can we render again unto God for you, for
all the joy wherewith we joy for your sakes before our God;
night and day praying exceedingly that we may see your face,
and may perfect that which is lacking in your faith?

6. **Even now.** This letter must have been written promptly
on Timothy's coming.—**Brought us glad tidings.**—The
same term elsewhere used for the proclamation of the "good
tidings of great joy." The glad tidings of Timothy to Paul were
I that their faith was standing the trial; (2.) that they showed
love to one another (Gal. 5:6); (3) that they remembered Paul
and were as eager to see him as he was to see them. This is
good news from redeemed men, answering to the good news
of God's redemption.

7. Therefore **were we comforted.** The word is the same
as that employed in 3:3. The tidings that their faith was
unshaken wrought for him the very comfort which he had
sent Timothy to give to them.—**In all our distress and**

316

affliction. "Some outward trial and affliction under which the apostle was then suffering" (Ellicott). Just at this time Paul was opposed by the Jews at Corinth and was "constrained by the word to testify" to them (Acts 18:5–10). His life at Corinth was marked by want and trial. The news of the progress of the Gospel in the hearts of his Thessalonians was a comfort to him.

8. The comfort and reward of a faithful pastor. No earthly gifts can console him, if his people flinch in the hour of trial or have the name of godliness without its power. (See Phil. 1:27; 4:1; Gal. 5:1.)

9. He rejoices in them **before God;** and again gives thanks for that joy. We see a glimpse of the hidden life of Paul before his God.

10. (Cf. 2:9, 13.) He prays night and day, (1) to see them again, and (2) to complete what is lacking in their faith. The word here used for "complete" sometimes is applied to military and naval preparation, "as of manning a fleet, of supplying an army with provisions" (Lightfoot).

11. Now may our God and Father himself, and our Lord Jesus, direct our way unto you:

11. Here, says Athanasius (Agt. the Arians, III. 11), Paul "guards the unity of the Father and the Son." He prays to the Father and the Son. He expects the answer from the Father and the Son.—**Direct our way.** It was the especial guidance of the Spirit of Jesus that had brought Paul to Europe and Thessalonica; and he could trust He would bring him to them again (Acts 16:6–10). God's providence in the past encourages us to believe that He will not leave us in uncertainty concerning duty in any case.

12–13. And the Lord make you to increase and abound

in love one toward another, and toward all men, even as we also *do* toward you; to the end he may stablish your hearts unblameable in holiness before our God and Father, at the coming of our Lord Jesus with all his saints.

12. He prays that the same love which he has for them may be made to increase and abound among them to each other, and to all men. Christian love goes out not to those only to whom we are indebted for a benefit, but to all our fellows, and overflows upon all men (2 Peter 1:7). The Thessalonians had shown such love in their prompt spread of the Gospel.

13. The *means* of their establishment in holiness is the growth of their Christian love. He wishes them to be blameless before God at the coming of Jesus (2:20; 4:13).—**With all his saints,** i.e. His holy angels and the spirits of just men made perfect (2 Thess. 1:7; Matt. 25:31; Hebr. 12:23. Also Ps. 89:5; Zech. 14:5; Dan. 4:10; Matt. 13:41; Mark 8:38; Luke 9:26).

22

1 Thessalonians 4

1–2. Finally then, brethren, we beseech and exhort you in the Lord Jesus, that, as ye received of us how ye ought to walk and to please God, even as ye do walk,—that ye abound more and more. For ye know what charge we gave you through the Lord Jesus.

1. **Finally.** (See Phil. 3:1; 4:8.) Marks the completion of the former part of the letter, and the transition to certain practical admonitions.—**We beseech and exhort.** He does not command; but, as one who has their heart, knowing that they have his, and in the mutual relations in which they stand **in the Lord Jesus,** he affectionately *asks* them.—**Exhort.** The same word translated *comfort* in 3:2, 7. (See on 2:3.) The "comfort" of the Holy Ghost is the "medium" of all Christian intercourse, like the hypothetical ether, whose vibrations in the natural world transmit light and heat.—**As ye received of us.** They not only had heard his instruction on this point, but had *accepted* it.—**To walk** (2:12; 1 John 2:6). The life of a Christian ought to put Christian principle into action, continuously, before the eyes of men.—**And please God;** so

as to please God.—**That ye abound more and more.** He
owns that they have heeded his precepts. But the Christian
life should also be a *progress.* Perfection is not to be looked for
in its beginning; imperfection and immaturity do not destroy
the title to the name of *Christian;* but a Christian cannot rest
in any degree of imperfection or immaturity.

2. **What charge we gave you:** i.e. What *precepts of
life.* It is evident that besides proclaiming the Gospel, the
apostle taught what manner of life accorded with it and
was pleasing to God. These precepts he gave them **through
the Lord Jesus** The substance of them was from Him, and
was solemnly imparted in virtue of the duty and authority
which belonged to Paul as Christ's messenger. The following
instance (ver. 6) shows that the apostle had criticised faults
of social life, in the name of the Lord. (See 4:11; 2 Thess. 3:4,
6, 10, 12.)

3–8. For this is the will of God, *even* your sanctification,
that ye abstain from fornication; that each one of you know
how to possess himself of his own vessel in sanctification
and honour, not in the passion of lust, even as the Gentiles
which know not God; that no man transgress, and wrong
his brother in the matter: because the Lord is an avenger
in all these things, as also we forewarned you and testified.
For God called us not for uncleanness, but in sanctification.
Therefore he that rejecteth, rejecteth not man, but God, who
giveth his Holy Spirit unto you.

3. **Even your sanctification:** i.e. God wishes and
intends your progress unto holiness. With this the laxity,
the uncleanness, the indecency, which the heathen allowed
and encouraged, was in conflict. Paul, in the name of Jesus,
forbade fornication (Acts 15:20). ("Speaking of the decay of

320

the Athenian people, Mr. Francis Galton says: 'We know, and may guess something more, of the reason why this marvellously-gifted race declined. Social morality grew exceedingly lax; marriage became unfashionable and was avoided; many of the more ambitious and accomplished women were avowed courtesans, and the mothers of the incoming population were of a heterogeneous class.' The same state of popular feeling with respect to marriage prevailed during the decline of the Roman Empire."—Kidd, Social Evolution, 316, n.)

4. The word translated **possess** means *acquire.*—**His own vessel** means *his own wife* (1 Peter 3:7). This passage may therefore be taken as a sanction of Christian marriage, and an injunction to marry instead of yielding to the common impurity of their time (1 Cor. 7:9). In contrast with the looseness of family life among the heathen, both then and now, a Christian is to form and maintain a home. He is urged to personal purity, to temperance, to respect for the restraints of law, and for the needs and rights of others. (Christian marriage rites are mentioned by Ignatius, ad Polyc. 5, and Tertullian, de Monogamia, 11; ad Uxorem, II., VIII.)

5. The knowledge of God produces an entirely different conception of the world and of life, and transports into a different sphere of moral ideas.

6. **In the matter.** This shows that, although *covetousness* and *uncleanness* are elsewhere ranged together by the apostle (Rom. 1:29; 1 Cor. 5:10; 6:10; Eph. 5:3, 5; Col. 3:5), he here refers to the same general subject that occupies the preceding verses. There he forbade uncleanness of life, and commanded the sanctification of a Christian's own home. Here he forbids adultery, the invasion and destruction of a brother's—i.e. a

neighbor's—home. He wrote from Corinth, a city proverbial
for its uncleanness of manners.—**The Lord is an avenger,**
etc. In those relations which are hidden in our homes, and
never are brought before human tribunals or told to any one,
the Lord sees, sifts and judges. He who forms the tie of man
and wife watches over it.

7. (See 4:3; 5:23.) "Holiness is to be the pervading element
in which the Christian is to move" (Lightfoot).

8. To reject these injunctions is to reject God, the Giver of
the Holy Spirit, whose "gifts" they enjoy, whose life animates
them, who makes them one.

9–10. But concerning love of the brethren ye have no need
that one write unto you: for ye yourselves are taught of God
to love one another; for indeed ye do it toward all the brethren
which are in all Macedonia. But we exhort you, brethren,
that ye abound more and more;

9. **Ye have no need.** Really an emphatic form of speech
(Philem. 19). "The thing is so necessary as not to require
instruction. For things that are very important are manifest
to all. By saying this he makes them more ashamed than if
he had admonished them" (Chrysostom).—**For,** etc. The love
of God shed abroad in their hearts taught them to love one
another. **Taught of God** (John, 6:45).

10. (3:6; 4:1.) "It is probable that in the interval between St.
Paul's departure from Macedonia and the writing of this letter
other Christian communities were established, at least in the
larger towns, such as Amphipolis, Pella, etc., either by the
instrumentality of the more active of his recent Macedonian
converts, or by the missionaries of his own sending, such
as Luke, Silvanus and Timotheus, all of whom seem to have
been actively engaged in Macedonia during this interval"

322

(Lightfoot).

11–12. And that ye study to be quiet, and to do your own business, and to work with your hands, even as we charged you; that ye may walk honestly toward them that are without, and may have need of nothing.

11. The Thessalonians were excited by the hope of the coming again of the Lord, and were tempted to lay aside their usual avocations, and spend their time in idle discussion. "A restless, meddling and practically idle spirit exposed them to the comments of those without" (Ellicott). Perhaps the great charity of some encouraged the idleness of others. Paul exhorts them to *set their ambition* on *being quiet,* attending to their own business, and working for their living. These symptoms of unrest, fanaticism and idleness had appeared while he was yet with them, and he had *charged* them on the subject. It is evident that *to follow Christ* does not require us to give up daily work, nor does it justify us in becoming busy bodies in other men's matters.

12. As a sufficient reason for this advice Paul instances (1) their reputation among **those without,** and (2) their duty to maintain their independence, as, in his own case, he had set them an example (2:9). A Christian should walk unblameably (2:10), and thereby may glorify the name of Christ (Matt. 5:13–16; 1 Tim. 3:7). But he may not make public opinion his rule of life (Matt. 5:11; 23:28.—**Of nothing.** This *may* be translated, *may have need of no man.* In both cases it enforces the duty of self-support, independence. If the Thessalonians had stopped working, they soon would have become a burden on the alms of the community and put the name of Christ to shame. On the other hand, they should work, to have to give to those who were in need (Eph. 4:28). This explodes the

theory of the sanctity of voluntary poverty, so praised by the
Mendicant Friars before the Reformation. "Let us therefore
renounce our parents, and kinsmen, and friends, and wife,
and children, and possessions, and all the enjoyments of life,
when any of these things become an impediment to piety"
(Const. App. V. 1, 5).

13–18. But we would not have you ignorant, brethren,
concerning them that fall asleep; that ye sorrow not, even
as the rest, which have no hope. For if we believe that Jesus
died and rose again, even so them also that are fallen asleep
in Jesus will God bring with him. For this we say unto you by
the word of the Lord, that we that are alive, that are left unto
the coming of the Lord, shall in no wise precede them that
are fallen asleep. For the Lord himself shall descend from
heaven, with a shout, with the voice of the archangel, and
with the trump of God: and the dead in Christ shall rise first:
then we that are alive, that are left, shall together with them
be caught up in the clouds, to meet the Lord in the air: and
so shall we ever be with the Lord. Wherefore comfort one
another with these words.

13. **But.** Although he has thus enjoined them to work
quietly among those who expected no coming of the Lord,
he will not leave the question which troubled their excited
hearts unanswered. They were distressed, lest those who had
died among them would have no part in the glories of Christ's
coming. (Lightfoot refers to a similar question in Clem. Rec.
I. 52, and says, "It is not necessary to suppose any lengthened
existence of the Church of Thessalonica at the time when this
letter was written, in order to account for this difficulty. If
only one or two of the converts had died in the meanwhile, it
was sufficient to give rise to this question.")—**Them that fall**

asleep. (Lightfoot: *Them that are lying asleep.*) Death is called a sleep, because from it we shall awake (Matt. 9:23).—**Even as the rest** (5:6; Eph. 2:3).—**Which have no hope.** Ancient literature and the inscriptions on ancient tombs show that they had no hope of an awakening.

14. **If we believe,** etc. "Observe that he says not, If you believe that Christ hath fallen asleep; but makes it harder with Christ's death than with ours, saying, If we believe that Christ *died;* while of us he says, not that we die, but that we *sleep.* Our death he calls not death but sleep; and Christ's death he calls a real death. So he ascribes to the death of Christ such power that in comparison with it ours is but a sleep. For this is the right way to comfort, viz., to snatch out of sight the death we suffer and to look only at the death of Christ. Paul as much as says with these words, Why do you think much of your death; look at Him who really is dead, in comparison with whom all others are not dead. If we would grieve let us grieve for the death of Christ. That is to be called a real death, not alone because it was so bitter, shameful and great, but also because it was so powerful that it baptized all the rest of the dead, so that henceforth they are to be called not *dead,* but *asleep.* He always leads our heart (because He cannot so lead our eyes) away from that which the eyes look on, to that which God says, and to Christ, that we may not at all doubt that He will bring us with Christ" (Luther).—**That are fallen asleep in Jesus.** The Greek has "through" Jesus, and seems to imply that through Him death has become a sleep. This verse is significant as one of the earliest recorded declarations of Christian faith, (1) in the resurrection of our Lord, and (2) that all those who sleep through Him shall live with Him. "Almighty God Himself will raise us up through

our Lord Jesus Christ, according to His infallible promise, and grant us a resurrection with all those that have slept from the beginning of the world; and we shall then be such as we now are in our present form, without any defect or corruption. For we shall rise incorruptible; whether we die at sea, or are scattered on the earth, or are torn to pieces by wild beasts and birds, He will raise us up by His own power, for the whole world is held together by the hand of God" (Const. App. V. 1, 7).

15. Paul proceeds to answer their question. His solemn appeal to **a word of the Lord,** and the carefulness with which on certain other occasions he tells that he is giving *his own judgment* (1 Cor. 7:25, 40), establish the fact that he received from God special revelations to guide him in his duty and teaching (Gal. 1:12; 2:2; Eph. 3:2; 2 Cor. 12:1). The Holy Scriptures of the New Testament as well as the Scriptures of the Old Testament (2 Peter 1:21; 2 Tim. 3:16) are a record of revelations from God. Paul's inspiration, however, must be defined as he defined it. In this verse he seems to include himself among those who would be alive and be left unto the coming of the Lord, and certainly did not know he would be among those "asleep in Jesus." Though the Lord enabled him to know what was essential for him to know for the well-being of the Church, He did not give him a full prevision of all that would befall him (Phil. 1:25. See 2 Kings 4:27). Neither were he and the other apostles raised above the need of exercising their conscience, reason and judgment.—**That remain.** He thus qualifies the preceding words, so as not to assert that he will survive until the coming of the Lord. "St. Paul himself shared in that expectation (that their Lord would come again in that very generation),

but being under the guidance of the Spirit of truth, he did not deduce therefrom any erroneous practical conclusions" (Conybeare and Howson, 314. See Mark 13:32; 1 Cor. 15:51; 1 Thess. 5:1, 2; 2 Thess. 2:2; 2 Peter 3:8). "Here Paul shows how Christians should comfort themselves when a father, or a mother, or another dear one, dies. They should not think as heathen do; for these think that such an one is gone forever. But Christians should know that they will come again and hereafter will live with them again in a better life. For just as Christ is risen from the dead, so shall all Christians also rise again, and there will be no difference between those who died, whether one died before or after the other. Such a hope should not only lessen our grief for those who are dead, and keep us from despondency, but also should make death soft and easy to us who remain" (Veit Dietrich). This verse is Paul's direct answer to the question of the Thessalonians, which they seem to have debated among themselves.

16. **The Lord himself shall descend.** (Acts 1:11.)—**With a shout.** The victorious cry summoning the dead to life (John 11:43). "Used of a cry addressed to a multitude" (Bengel).—**The voice of the archangel.** (Cf. Matt. 24:31; 25:31; 2 Thess. 1:7.)—**And with the trump of God.** Compare the sound of the trumpet on Sinai, Ex. 19:16. Among the Jews the New Moon that ushered in the seventh month was called the Feast of Trumpets. The seventh month of every year was intended to repeat, intensify and explicate the thought presented in the Sabbath day: the Feast of Trumpets declared the Last Judgment, the Day of Atonement showed the need of repentance and promised the Sacrifice once for all, and the Feast of Tabernacles prefigured the joyous harvest home, when God shall gather His wheat into the garner. The year of

Jubilee also began with a progress of the priests throughout the land, blowing trumpets. Its characteristic thought was the homecoming of every one, the Sabbath of the world (Numb. 10:2; 31:6; Joel 2:1).

17. He states *the order* of that great event: (1) the resurrection of those fallen asleep in Christ, (2) the change of those still living upon earth at that time (1 Cor. 15:51); and (3) that both alike shall be taken to dwell with the Lord forever.—**The dead in Christ.** He is not speaking here of the general resurrection, but particularly of those who had fallen asleep in Christ. These remain *in Christ,* though they have passed from our sight.

18. Here is material of comfort. But we are to comfort one another with **these words** of the Lord.

23

1 Thessalonians 5

1–3. But concerning the times and the seasons, brethren, ye have no need that aught be written unto you. For yourselves know perfectly that the day of the Lord so cometh as a thief in the night. When they are saying, Peace and safety, then sudden destruction cometh upon them, as travail upon a woman with child; and they shall in no wise escape.

1. **The times and the seasons.** *The times* is a general term; *the seasons* is definite, meaning "the right or fitting time." Lightfoot says, " 'Times' points to the *date;* while 'seasons' refers to the occurrences which will mark the occasion, the signs by which its approach will be ushered in" (Matt. 16:3).—Ye have no need. (See 4:9.) He had told them before that the Lord had said they were not to know just when He will come again (Matt. 24:4, 42; Acts 1:7).

2. Matt. 24:43; Luke 12:39; 2 Peter 3:10; Rev. 3:3; 16:15.—**Day of the Lord.** Many MSS. omit the article before *day. Day of the Lord* is a technical term in the Hebrew prophets for the revelation of God's just judgment (Isai. 2:12; Jer. 46:10; Ezek. 7:10; 13:5; Joel 1:15; 2:11; 3:14; Zeph. 1:14:

Mal. 4:5). Paul may here remind them of a "general law" of such final judgments on nations and systems of corruption which God has tolerated with much longsuffering: Ye know perfectly that a day of the Lord comes suddenly, unexpectedly, without announcement, stealthily, **like a thief in the night.** Paul's words seem to imply (1) their knowledge of the Old Testament Scriptures, and (2) their familiarity with our Lord's declarations on the subject.

3. **When they are saying** (Ezek. 13:10, 16; Matt. 24:36–39; Luke 17:26–30).—**Sudden destruction** (Luke 21:34, 36). Such it will be to those who look not for it. The point is, its suddenness, and the utter impossibility of escaping it.—**As travail.** (See Ps. 48:6; Jer. 6:24.)

4–11. But ye, brethren, are not in darkness, that that day should overtake you as a thief: for ye are all sons of light, and sons of the day: we are not of the night, nor of darkness; so then let us not sleep, as do the rest, but let us watch and be sober. For they that sleep sleep in the night; and they that be drunken are drunken in the night. But let us, since we are of the day, be sober, putting on the breastplate of faith and love; and for a helmet, the hope of salvation. For God appointed us not unto wrath, but unto the obtaining of salvation through our Lord Jesus Christ, who died for us, that, whether we wake or sleep, we should live together with him. Wherefore exhort one another, and build each other up, even as also ye do.

4. **As a thief.** Christians will not be taken at unawares, because they always are heeding our Lord's injunction *to watch* (Luke 21:36). Some MSS. read **thieves;** as if Paul meant to liken ungodly and unbelieving men to those doing evil in the dark, and revealed at their mischief by sudden light.

5. 1 John 1:5–7; Eph. 5:8–11; John 3:19–21; 12:36; Luke

16:8. (Cf. Luke 1:78; 2:32.)

6. **Let us not sleep.** Let us neither remain unconcerned and unprepared, nor pass our time in levity and carousing. But let us be awake and watching, "with all our senses and capacities in full exercise" (Ellicott). "It is in our power always to have it day" (Chrysostom).

8. The figure of an earnest soldier, arming himself for battle, with full preparedness of soul, not with the light eagerness of one untried. (See Rom. 13:12, 13).—**Putting on.** Isai. 59:17: Putting on the armor of God. The figure is expanded, Eph. 6:10–17. (See also Rom. 13:12; 2 Cor. 10:4.) The armor consists of Faith, Love and Hope. (See 1:3.) Faith and Love are the breastplate, or coat of mail, corresponding to God's righteousness. Faith lays hold on the righteousness of God. The Christian wears the righteousness which is from God by faith (Phil. 3:9). Faith works through love (Gal. 5:6). God's helmet is salvation. We put on a hope of salvation. This is our crest.

9. This is our warrant for thus putting on the armor of God. God intends that we shall **obtain** salvation through our Lord Jesus Christ.

10. **Who died for us.** (See on Col. 1:20.) Our salvation is founded on the *death* of Jesus Christ *for us.* As our future life is assured by His resurrection (4:14), so our deliverance has been wrought by His death. (See 1:10.) Paul had taught the Thessalonians the doctrine of Christ's atonement for our sins.—**Whether we wake or sleep.** This is said with reference to the question of 4:13–17.

11. **Wherefore.** Because of this assurance of salvation.—**Exhort** (2:3; 3; 2).—**Each other.** *Each* is here urged to encourage and build up his fellows singly.—**Build up** (Eph.

2:20; 1 Cor. 3:9, 16; 8:1; 10:23; 2 Cor. 6:16). *Edification*
is proposed, the edification of each one, rather than "the
building-up" of the congregation in numbers and influence.
And this is made a duty of each and all. "The full meaning is,
'build one another up that you may all together grow into a
temple of God'" (Conybeare and Howson).

12–13. But we beseech you, brethren, to know them
that labour among you, and are over you in the Lord, and
admonish you; and to esteem them exceeding highly in love
for their work's sake. Be at peace among yourselves.

12. (See Eph. 4:11; 1 Tim. 5:17.) At this early period the
Church at Thessalonica had *officers:* persons who presided
over them, labored among them, and admonished them.
There were several who shared this office of oversight
and responsibility, as at Philippi (Phil. 1:1); there was not
one bishop only. (See also Acts 11:30; 14:23; Eph. 4:11.)
They presided in their common worship. (See Justin's First
Apology, LXV.: "There is then brought to the president (or
to that one of the brethren who is presiding) bread and a
cup of wine mingled with water; and he, taking them, gives
praise and glory to the Father of the universe, through the
name of the Son and of the Holy Ghost, and offers thanks at
considerable length for our being created worthy to receive
these things at His hands. And when he has concluded
the prayers and the thanksgivings, all the people present
express their assent by saying Amen.") They also conducted
their common affairs "in the Lord." They **laboured** among
them: the word showing that their office demanded toil
and weariness. (Polycarp, in his letter to the Philippians,
VI., besides speaking of the necessary moral qualifications
of such officers, says: "Let the presbyters be compassionate

and merciful to all, bringing back those that wander, visiting all the sick, and not neglecting the widow, the orphan or the poor.") And, besides, it was their office to **admonish** by word each according to his need. These presidents or presbyters did not lay down their ordinary avocations, and live upon the contributions of the Church. "The bishops and presbyters of those early days kept banks, practised medicine, wrought as silversmiths, tended sheep, or sold their goods in open market" (Hatch). (See Socrates, History, 1:12; 7:28; Greg., M. Ep. 13:26; Basil, Ep. 198; Epiphanius, Heresies, 80:6.) The apostles found it necessary from the beginning to appoint such responsible officers in every congregation (1 Ep. of Clement, XLIV.). Those who had been newly won to the Gospel needed to be held in fellowship with their brethren, and to be edified by further instruction and pastoral care. So do old established congregations need the continual service of the Christian ministry. They need not only the offices of ministering love, but the admonition of the Word. Paul exhorts the Thessalonians to **know** those thus laboring among them; i.e. to appreciate and acknowledge them. We may infer that this admonition was needed. Some were disorderly (5:14; 2 Thess. 3:6). In the next generation, St. Clement wrote a letter to the Corinthians, who were inclined to displace a presbyter. The success of the ministry depends in great measure on the openness with which their admonition is received. Their work is laborious, responsible and of the highest worth.

13. They are to **esteem them in love.** The tie between them and the officers of their community is to be the common tie between all the members of the body of Christ, with especial recognition of their office.—**Be at peace**

333

among yourselves The Vulgate has *with them;* and so Luther translates it. There may have been a difference of opinion among the Thessalonians, which threatened division, some esteeming the presidents, some standing aloof. Paul intimates the danger, and the necessity of preserving the unity of the community.

14–18. And we exhort you, brethren, admonish the disorderly, encourage the fainthearted, support the weak, be longsuffering toward all. See that none render unto any one evil for evil; but alway follow after that which is good, one toward another, and toward all. Rejoice alway; pray without ceasing; in everything give thanks: for this is the will of God in Christ Jesus to you-ward.

14. He indicates the causes which may have occasioned the danger. Some have thought that here he specially addresses the presbyters (so Conybeare and Howson, who, however, add, "It must be admitted that many of the duties here enjoined are duties of all Christians"); but he continues to address those whom he has exhorted to maintain peace. There were among them some **disorderly** (Wiclif: "unpesible"; Tyndale: "unruly"; Rheims: "unquiet"); i.e. persons who were not willing to submit to the order established and acquiesced in by the others. "Such are not wanting even in the most flourishing Church" (Bengel). They would not "keep in line." They were to be **admonished** by their brethren. This means, that the rest were to speak to them, and show them how improper was their perversity. There were also **fainthearted** ones. (Ellicott: "Feeble-minded, unduly anxious and sorrowful about the state of those that were fallen asleep.) Septuagint: Isai. 57:15; Eccles. 7:10; Prov. 18:14. Such they were to **encourage** (2:11). And some were

334

weak (Rom. 4:19; 14:1, 2; 1 Cor. 8:7, 10; 9:22; 11:30). It may mean that some among them were as yet very imperfect, and therefore unstable against either temptation or persecution; and Paul exhorts the rest not to abandon such, or to despise them, but to keep near them and support their wavering faith. They were *to lift them up* (Cranmer.) The word here used is in other passages translated *hold to* (Matt. 6:24; Luke 16:13; Titus. 1:9).—**Be longsuffering towards all.** The confessors of the truth might be tempted to despise the weak. Wiclif: "Have continual patience towards all men." "There is no one to whom longsuffering cannot be shown; no one to whom a believer ought not show it" (Bengel).

15. Some had to suffer wrong from others of their own number. But Rom. 12:17–19; 1 Peter 3:9. This injunction is enough for every Christian conscience.

16. **Rejoice alway** (Phil. 4:4).

17. **Pray without ceasing** (2:13; 3:10; Eph. 6:18; Col. 4:2). A man may pray while engaged in his work. Paul does not mean that we should continually be saying words of prayer, but that we should always live in the presence of God, so that at any moment we can lift up our hearts and speak our thought into His ear (Ps. 34:15).

18. **In everything give thanks** (Phil. 4:6; Col. 1:3; 3:15; 2 Cor. 4:15; 9:11, 12). He describes the sphere of Christian worship, *always, without ceasing, in everything.* It is the will of God that His people should always live in praise and prayer. "The trades of the faithful are works by the by, but the worship of God is their great work" (Const. App. LXI.).

19–21. Quench not the Spirit; despise not prophesyings; prove all things; hold fast that which is good;

19. **Quench not the Spirit.** These letters of St. Paul admit

us into the varied life of the infant Church. There were not
only the offices of mutual love, and the labors of the elders,
but there was discontent too, threatening disorder; questions,
perplexities, conflicting counsels. Some at Thessalonica had
received special gifts of the Spirit (4:8). Others shrank from
these exhibitions, which sometimes led to disorder, perhaps
to deceit, and were not always edifying. (See 1 Cor. 14.)
They were tempted to resist and check the utterance of the
Spirit through themselves or others. Paul warns against this
extreme judgment.

20. **Despise not prophesyings.** "Like him who spake with
tongues, the prophet also uttered the speech of the Spirit
(Acts 19:6), but with his own consciousness wide awake, and
with reference to the congregation (1 Cor. 14:3, 4). What
he immediately received from the Lord was *revelation.* But
not simply revelation of the future (Acts 11:27; 21:10). The
spiritual gaze of the prophet penetrated the depths of the
soul (1 Cor. 14:25), the mind of the spirits (1 Tim. 1:18;
4:14), the real wants of the congregation (1 Cor. 14:3–5).
The peril of knowledge was obscurity (1 Cor. 8:1); the peril
of the gift of tongues lay in self-satisfaction and vanity; and
the peril of prophecy, in the temptation to go beyond the
basis of faith (Rom. 12:6). The prophet, who, inspired by
the faith, spoke forth from the fulness of life, built up the
life of the congregation in the faith (1 Cor. 12:3–5). The
three classes of spiritual gifts therefore correspond to the
three momenta around which the life of the congregation
is disposed, *doctrine,* moral common life or *fellowship,* and
cultus (Acts 2:42)" (Kahnis, Doct. of the Holy Ghost, 75).
"According to the classical usage, the meaning is that of
forthtelling rather than of *foretelling.* The Hebrew term

336

nabi originally signified nothing more, though the idea of prediction is more frequently associated with it. In the New Testament the notion of foretelling is kept in the background, rarely appearing (as in Acts 11:28) except in reference to the prophets of the Old Dispensation. When any of these words are used by St. Paul of the special gift of the Spirit, there is not the slightest allusion to the anticipation of future events. Prophecy is, in short, the impassioned and inspired utterance of the deep things of God" (Lightfoot). The rich use which the early Church, many of whose members had been recently won from heathenism, made of the Old Testament Scriptures, and the skill with which they interpreted them of Christ, leads to the conclusion that many of "the prophets" were inspired to expound these Scriptures and apply them. So Erasmus says on this passage, "Prophecy is the declaration of the secret, hidden meaning of the Scriptures." Doubtless the enthusiastic addresses of the prophets had had a part in begetting the unrest and expectation which had been reported to Paul, and which he had already rebuked (4:11). Notwithstanding, he does not give his sanction to a contempt for this extraordinary instruction.

21. If a usage proved not unto edification, they might discard it (1 Cor. 14:26–28). When the prophets poured forth their wonderful utterances, the rest were to *discern,* and not to accept everything that was said (1 Cor. 12:10; 14:29; 1 John 4:1). The discernment of spirits was a spiritual gift, as well as prophecy. All hearers should try by the Word of God what they are taught. "They should hear with understanding, and judge and try whether it agrees with the truth and the Spirit of God, who speaks in the Holy Scriptures" (Erasmus). "The simple fact of a preternatural inspiration is not enough

to establish the claims of a spirit to be heard. There are inspirations from below as well as from above (1 John 4:1).... The earliest Christian writers have preserved in connection with this injunction an alleged saying of our Lord, which has not been recorded in our gospels—Be ye approved money-changers" (Lightfoot). "See, here he will have no doctrine or proposition held, except it be tried by the congregation hearing it, and be by them approved. This 'proving' does not belong to the teachers, for they first must say what the others are to prove. So the judgment is taken from the teachers and given to the disciples among the Christians, so that among them it is just the opposite to the way of the world. In the world masters bid as they will, and those under them must receive it. But among you, says Christ, it shall not be so, but every one is the judge of the other, and again every one is subject to the other" (Luther).

22. Abstain from every form of evil.

22. He lays a direct responsibility on every conscience. They were to try the doctrine they received. They were not to allow themselves to be led into any kind of evil. This and the preceding verses are quoted by early Christian writers in direct connection with an alleged saying of our Lord—"Be skilful money-changers."

23–24. And the God of peace himself sanctify you wholly; and may your spirit and soul and body be preserved entire, without blame at the coming of our Lord Jesus Christ. Faithful is he that calleth you, who will also do it.

23. God is called **the God of peace,** in reference to the elements of discord which have just now been considered. 1 Cor. 14:33: *God is not a God of confusion, but of peace.* He gave those gifts in order to minister peace. They are to be received

and tried and used in the spirit of peace. On this verse Tertullian says (de res. Carnis, XLVII.): "Here you have the entire substance of man destined to salvation, and that at no other time than at the coming of the Lord, which is the key of the resurrection." The *spirit* of a man is that part of his being in which God enters into communion with him. The *soul* is his intellectual nature, including his feelings and impulses. (See on Phil. 1:27.) The apostle has had reason to admonish them with reference to the *body* (4:1–8); and also in reference to their life in fellowship with one another and before the eyes of those without; and again, as to the extraordinary manifestations of the Holy Spirit. As if summing all up, he prays that God may sanctify them wholly, and present them perfect and without blame, at the coming of the Lord.

24. 1 Cor. 1:9; Rom. 8:30; Phil. 1:6; 1 Peter 5:10. God's *call* brings an assurance of His *purpose*. It is a promise (1 Thess. 3:3). This may have been a "watchword" of the time.

25. Brethren, pray for us.

25. He desires their prayers (Col. 4:3). After having admonished them and prayed for them, he says, I also need *your* prayers. Deny them not to me.

26. Salute all the brethren with a holy kiss.

26. Rom. 16:16; 1 Cor. 16:20; 2 Cor. 13:12; 1 Peter 5:14; Tertullian, de Oratione, XVIII.; Justin, I. Ap. LXV. The *kiss* was an ordinary mode of friendly salutation, as it now is between women in some countries, and in some countries between men. In the Christian service of worship, before the administration of the Holy Supper, it was given by one to the other in token of mutual reconciliation and unclouded friendliness. Thus in the Const. App. II. 57: "Let the deacon say, Let no one have any quarrel against another; let no one

come in hypocrisy. Then let the men give the men, and the
women give the women, the Lord's kiss. But let no one do
it with deceit, as Judas betrayed the Lord with a kiss." The
custom is said to have continued in the Western Church until
the thirteenth century, and in the Coptic Church to this day.
The *Pax* in the Lutheran service is a memorial of this rite. St.
Paul here insists upon this entire mutual reconciliation in
all their assemblies for worship. However Christians may
differ from each other on matters of opinion, they should let
nothing come between their hearts (Matt. 5:23, 24). "Greet all
the brethren with the kiss, not with the kiss that is customary
among men, but with the pure, holy kiss that befits Christian
love" (Erasmus).

27. I adjure you by the Lord that this epistle be read unto
all the brethren.

27. This solemn adjuration seems to imply that there was
a possibility that some would think of excluding others from
direct communication with the apostle. Perhaps the *presidents*
may have been charged with shutting others out; perhaps
their friends may have kept apart from their critics; but Paul
requires that his letter should be read to every one. Like
our Lord's special direction that *all* should drink of the Cup,
this seems to witness against the Romish prohibition of the
Scriptures to the laity.

28. The grace of our Lord Jesus Christ be with you.

28. The *Salutation* and *Benediction.*

V

2 Thessalonians

ANNOTATIONS
ON THE
SECOND EPISTLE
TO THE THESSALONIANS

BY

EDWARD T. HORN, D. D.

24

Introduction

The messenger who took the First Epistle to the Thessalonians must have brought back word, that, while the Thessalonians were steadfast under persecution, some of the troubles Paul had referred to were more threatening than ever. Some of the believers still neglected their daily work and, idle, discussed trifles. A new question was debated—viz. whether the day of the Lord was not just at hand; and it is probable that some even alleged the authority of the apostle for their contention that the end of all things was so near that it was useless and foolish to continue in the ordinary occupations of earthly life. There were some also who were not at all prompt to yield to the injunctions of the former letter.

Therefore we observe in this letter a tone of positive commandment on the part of the apostle, beyond his manner in other letters. He insists on their submission to order. He emphasizes the example of daily work and consequent independence he had set them. He teaches that the day of the Lord is not just at hand, but that certain developments must be completed before it will come.

It was written while Silas and Timothy were with him. The condition of things at Thessalonica was not very different from that which occasioned the former epistle, and it exhibits the same line of thought. It was written after churches had begun to be in the neighborhood of Corinth (1:4), and in the midst of sufferings at the hands of Jews; probably in the beginning of a.d. 54.

25

2 Thessalonians 1

1–2. Paul, and Silvanus, and Timothy, unto the church of the Thessalonians in God our Father and the Lord Jesus Christ; Grace to you and peace from God the Father and the Lord Jesus Christ.

1. (See on 1 Thess. 1:1.)

2. The best MSS. read, *Our* Father. (See 2 Thess. 1:12. So 1 Cor. 1:3; 2 Cor. 1:2; Eph. 1:2; Phil. 1:2; Col. 1:2; Philem. 3.)—**Grace and peace.** (See on Col. 1:2.) Ellicott quotes Thomas Aquinas: "Grace is the source of every good thing; peace is the issue of all good things." Grace and peace come to us from the Lord Jesus Christ, who is here spoken of in the unity of the Father.

3. We are bound to give thanks to God alway for you, brethren, even as it is meet, for that your faith groweth exceedingly, and the love of each one of you all toward one another aboundeth;

3. (See 2:13; also Phil. 1:3: Col. 1:3.) The apostle here confesses that the thanksgiving which always rises when he thinks of his converts, is also a duty. "We may take it as a

settled principle, that in the communion of the Christian
with God, his petitions should always take the second place,
and thanksgiving the first. Many a sin is committed in *asking*
rather than *giving thanks*" (Frank, Hy. and Critique of Recent
Theology, 322).—**Alway.** It is not enough to acknowledge
each gift of God when it comes to us, but we should abide
in thankful praise of His grace. (See the Preface in the
Communion Service.)—**As it is meet,** etc. He proceeds to
give the special reasons which justify thanksgiving in this
instance. This is not flattery, but a proof of the prosperity
of the Church of the Thessalonians. Paul had commended
their love in his former letter (1 Thess. 1:3; 3:6; 4:9, 10),
and wished that it might abound more and more, and he has
now received information that their faith *groweth exceedingly,*
and the love of *each one toward one another aboundeth.* He
gives thanks that his prayers for them are heard. "The words
(*groweth,* etc., and *aboundeth*) are carefully chosen; the former
implying an internal, organic growth, as of a tree; the other a
diffusive, or expansive character, as of a flood irrigating the
land" (Lightfoot). There is in this letter abundant evidence
that the Thessalonian Christians still were imperfect; but
here is proof of the presence of the life of God among them.
Paul uses an emphatic word to describe the growth of their
faith. Christians should grow in conviction of the truth of the
Gospel, in appreciation of what God has done and is doing for
us, and in patient fidelity to Him and His cause and the duties
with which the Gospel endows us. The **love** here spoken of
is love towards one another. It characterized every member
of that Church. It embraced as its object every member of
the Church. Even those who were faulty were not destitute
of this affection for their fellow-believers. The love which

covers a multitude of sins is not, therefore, an infallible proof of present perfection.

4. So that we ourselves glory in you in the churches of God for your patience and faith in all your persecutions and in the afflictions which ye endure;

4. (See 2 Cor. 8:1, 2; 9:1, 2.) It was natural for Paul to tell everywhere the good news that came to him of the steadfastness and growth of his churches, and to stir up some by the example of others. He gloried in their **patience;** i.e., their brave endurance, their steadfastness; and in their **faith.** Faith here manifested itself in *fidelity,* unshaken by the perils to which it exposed them. In spite of what they had to endure, they persisted in the obedience of Christ. (For *faith* used in the sense of *faithfulness,* see Gal. 5:22; Rom. 3:3; Titus 2:10. Cf. also the adjective, 1 Thess. 5:24; 2 Thess. 3:3; 1 Cor. 1:9; 10:13; 2 Cor. 1:18; 2 Tim. 2:13; Luenemann.) For at that very time they were enduring not only the **afflictions** which their separation from their own people naturally brought about, but also positive **persecutions** at the hands of Jews and Gentiles. We here learn that *afflictions,* from which no men are free, though a trial, are the sphere in which Christian faith finds exercise and may grow exceedingly. While our brethren in the world suffer under them (1 Peter 5:9), we are sustained in them by the grace of God, and they work out for us the far more exceeding and eternal weight of glory (2 Cor. 4:17). Christ did not promise, and Paul did not pray, that His followers might be exempt from affliction (Acts 14:22).—**In the churches of God.** Either the zeal of Paul and his fellow-workers must already have been rewarded by the formation of *churches* in the neighborhood of Corinth (Cenchreæ), or he must have "gloried" in other letters of this period, which

have not been preserved to us.

5. *Which is* a manifest token of the righteous judgment of God; to the end that ye may be counted worthy of the kingdom of God, for which ye also suffer:

5. **A manifest token.** (See Phil. 1:28; Rom. 8:17; 2 Tim. 2:11, 12.) Their patient endurance and courageous faith under affliction and persecution, being a gift of God, is an earnest of His present interest in them, and of His final reversal of the injustice of the world (Rom. 2:5–11). The same righteous judgment that now upholds them under persecution, and enables them to persevere, will also acknowledge their title to the kingdom of God, for the sake of which they now are suffering.—**The kingdom.** (See Rom. 14:17.) "The new order of things as established under Christ, though with a special reference to its final and perfect development in His future kingdom" (Lightfoot). At the great day of final account, men shall receive that which they really make the object of their lives (Rom. 2:7). St. Paul's argument here rests upon a fundamental confidence in the righteousness and fairness of God. This underlies the New Testament and the Old (Gen. 18:25; Luke 11:13; 18:7. Also Luke 16:25).

6. If so be that it is a righteous thing with God to recompense affliction to them that afflict you,

6. **If so be.** Equivalent to, *for it is just with God* (Rom. 8:9, 17; 1 Cor. 8:5). The Christian relies upon the character of our Heavenly Father.

7. And to you that are afflicted rest with us, at the revelation of the Lord Jesus from heaven with the angels of his power

7. **Rest.** The word, used also in 2 Cor. 13:7; 7:5, means *relaxation* after conflicts, as when the strings of a harp are loosened after playing. The *rest* which Paul is confident of

enjoying (**with us,** 2 Cor. 1:7; Phil. 1:30), and which he is as confident that God will give to the persecuted Thessalonians, is here put in contrast with the present tension and effort of their trial. It is "the immediate aspect of heaven to the suffering, rest to the weary and worn-out, release from all the disquiet, pain and sorrow of the earth, stillness after turmoil, the quiet haven after the tempest" (Eadie). Every servant of God may comfort himself with this assurance of a part in the inheritance of the saints in light (Rev. 3:20). This waits until **the revelation of the Lord Jesus from heaven.** We are in this world as He was. But those who share His humiliation shall also share His glory. (See Col. 3:3, 4; 1 John 3:1–3; Rom. 8:17; Rev. 7:13–17.) The second coming of our Lord is spoken of as a revelation, for then He shall come in His glory. The exaltation of our Lord had not yet been fulfilled. Risen and ascended, at the right hand of God, having all power in heaven and earth, He is yet to come again, manifesting His power as well as his grace, judging the quick and the dead, and to be glorified in them that believe. The second coming of our Lord was eagerly expected by the apostles (2 Peter 3:12), and formed a principal topic of their preaching (Acts 3:20; 10:42; 17:30, 31), as well as of their more intimate communications to believers (2:5, 6). It occupied St. Paul's mind at this time, as well as the minds of his Thessalonian converts; and it was to strengthen their expectation of it, as well as to remove false views concerning it, that he wrote this letter. The coming of our Lord with power and great glory, He Himself had promised (Matt. 24:30; 25:31). The **angels** are the ministers of His **power.** (See Matt. 26:53.)

8–10. **In flaming fire, rendering vengeance to them that know not God, and to them that obey not the gospel of**

our Lord Jesus: who shall suffer punishment, *even* eternal
destruction from the face of the Lord and from the glory of
his might, when he shall come to be glorified in his saints,
and to be marvelled at in all them that believed (because our
testimony unto you was believed) in that day.

8. **In flaming fire.** (See Ex. 3:2; 19:18; Deut. 4:11;
Ps. 68:17; 104:4; Isai. 66:15; Dan. 7:9, 10; Mal. 4:1.)
Paul here ascribes to our Lord the same manifestations of
divine majesty which the Old Testament ascribes to Jehovah.
Two classes of persons are here mentioned as destined to
feel **the vengeance of God:** them **that know not God;**
viz. the heathen, or the Gentiles (1 Thess. 4:5; Gal. 4:8;
Eph. 2:12); and **them that obey not the gospel;** viz. the
unbelieving Jews (Rom. 10:3, 16, 21), including also those
Gentiles who, in spite of instruction, rejected the Gospel. It
is noteworthy that those who have, but disregard, the light,
join with those who sit in darkness to persecute those who
have and bring the light (John 3:19–21). Both love darkness
rather than light, and therefore are condemned to darkness
(Jude 13). Salvation is impossible without knowledge of
God. To know Him is eternal life (John 17:3, 25). Many
are responsible for their ignorance (Rom. 1:28). Many
refuse and persecute the Gospel which comes to make God
known to them (Jer. 10:25). Ignorance does not excuse sin.
Though Peter said that the people of Jerusalem had slain
Christ "through ignorance" (Acts 3:17), he shortly before
had declared that they did it "with wicked hands" (Acts
2:23). Though Paul says he obtained mercy because he
had persecuted the Church "ignorantly in unbelief," he still
declares that in his rage against the Church he was "the chief
of sinners." The infanticide of India, the fearful excesses of

devotees, the calm face with which an inquisitor could watch the sufferings of a Protestant on the rack, will show that a man may do wrong ignorantly, but not innocently. All want of conformity to the law of God is sin. There are, however, degrees of sin. So our Lord compared Capernaum and Bethsaida with Sodom; the servant who knew his master's will and did it not, with those who say, I see; those who delivered Him to Pilate with the governor himself. In the Old Testament God provided a sacrifice for sins of ignorance. The sacrifice on the great day of atonement was intended to take away the sins the worshippers had not been able to confess. The heathen are in a state of guilt. They not only are strangers to the covenant of promise, and know not God; but they choose to act against conscience. The Jews are deaf to their own Scriptures (John 5:39), and obey not the Gospel of Christ. For many of our sins of ignorance we are responsible. Though the Lord has promised to give His Spirit to them that ask Him, we do not ask. We do not use the opportunities God gives us to grow in spiritual understanding. We should humbly mourn the sins into which we fall ignorantly, and ask God to forgive them. But though we are much worse than in our most earnest and rigorous moments we imagine ourselves to be, and are guilty of sins and shortcomings we never dreamt of, all these are covered and forgiven by the great atonement of our Saviour and the mercy of our Father in heaven (Luke 23:24; Matt. 5:21–22; 10:15; 11:21–24; 12:31, 32; Luke 12:47, 48; John 19:11 (see Tholuck); Acts 2:23; 3:17; 13:27; 17:30; Rom. 2:9; 1 Cor. 2:8; 1 Tim. 1:13; 1 John 5:16; 1 Kings 8:46; 2 Chron. 6:36; Ps. 19:12. Also Mueller, Christian Doctrine of Sin, I. 203; Gerhard, Loci, II. 10; VI. 23; XX. 92; J. H. Newman, Parochial Sermons, I. 7).

The **gospel.** The good news of salvation, of the mercy and
fatherly care of God, comes only in and through **our Lord
Jesus.** It cannot be obeyed, without obedience to Him.

9. **Eternal destruction.** The word *eternal* places the
doom of the condemned beyond all time. No notions of
succession or measurement apply to it. It certainly conveys
the meaning of hopeless exclusion from the presence or favor
of God.—**From the face of the Lord.** (See Isai. 2:10; Jer.
4:26.) Those who clamor against the doctrine of unending
punishment for those who forget God, really desire an eternal
life which is not before His face, in His presence. God blesses
His people with the assurance that His face will shine upon
them, the light of His countenance will be lifted up upon them
(Numb. 6:25, 26). The wicked, the worldly, desire nothing
so much as to hide from the face of Him that sitteth upon
the throne (Rev. 6:16). God will fulfil the desire of every
heart. Some shall see Him (Matt. 5:8; 1 John 3:2); others shall
suffer eternal destruction from His face. Paul also accounts
it suffering to be destroyed **from the glory of his might.**
While the power of the Most High fills His enemies with
terror, it fills His children with awful joy.

10. **When he shall come,** etc. (1 Thess. 3:13; Phil.
3:20). Observe the parallelism in this verse, indicative of the
exaltation of St. Paul's spirit as he dictated it. We have here
another step in the exaltation of our Lord. Not only shall He
be revealed with His power and glory and surrounded by His
holy angels, but He shall be glorified in His saints; the Body
of Christ, of which He is head and all we are members, shall
be glorified with Him. As He is, so shall redeemed mankind
be, unblameable in holiness. The glorious completion of His
redemption of mankind is essential to His great glory.

"Thou to our woe who down didst come,
Who one with us wouldst be,
Wilt lift us to Thy heavenly home,
Wilt make us one with Thee!"

Consider, then, the history of a "saint." He is (1) a poor sinful man, consecrated to God, and admitted to the new covenant with Him in Holy Baptism. (2) He becomes thereby a member of the Body of Christ. (3) He therefore suffers with Him. (4) He is made like Him. (5) He reigns with Him, is glorified together with Him. God's great day is the day not only of the revelation of the Lord Jesus, but of the manifestation of the sons of God (Rom. 8:19).—**In all them that believed.** "The results of faith are so marvellous" (Eadie).—**Because our testimony unto you was believed.** The position of the verb in the original renders it emphatic. Paul gratulates himself upon the readiness with which they had received his testimony. (See 1 Thess. 2:1, 13.)—**Our testimony.** The particular testimony Paul and his companions had borne, concerning God and Jesus, and "that day."

11–12. To which end we also pray always for you, that our God may count you worthy of your calling, and fulfil every desire of goodness and *every* work of faith, with power; that the name of our Lord Jesus may be glorified in you, and ye in him, according to the grace of our God and the Lord Jesus Christ.

11. **To which end:** refers to the happy issue described in the preceding verse. Knowing what God had called them to, Paul continually prayed that they might attain to it.—**Always.** To be taken literally, Paul never ceased to pray for those who had believed through his word.—**Our God.** (See 1 Thess. 3:3.)—**May count you worthy,** etc.

(See Rev. 3:16.) The prayer is, that they may continue
to have God's approval (1 Thess. 2:12; 4:1). The **calling**
includes not only the first call addressed to them, but the
whole purpose of God in calling them.—**Every desire of
goodness:** refers to the fresh youthful aspirations of the
Thessalonian believers. He prays that God will not let those
desires be disappointed, but will bring them to fulfilment.
Goodness here is not *beneficence,* but *moral goodness* (Gal. 5:22;
Rom. 15:14; Eph. 5:9). "It is something to do good, but
it is a higher stage of moral progress to delight in doing
good" (Lightfoot).—**Work of faith** (1 Thess. 1:3). We here
are admonished to expect from God the fulfilment of our
good desires, and the performance of the works to which we
are urged and bound by faith.—**With power.** These words
belong to **fulfil.** Paul wishes for them a *mighty* operation and
performance of God.

12. **That:** so that: i.e. the fulfilment of every good purpose
of His followers and the energetic work of faith are the means
of the glorification of our Lord on earth.—**The name.** Not
Christ, but His Name; showing that Paul has in mind not the
certain revelation of the last day, but prays that on earth, and
now, the name of Jesus may be glorified in His followers, and
they in Him, or *in it* (Luenemann, Hofmann). John 17:23;
2 Cor. 3:18; Acts 3:16; Phil. 2:9; Heb. 1:4. "The Name
of God is hallowed when the word of God is taught in its
truth and purity, and we, as the children of God, lead holy
lives in accordance with it. But whoever teaches and lives
otherwise than God's word prescribes, profanes the Name of
God among us" (Catechism).

26

2 Thessalonians 2

1–2. Now we beseech you, brethren, touching the coming of our Lord Jesus Christ, and our gathering together unto him; to the end that ye be not quickly shaken from your mind, nor yet be troubled, either by spirit, or by word, or by epistle as from us, as that the day of the Lord is *now* present;

1. **We beseech you.** (See 1 Thess. 4:1.) "A transition from his request for them to his request of them" (Eadie). He grounds this request on the *coming of the Lord* and their *gathering together unto Him.* (See 2 Peter 3:11. Also 2 Macc. 2:7; Matt. 24:31; Mark 13:27.) He says, We beseech you *for the sake of* the coming. This was a prime motive of the early Church.

2. **From your mind.** Lightfoot: "Judgment, reason, sober sense, as opposed to any fit of enthusiasm, or any feverish anxieties and desires." From your fixed Christian purpose, which had shown itself in faith and patience, and in the desire of goodness and work of faith.—**Troubled.** "Nor yet be confused" (Lightfoot).—**By spirit;** i.e. by false prophecy (1 Thess. 5:19–21).—**By word.** Some have interpreted this

355

as meaning computation, and have referred it to calculations based on the predictions of the Old Testament. But it means a report of an *alleged saying* of the apostle.—**By epistle as if from us.** "Such forgeries were not at all uncommon in this century after the beginning of the Alexandrian period of literature, and their authors were very adroit in justifying such deceptions for the sake of giving currency to certain principles and opinions" (Neander, Planting, etc., I. 208; Eusebius, History, IV. 23). The apostle found it necessary to give in this letter a token by which they might discriminate a genuine from a spurious epistle (3:17). We now come to the particular error which he means to correct, and for which a special revelation, or a misconstruction of something he had said, or a forged letter, or a false inference from his former letter, may have been pleaded; viz. **that the day of the Lord is present,** is commencing, has come. Against this view, he tells them what must occur before the coming of that day.

3. Let no man beguile you in any wise:

3. These words seem to imply that some were trying to deceive them.

3–9. For *it will not be,* except the falling away come first, and the man of sin be revealed, the son of perdition, he that opposeth and exalteth himself against all that is called God or that is worshipped; so that he sitteth in the temple of God, setting himself forth as God. Remember ye not, that, when I was yet with you, I told you these things? And now ye know that which restraineth, to the end that he may be revealed in his own season. For the mystery of lawlessness doth already work: only *there is* one that restraineth now, until he be taken out of the way. And then shall be revealed the lawless one, whom the Lord Jesus shall slay with the breath of his mouth, and bring to naught by the manifestation of his coming; *even he,* whose coming is according to the working of Satan with all power and signs and lying wonders,

3. Paul foretells an **apostasy,** *the* apostasy, evidently from the truth of God, from the Gospel of Jesus. "The revolt, the rebellion, springing up from within rather than from without" (Lightfoot). So our Lord said, When the Son of Man cometh, shall He find faith on the earth? Such an apostasy occurred, for instance, in the great spread of Gnosticism in the early centuries, and in the secularization of the Church which coincided with the Christianization of the Empire, and in the victory of Islam throughout Western Asia, and in the revival of essential heathenism in the Roman Church.—**The man of sin.** Sin is "lawlessness." His coming is described as a *revelation,* for the mystery of lawlessness already is at work (verse 7), but its revelation is not yet (verse 8). Paul refers to something he had told the Thessalonians while he was with them, which would make these words clear to them (verse 5). There were current among the Christians of that time criticisms on the ruling powers in the state and prophecies of their overthrow, which would bring about an entire change of the social world, which, however, were spoken of darkly, and under cryptograms. See, for instance, "the number of the beast" in the Revelation. Apocalypses, after the pattern of Daniel and Esdras, were current among the Jews at that time. Such Christian Apocalypses are the Revelation of John and, later, the *Shepherd* of Hermas. Paul, probably, had communicated to the Thessalonians and explained to them our Lord's prediction of the catastrophe of the Jewish state and the end of the world. The phraseology in this passage is based on the revelations of Daniel (see Dan. 7:25;

11:36), which commonly are referred to Antiochus Epiphanes and his persecutions.—**The son of perdition** (John 17:12). "When lawlessness increaseth, they shall hate and persecute and betray one another, and then shall appear the world-deceiver as the Son of God, and shall do signs and wonders, and the earth shall be delivered into his hands, and he shall do iniquitous things which have never yet come to pass since the beginning" (Teaching of the Twelve Apostles, XVI.).

4. Dan. 11:36. He exalts Himself in the very sanctuary. "In the temple; i.e. becomes in the Christian Church a regent and king, a preacher. There will he sit, and will exalt himself and resist God, not aiming at exceeding God in majesty, but exalting himself above God as He is preached and worshipped. That is, he will put himself higher than God is, not in majesty but in his words. When the Holy Scripture bids something, he will not regard it as God's Word to him. The doctrine of the pope is nothing but an exaltation above God and resistance to Him, not as He is in His majesty, but as He has revealed Himself to us in His Word, or as God is preached to us. The Turk does not sit in the Church, but the pope handles both Word and Sacraments. Yet with all violence he sets himself against them, and will have it that the Divine Word and Sacrament are not right, but that lies and the devil are" (Luther, on John, 3:47, 147). "So Gregory the Great saw at least "the forerunner of Antichrist" in John the faster, patriarch of Constantinople, because he claimed the title of "Universal Bishop" (Ep. VII. 33).

5. (See on 5:3; 1 Thess. 3:4.)

6. That which **restraineth.** There was *something*, or, as the next verse has it, *some one*, who then hindered the revelation of the man of sin, though the mystery of lawlessness already

358

was at work. Some earlier commentators found here a Greek rendering of the Latin name of the Emperor Claudius. They referred this to the Roman state. "What obstacle is there but the Roman state, the falling away of which, by being shattered into kingdoms, shall introduce Antichrist?" (Tertullian, de Res. Carnis, 24). "This aforesaid Antichrist is to come when the times of the Roman Empire shall have been fulfilled, and the end of the world is drawing near" (Cyril, Catech. XV. 12.) Dan. 10:13, 20.

7. The "restrainer," being described here as a person, and in verse 6 as a thing, may be a principle, or an organization, or a system of things, of which a man is the representative before the world.

8. (Isai. 11:4.)

9. "He concentrates in himself every satanic error" (Irenæus, 5:25). Miracles alone do not guarantee the truth of him who does them. (See 1 Tim. 4:1–3; 1 John 2:22; 4:1–3.) This prophecy of St. Paul has not yet been completely fulfilled. It is not necessary to suppose that he had so clear a prevision of the Antichrist that he could have described him to us in every detail. He describes the essential characteristics and general features of the Antichrist. The Old Testament prophets did not know what time, or what manner of fulfilment, God intended when He spoke through them; and there is no reason to suppose the New Testament prophets had or could have a more definite knowledge. In the Old Testament a prophet foretold an event near to his own time and intelligible to his own age, which the progress of revelation has shown to refer to a greater event far more remote (Isai. 7:14, 53; Jer. 31:15). The supposition that this may be the case here is strengthened by the fact that Paul

359

borrows his phraseology from the Old Testament. Such a prophecy might even have a series of fulfilments, identical in principle and expressive of the continual opposition of the kingdom of God and the kingdom of evil.

St. Paul here uncovers a fundamental spiritual fact. Side by side with the *mystery of the Gospel* (Col. 1:26–28) *the mystery of lawlessness* is working. It will culminate in an uncovered and shameless, direct and definite opposition to our Lord Jesus Christ. Before that culmination there will be an apostasy. And when the man of sin is revealed, he will be found enthroned in the sanctuary of God, of the Church and of the faith, setting himself forth as God. It is not necessary to confine this interpretation to one person (1 John 2:18). The description might fit such a system as the Papacy, which never is without a representative, but hands down an unbroken policy and process of assumption from pope to pope. Tertullian applied it to Marcion (adv. M. III. 8), Athanasius to Constantius (Ep. ad Solit. Vit. Agent. 842, 852).

It is to be remembered that in the Papacy has culminated that earthly organization of a church, which contradicts the spiritual conception of Christ; which substitutes its laws and canons, its decisions and traditions, its hierarchy, for the teaching and the spirit of our Master; which has proceeded from the claim of sole and universal authority to the declaration that when the pope speaks *ex cathedra* his is the voice of God, and that the Holy Scriptures are to be received only according to his interpretation; and which claims the power to open to and shut against souls the kingdom of heaven. His dictum, it is said, cannot be reversed, and even may not be examined, in spite of conscience.

360

Therefore, while we cannot say that there may be no other manifestation of Antichrist, we must say of Rome, *Here is Antichrist.*

This passage warns us against too great readiness to admit theories of the nearness of the advent of our Lord. And it also warns us not to be of those who grow cold and fall away. We must resist the mystery of iniquity that already is at work. There are too many optimistic Christians, who hail every new manifestation as a foregleam of the millennium. It also puts us on our guard against a merely formal and outward Christianity, that sees the kingdom of heaven only in outward organization, in numbers and power, instead of in righteousness, peace and joy in the Holy Ghost (Rom. 14:17).

10–12. And with all deceit of unrighteousness for them that are perishing; because they received not the love of the truth, that they might be saved. And for this cause God sendeth them a working of error, that they should believe a lie: that they all might be judged who believed not the truth, but had pleasure in unrighteousness.

10. The deceit of unrighteousness deceives those that are perishing, *because* they received not the love of the truth. They might have been saved, but would not. "The truth might be received in some so lightly, and understood so superficially, that no true love for it might coexist; and where this love for it is absent, the mind is open to assaults and hesitations" (Eadie).

11. Upon such, and for this cause, God sends the working of error, etc. (Rom. 1:32). He says that they should believe **the lie;** that is, the fundamental, soul-destroying lie of the adversary of Jesus. The natural consequence of their rejection of the truth, which is its just punishment also, God lets come

361

upon them, *sends* it on them (Ps. 51:4). A fearful warning
to those who are tempted to acquiesce in decrees of earthly
authority (for instance, of the pope, etc.) *against* conscience.

12. They rejected the truth—and, therefore, *believe the
lie.* The one involves the other. They had pleasure in
unrighteousness—and therefore fall victims to *the deceit of
unrighteousness.* Salvation is impossible in unrighteousness,
and without the truth; and they who prefer unrighteousness
and falsehood thereby perish. This also is the righteous
judgment of God. " 'Truth' and 'falsehood' are terms
belonging not more to the intellectual than to the moral
world. Wrong-doing is a lie, for it is a denial of God's
sovereignty; right-doing is a truth, for it is a confession of
the same" (Lightfoot).

13–14. But we are bound to give thanks to God alway
for you, brethren beloved of the Lord, for that God chose
you from the beginning unto salvation in sanctification of
the spirit and belief of the truth: whereunto he called you
through our gospel, to the obtaining of the glory of our Lord
Jesus Christ.

13. He resumes the thought of 1:3.—**Beloved of the Lord.**
1 Thess. 1:4, he says, Beloved of God.—**For that God chose
you.** For the proof that they had been chosen by God, see
1 Thess. 1:5.—**From the beginning.** (See 1 John 1:1; 2:13;
Eph. 1:4; 3:9; Col. 1:26.) The choice and purpose of God
are not found *in time,* in consequence of other operations,
and to meet unforeseen exigencies; but, though manifest in
the course of the world's history, are, by their nature, eternal.
Those whom He chooses, He chose before the foundation
of the world.—**Unto salvation.** This is the purpose of God
in choosing them. This salvation consists in **sanctification**

by the Holy Ghost, and belief of the truth. Our *faith* is a part of the purpose and work of God, and is included in sanctification by the Spirit. If we have faith, it is a gift of God, and a proof that we are chosen by Him in His Beloved.

14. **Whereunto;** i.e. to which salvation, thus described, He called you. The eternal choice of God is manifested in our lives, by the call, which comes to us through the Gospel. (Catechism, Third Article of the Creed.) To whomsoever the Gospel comes, thereby the call of God comes to him, which if he receives (1 Thess. 1:6), he makes his calling and election sure. No one need debate whether he is chosen of God or not: if he heeds God's call, he may know he is chosen. **Our gospel;** i.e. through the Good News which Paul and Silas and Timothy told. He has no doubt of the eternal truth of that which he preached. It was the voice of an eternal purpose of God. And wherever that Gospel is proclaimed, there sounds forth the call of God.—**To the obtaining of the glory,** etc. This is parallel to the former verse. The outward glory answers to the inward salvation; if, indeed, the glory of our Lord Jesus Christ be not rather inward also (1 Thess. 1:5; 5:9; Rom. 8:17, 29; John 17:22).

15. So then, brethren, stand fast, and hold the traditions which ye were taught, whether by word, or by epistle of ours.

15. **So then, stand fast** (1 Thess. 3:8; Phil. 2:12–16). They must abide in the calling and salvation of God.—**And hold the traditions,** etc. Paul refers to the instructions he had given them while he was with them, and those contained in his former letter. This is evident, because in this letter he repeats and emphasizes them.—**Traditions.** On the word, see Matt. 15:2; Mark 7:3; Gal. 1:14; Col. 2:8. " 'Tradition' in the scriptural sense of the word may be either written

or oral. It is a synonym for 'teaching,' implying on the part
of the teacher a confession that he was not expressing his
own ideas, but *delivering* or *handing on* a message that he
had received from heaven" (Lightfoot). It is evident that
Paul gave the Thessalonians, while he was with them, very
thorough instruction, in Christian doctrine, in the Christian
hope, and in the particulars of Christian conduct (2:5; 3:6,
10; 1 Thess. 3:4; 4:6, 11; 5:2. Also 1 Cor. 11:2, 23; 15:3). The
instructions which he gave, and could refer to thus, were not
traditions of men (Col. 2:8), but had the authority of the Lord
Jesus Christ (3:6). While the Thessalonians necessarily had to
read and understand this letter in the light which St. Paul's
recent teachings cast upon it, and, on the other hand, had to
correct the exaggeration and misinterpretation of his oral
teaching (of which some were guilty) by the more detailed
explanation which he writes, it is manifest that *we* cannot
interpret this letter by those traditions, because we do not
know what instructions he gave, except in those cases in
which he has repeated them in the letter. Romanists hold
that Holy Scripture does not contain everything that pertains
to faith and piety, but that many things necessary to faith
and practice, which are not taught in the Scriptures, and
cannot be proved from the Scriptures, must be accepted on
the authority of unwritten tradition. Therefore they teach
that the Holy Scriptures are to be received only as they are
interpreted by the tradition of the Church. Their contention
shatters on the impossibility of an infallible depository of
that tradition. If it be argued that that is true which survives
in the belief of the Church after ages of debate (*securus judicat
orbis terrarum*), we are left without any decision at all, for
we never know whether the end of the process has been

reached. If it be contended that this tradition is entrusted to the universal episcopate, we find (1) that Rome confines it to the episcopate so far as the bishops are in communion with Rome; and (2) that Councils of the Church have disagreed with and anathematized each other. And finally, Rome has declared that the decision of a Council requires the approval of the bishop of Rome, and that he only is the infallible final interpreter of the word of God. Yet popes have disagreed with and anathematized popes. A far better rule is found in Gal. 1:8. By this every doctrine, inference, custom and tradition must be tried.

Chemnitz ennumerates different sorts of traditions: (1) the words of Christ and of His apostles, which afterwards were written down by apostles and evangelists; (2) the testimony to the authenticity of the New Testament Scriptures, given by the Primitive Church; (3) the witness of antiquity; (4) the consent of the early Church as to the exposition, true sense and native meaning of the Scriptures; (5) those dogmas, which are not in so many letters and syllables written down in Holy Scripture, but are collected from its plain testimony by good, certain, firm and manifest reasoning; (6) the Catholic consent of the Fathers; (7) the rites and ancient customs which antiquity referred to the apostles, among which certainly are some added since the apostolic age, for the sake of edification, order and decency; and (8) popish traditions concerning faith and morals, which have not the approval of the Scriptures. Of these he says, that those which agree with the Scriptures are to be approved, but among the others are to be found mistakes of good men and impostures by the bad. It is not enough to allege that a tradition is *Apostolic* or from *the Fathers.*

16–17. Now our Lord Jesus Christ himself, and God our
Father which loved us and gave us eternal comfort and good
hope through grace,—fort your hearts and stablish them in
every good work and word.

16. St. Paul wishes and expects comfort and strengthening
from the power of the Lord, as from the Father. He prays
to Him, and confesses that He is the hearer and answerer
of prayer.—**Which loved us,** etc. Refers to *the Father* (John
3:16; Rom. 8:32, 37; Gal. 2:20). In our tribulations and
afflictions God gives us **eternal comfort;** in our weakness,
eternal *encouragement.* He admits us into fellowship with Him
and His Son in the Eternal Spirit (John 14:23).—**In grace.**
The grace of God is the element in which we live and move
and have our being; in which we enjoy His eternal comfort
and have a good hope.

17. (See 1:11.)

2 Thessalonians 3

1. Finally, brethren, pray for us, that the word of the Lord may run and be glorified, even as also *it is* with you.

1. **Finally** (Phil. 3:1; 4:8; 1 Thess. 4:1). "Suffice it to say, that the use of the phrase implied that the primary object of the writer has been gained; that what especially prompted him to compose the epistle has already found a place in it, and that what follows is more or less supplementary in its nature: 2 Cor. 13:11; Eph. 6:10" (Eadie).—**Pray for us.** He had just now prayed for them, and in return asks their prayers. So pastor and people, the ministry and those Christians who are engaged in secular occupations, missionaries and the churches at home, and all Christians indeed, are knit together by prayer for each other. The *General Prayer* of the Christian service of worship, the prayer for all estates and conditions of men, not only is becoming, but is the natural pulsation of the common life of the Church (Phil. 4:6; Col. 4:3). Paul asks them to pray for him and his associates, but not for their personal advantage, but that the word of the Lord may run and be glorified. The "word of the Lord" is the good news

of salvation through Christ. It *ran,* when, conquering all
impediments, it became known further and further. It was
glorified, when the story of its triumphs was told far and near
(1 Thess. 1:7, 8; 2:1, 13; Acts 13:48). Those who have received
the Gospel should pray that it may be preached to all men,
and may meet with like triumphs everywhere.

2. And that we may be delivered from unreasonable and
evil men; for all have not faith.

2. **And that we may be delivered,** etc. (Rom. 15:30,
31; Acts 18:6, 12–17). Just at this time the apostle and his
associates were vexed and threatened by the persistent and
unreasonable opposition of Jews at Corinth. Paul describes
them as **unreasonable** and **wicked.** The former word, by
which the penitent thief described his evil deeds, "This man
hath done nothing *amiss*" (Luke 23:41), seems to denote
persons who are utterly aimless and, having no intelligent
principles, cannot be reached by reason at all. They are
"impracticable." In answer to Paul's proof that Jesus is the
Christ, they *railed at* him, and acted *with one accord,* and
therefore with no exertion of their own conscience, in the
senseless and ineffectual tumult made against him. They were
also *wicked;* not thoughtless only, but positively bad. It is to
be observed that though the apostles had difficulty enough
to bring their message to the hearts of thoughtful and sincere
men, who would be slow to embrace a faith which required
them to be born again and become as little children, and the
success of which would involve the necessary dissolution
of the existing order of the world, their principal sufferings
were caused by the clamor and tumult of lewd fellows of
the baser sort. The power of "unreasonable" men to force
others to combined wrong-doing is a continual shame to

mankind.—**For all have not faith.** Does this mean merely, Not all the Jews here at Corinth believe,—a mere statement of fact, an item of news? Or is it a sorrowful reflection of the apostle—the recognition of the sad fact that some seem incapable of faith, a barren soil on which though the Divine Seed falls it cannot enter, utterly deaf to and impenetrable by the Spirit of God? It certainly is true that some, many, seem to have no side at all for spiritual verities. These, however, are not such as the Berœans (Acts 17:11), but unreasonable and wicked men. Not all have faith; therefore we, who, by the grace of God, believe, should be thankful that this grace has been wrought in us, and should keep our faith reverently.

3. But the Lord is faithful, who shall stablish you and guard you from the evil *one*.

3. **The Lord is faithful** (Phil. 2:13; 1 Thess. 5:24). This is the guarantee of our faith. We have it, because He gave it; we will be stablished and guarded, because the Lord is faithful. Very probably this was a commonplace, a watchword of the Church, like 1 Cor. 16:23; 1 Cor. 1:9; Phil. 1:6. The *Lord* is Christ. Paul teaches not only, that He went up into heaven, and possesses all power, but that He regards and takes care of all His followers (Matt. 28:18–20). He establishes them in the faith, and guards them against the assaults and guile of the evil one (Eph. 6:16; Matt. 13:19).

4. And we have confidence in the Lord touching you, that ye both do and will do the things which we command.

4. Gal. 5:10; Phil. 2:24. His confidence was not in anything in them, but in the Lord. The good thing we desire of any one in the Lord, we must seek of Him. We have a right also to believe that He intends to accomplish in every Christian that which ought to be. The particular grace which Paul here

expects the Lord to work in them, is a readiness to do what
he now bids them do. Obedience to those whom God has
called and set to instruct us, is a Christian grace. Paul, far
distant from them, because of his confidence in the Lord, does
not doubt that the Thessalonians are even now observant of
what he had enjoined on them, and will continue to heed his
bidding.

5. And the Lord direct your hearts into the love of God,
and into the patience of Christ.

5. The aim of his commandment was their growth in the
love of God and the patience of Christ. He prays that the Lord
will always open and incline their hearts to such instruction.
The **patience of Christ** is a patience like Christ's; and **the
love of God,** a love patterned after God's. (See 1 Thess. 1:3;
1 John 4:7–20.) The earlier English versions agree with this;
the patient waiting for Christ appears in the Genevan Version,
1557.

6–15. Now we command you, brethren, in the name of our
Lord Jesus Christ, that ye withdraw yourselves from every
brother that walketh disorderly, and not after the tradition
which they received of us. For yourselves know how ye ought
to imitate us: for we behaved not ourselves disorderly among
you; neither did we eat bread for nought at any man's hand,
but in labour and travail, working night and day, that we
might not burden any of you: not because we have not the
right, but to make ourselves an ensample unto you, that ye
should imitate us. For even when we were with you, this
we commanded you, If any will not work, neither let him
eat. For we hear of some that walk among you disorderly,
that work not at all, but are busybodies. Now them that
are such we command and exhort in the Lord Jesus Christ,

370

that with quietness they work, and eat their own bread. But ye, brethren, be not weary in well-doing. And if any man obeyeth not our word by this epistle, note that man, that ye have no company with him, to the end that he may be ashamed. And *yet* count him not as an enemy, but admonish him as a brother.

6. After such an affectionate and impressive introduction, he proceeds to *command* them. Observe the positive and uncompromising manner in which he here insists on their duty. It is evident he means that his bidding shall not be misunderstood or be liable to any misinterpretation (2:2). (See verses 10, 12.) There arc duties which no Christian dare disregard. St. Paul here solemnly commands an exercise of Church discipline. This, not merely because in his opinion salutary, but **in the name of our Lord Jesus Christ** (1 Cor. 5:4). Therefore, by revelation. *They were to withdraw themselves from every brother that walketh disorderly.* In 1 Thess. 5:14, he had bidden them *admonish* such. The admonition having proved fruitless, they were to withdraw from association with him (verse 14), while still holding him as an erring brother, not an enemy (verse 15). A **disorderly** man was one who would not keep in line with the rest; would not submit to the regulations which the apostle had given them, or they made for the order of their community; who insisted on his own way, over against the common sense of the rest or the teaching of the Lord (1 Thess. 5:14). So were they to treat those who would not observe "the traditions" which Paul had given them. It is evident, therefore, that Christian congregations should punish with exclusion from their communion not only such as deny the faith, and commit notorious sins (1 Cor. 5:9–11), but those also who will not

submit to just order and to those regulations of conduct
which the apostles have given in the name of Christ. The
Gospel is not merely a theory, or a promise, it is also a life.

7–9. Phil. 3:17. Paul confidently refers to his example
(1 Thess. 2:9). And it appears that he had preserved
his independence of their charity, that he might be an
example to them. We discover how keen he was to detect
the characteristics of those he labored among. He had
seen the disorderly disposition of some who were ready
to listen to and follow him. They were light-minded men,
prone to disagree with others, and proud of singularity, as
if it betokened exceptional wisdom; and they welcomed
an opportunity of getting out of line and concentrating
on themselves the attention of others. Such spread the
fanatical reports of the present end of the world, forsook the
avocations by which they ought to have earned a livelihood,
and became a charge to the Christian community. Our
missionaries are troubled by such converts now; such gather
round every new sectary in Christendom; and such are to
be found in every parish. The salvation of their own souls
depends on their receiving admonition from the Church, and,
if they will not heed it, severer discipline. Christians show
their obedience to the apostolic tradition, not by "forsaking
the world" after the manner of those ascetics who gave their
all to the poor, abandoned their families and callings, and
retired to deserts and caves in the mountains; but by diligence,
that they may maintain their own, and have to give to him
that needeth. "The Lord our God hates the slothful. For no
one of those who are dedicated to God ought to be idle" (App.
Const. II. 63).

11. Here we have a definition of their *disorderliness.* They

did no work, but they were continually *at work* in what did not concern them (Acts 19:19; 1 Tim. 5:13). Those who are conscientious in the discharge of their own duty will not be tattlers and busybodies. (See Phil. 3:3. Also 1 Cor. 7:31; 2 Cor. 1:13; 6:10; 10:12; Hebr. 5:8.)

12. Paul addresses himself to these erring brethren again. He commands them again (1 Thess. 4:11); he exhorts them. He exhorts them to quietness. It is an admonition to those busy Christians, who always wish to be observed and talked about. He rebukes their willingness to be supported by the rest. They were what are called in the East *Rice-Christians*: such as join the Church for worldly profit. (See Teaching of the Twelve Apostles, XI., XII.; Eusebius, History, V. 18, 2.) In our own day many profess to follow Christ, or, denying duty, go from congregation to congregation, for the sake of trade or of social advancement.

13. But now he turns to the whole body again, as much as to say, Though they may not do right, and you often are disappointed to find those on whom you have lavished your confidence untrustworthy, still **be not weary in well-doing.** Do not let it discourage you from charity, though the objects of your almsgiving are found to be undeserving.

14–15. He returns to stern command. If any one persists in disobedience to the clear word of this letter, let him be a *marked* man, one to be avoided. Not that he is an enemy, but because he is a brother; for he must be taught in what a perilous case he is, and must be made ashamed, that he may be saved. The end of Church discipline is not the purification of the community, much less is it the preservation of its good name, but the rescue and sanctification of the offender. Christian charity requires that a persistent sinner, deaf to

every admonition and remonstrance of the Word of God
and the Christian congregation, should be excluded from the
fellowship of the Church.

16. Now the Lord of peace himself give you peace at all
times in all ways. The Lord be with you all.

16. **The Lord of peace himself,** i.e. Christ. In 1 Thess.
5:23 the Father is spoken of as *the God of peace.*—**Give you
peace** (Phil. 4:7; Col. 3:15; John 14:27).—**At all times, in all
ways.** God can give peace in the midst of tribulations and
labors, as well as in a time of tranquillity.

17. The salutation of me Paul with mine own hand, which
is the token in every epistle: so I write.

17. Paul wrote his letters by the hand of an amanuensis
(Rom. 16:22), but thus early adopted the habit of adding his
Salutation in his own handwriting, as a token of the genuineness of the letter; doubtless led to this by the ascription
to him of forged letters or false teaching. (See 2:2; Gal. 6:11.)
This is, so far as we know, only the second in order of those
letters of St. Paul which have come down to us; but his words
make it not improbable that before this he had written more
than one. (See on Phil. 1:4; 3:1.) This apostolic signature is
the first step towards fixing the New Testament Canon of
Holy Scriptures. The genuineness of this epistle is attested by
its own contents, by its relation to the former epistle, and by
Polycarp (Phil. 11), Justin Martyr, Irenæus (Adv. Hær. 3, 7, 2),
Clement of Alexandria (Strom. 5), Tertullian (de res. Carnis,
24), the Muratorian Fragment, the earliest Syrian Version
(the Peschito), and by the quotations of the heretic Marcion.

The canonical authority of this letter is grounded on its
apostolic origin and the fact that Paul in it utters the Word
of God. These are the two marks he has affixed to it and to

374

all his epistles. The Church, or the scholars in it, or the men composing it, weighs the historical evidence concerning the preservation and authorship of a sacred book, the evidence of its own contents, its relations to other scriptures, and its consonance with the whole Gospel. But that which gives a book authority is, that it was written by one whom Jesus called to witness directly to His truth.

18. The grace of our Lord Jesus Christ be with you all.

18. The Apostolic Benediction. He wishes that the grace of Christ may be with them **all.** That they receive that grace, is enough; that it abide with them, will be enough forever.